Chloé

CATWALK

Chloé

CATWALK

The Complete Collections

Preface by Suzy Menkes

Text by Lou Stoppard

With over 1,000 photographs

Yale University Press

Contents

The Collections

GABY AGHION & STUDIO

MARTINE SITBON

KARL LAGERFELD

Preface

The silvery water cascaded over a fiery red and deep blue bodice, and then flowed down the black skirt. Who could have imagined, as the models sashayed down the Paris runway, that these striking outfits were all beaded with needle and thread?

I remember the Chloé woman dressed by Karl Lagerfeld in 1983–1984 as an example of the witty and original designs that personified the company's Parisian style. The irony is that Karl – to be followed at Chloé by a powerful line-up of designers from Gabriela Hearst today to Stella McCartney back in 1997 – was one of the company's rare males. Even before Karl brought his fantasy and exuberance to Chloé in 1964, there had been strong women, like Maxime de la Falaise, in the design department. Not least, there was Gaby Aghion, the founder of the brand, who was powerful, imaginative – and female. As a junior reporter, I was at the receiving end of her firm vision of how the clothes and the shows (seen from my back-row position) should be.

I remember Chloé in so many ways: the wit of Karl in those early days before he joined Chanel (he returned briefly to Chloé in 1992). He found at Chloé his own power women, like Inès de la Fressange, with her long, lean silhouette and kooky smile. The forward march of creative directors continued to raise the pace of modern fashion and its desire for women to be in charge – and that attitude included 'It' bags, so appropriate for busy working lives. Each designer found an individual way of expressing a female attitude. I remember Martine Sitbon, selected as a lively French designer, choosing powerful models like Linda Evangelista and Claudia Schiffer to push forward Chloé's vision of modern femininity.

Perhaps the most striking fact that pulled the different designers together was a female friendliness. There was no vulgarity in the easy looks that I noted among the British creatives Phoebe Philo and Clare Waight Keller. They brought to the runway a womanly solidarity. Those designers were followed by Natacha Ramsay-Levi, French and dynamic, underscoring the fact that Chloé was about attitude – both powerful and with something to say.

The changing spirit, including nationality and originality, has emphasized the importance of attitudes. Gabriela Hearst is a leader of thoughtfulness put into action. She can recount the details of fabric, the power of human hands and the strength of mindful creation. How I would love for her to gather all the former Chloé creatives as a statement about women in fashion ... and about intelligent designers who insist that they should have a powerful place.

Suzy Menkes

Introduction

A New Vision of Femininity

Today, it is commonplace for fashion brands to extol their supposed feminist credentials; positioning themselves as the makers of clothing that 'empowers' women, or promoting the fact that they employ female creative directors, or have fostered female talent and stories through their campaigns and content. And yet, few – despite myriad attempts at invention and assertion – can compete with the history of Chloé, when looking to boast of being a women-led brand built around female stories, around new visions of femininity, around questioning societal norms and the status quo. Indeed, today's intersection between fashion and feminism feels overdue, given that, back in the 1950s, founder Gaby Aghion envisaged her house as a hub for modern women, keen to shrug off post-war restrictions, and as a bastion of new ideas regarding presentation, formality, image and social structure. 'I think my actions went a small way toward liberating women,' Aghion wrote in 2013. 'Women in France were very timorous. The French woman had no freedom; she was like – and this may sound shocking – her husband's servant. I always thought that as women we could succeed independently. I fought for this personal freedom of choice.'

Not only did Aghion pave the way for other dynamic French female-led ready-to-wear brands, such as Sonia Rykiel and Chantal Thomass, but also, from the start, she did much to propel the status of – and opportunities for – women in design. Quickly, Chloé became known as a talent factory for bright young stars. Two of today's most applauded female designers, Stella McCartney and Phoebe Philo, got their breaks at the house, with the former becoming creative director in 1997, aged just 25 and only two years out of Central Saint Martins, and the latter taking on the top job at 27 in 2001. Other respected female designers to have contributed to the house include, in the early days, Maxime de la Falaise, Christiane Bailly, Michèle Rosier and Graziella Fontana, and later, from the 1990s onwards, Martine Sitbon, Hannah MacGibbon, Clare Waight Keller, Natacha Ramsay-Levi, and today Gabriela Hearst, a designer known for being one of fashion's most committed, and most inventive, sustainability advocates.

★

Chloé's story, then, is one of being ahead of the curve. '[I]n 1952, there was only couture or basic ready-to-wear,' wrote Gaby Aghion. 'There was no luxury ready-to-wear; well-made clothes, with quality fabrics and fine detailing, did not exist. A lot of things did not exist in France. Everything was yet to be invented, and this thrilled me.' Aghion was, back then, surrounded by the couturiers: Christian Dior, with his full-skirted New Look silhouette; Jacques Fath, with his strict, meticulously

tailored dresses; Cristóbal Balenciaga, with his sculptural forms. And yet
Aghion felt that these clothes did not suit the scene; did not suit reality.
She and her husband were part of the dynamic crowd of artists and
intellectuals who hung around the cafés of the Left Bank. 'We were very
avant-garde. It was after the war: you could remain as you were, but you
also had the freedom to invent,' she wrote. 'The world was opening up
before my eyes, and I believed I could do anything. I felt I had wings.'
She needed clothes that could keep up.

Thus, Chloé's very foundation is testimony to shifts, both societal and
cultural. It contributed to, and evolved from, a change in mood in fashion
and approach to dressing – the march of the casual, the freeing, the
playful, the quick. Yves Saint Laurent is regularly applauded as the key
pioneer of French ready-to-wear, of a new style of dress and shopping
(in 1966 he became one of the first couturiers to open a ready-to-wear
boutique under his own name), but too little attention is given to Aghion,
as an innovator working ahead of the French prêt-à-porter boom (she
founded her house in 1952, and held her first show in the autumn of 1957).
She should be credited as a radical forward-thinker; a champion of
youthful spirit – something with which Chloé has been synonymous ever
since. Aghion, like many of the designers who would follow her, was
interested in the new, the next. She was excited by change, and part
of her self-defined commitment in founding Chloé was to provide
women with the clothes they needed to face, and enjoy, all coming
shifts and modernizations.

The name Chloé belonged to a friend – Chloé Huysmans. 'I asked if
I could borrow it,' Aghion later explained, claiming that she liked the
elegant roundness of the letters. She also admitted a more pragmatic
reason: her family were grumbling about the fact that she was working,
and she was sure they would disapprove of her using her own name.

Part of Aghion's skill was knowing what she could do (provide a coherent
vision, attract press and clients) and what she couldn't (cut and sew).
Almost immediately, she hired seamstresses and a growing team
of talented young designers. She was a visionary entrepreneur. Long
before the explosion of marketing and intense control around logos
and ownership, she understood the importance of protecting – and
promoting – the Chloé name. She realized that reputation would come
with recognition, and so refused to let boutiques take the Chloé labels
off her clothing and replace them with their own, as was the practice
at the time.

Chloé's early shows were held in the same Left Bank cafés where the
idea for the brand had first germinated, and where the kinds of liberated
women for whom the label was intended hung out. The message was
modernity: ease, vibrancy, optimism, freedom. 'All I ever wanted was

for Chloé to have a happy spirit and to make people happy,' Aghion said in 2011. She found in Chloé an outlet, a focus, a means of achievement, fulfilment, independence, confidence. Thanks to Chloé, 'I was responsible for my own life', she said in 2013.

In 1958, Aghion hired Gérard Pipart, then 25, who was credited by the press as a key player in Chloé's early success. Also on staff in the early years was Tan Giudicelli, as well as Christiane Bailly, Michèle Rosier, Graziella Fontana and Maxime de la Falaise, whose employment pre-empted the arrival of cool British 'It' girls – such as Stella McCartney – decades later.

★

Gaby Aghion's prescient vision is also notable in her role as an early champion of Karl Lagerfeld. She gave him a big break in fashion, employing him as a designer when he was a relative newbie, with just a few years' experience at Pierre Balmain and Jean Patou. At Chloé, Lagerfeld developed the signatures that would go on to define his six-decades-long career. It was here that he was encouraged to explore his interest in nostalgia, in irony, in art, in playful catwalk theatrics, in quips about modernity and modern life, in shrewd readings of society and commerce, and in the constant quest for the new and the surprising.

Lagerfeld joined Chloé in 1964, initially working as part of the team of designers who delivered sketches and ideas to Aghion. After the other names eventually departed their roles, he was left alone, working alongside Aghion directly, and quickly rose to become the spokesperson and face of the collections. His two stints at the house (1964–1984, and 1992–1997) would crystallize the identity of Chloé as a house that championed easy movement and femininity, setting out codes – blouses, light long-line gowns, lace, billowing silk, artful layers, pleats, cut-out backs, even the signature Chloé pinky-beige – that could be repeated and reworked by other creative directors at the house for years to come.

Lagerfeld was a true pioneer. Working with the small Parisian atelier run by Nicole Lefort, he quickly introduced dynamic hand-painted motifs that now seem to encapsulate the trippy vibrancy of the 1960s. He also, in the early 1970s, played with branding, using the Chloé name and the 'C' across prints and embroideries: such logocentricism would not be repeated, and the house would not become known for overt branding, but these early designs show how ahead of the tempo Lagerfeld could be. Magazine editors and photographers were swiftly enamoured with Chloé, thrilled with the narratives they could build in countless editorials around the clothes; the visual plays they could make with the bold colours and prints, or the graphic cuts and embellishments.

Perhaps most interesting to observe in Lagerfeld's first stint at Chloé is the evolution of his signature wit. Throughout the archives, one finds playful motifs and patterns that nod to the developments, preoccupations and ambitions of the age: robots, rocket ships, clocks, speed dials. One also finds surreal trompe-l'œil embellishments: sewing scissors, needles and thread, dripping taps, showerheads.

By the 1970s, Chloé had cemented its reputation among a wide international audience, with American stores buying the collections and international press clamouring for tickets to the shows. Lagerfeld showed a keen awareness of the way the industry was changing – the increased media scrutiny, and the role of fashion shows as branding exercises and advertisements, rather than simply trade shows to sell clothes. Indeed, for A/W 1980–1981, he staged his show against the backdrop of a giant television set (see p.172) – a nod to the changing role that technology was playing in popularizing and democratizing fashion. Lagerfeld understood the power of spectacle, of icons and 'fashion moments'. From the 1970s, his shows were full of 'faces' – Jerry Hall, Pat Cleveland, Iman – models whose recognizability put them closer to celebrity than mannequin. And backstage, he would regale journalists with quippy, provocative lines, to be spread worldwide in their reports. 'I'm like a building with all sorts of TV antennas, like the ones you see in the USA; I can receive all the channels,' he said in 1984.

*

That year, Lagerfeld left Chloé for Chanel, and another period of teamwork started. Featuring Guy Paulin, Philippe Guibourgé, Peter O'Brien, Luciano Soprani and Carlos Rodriguez, this was a time of instability for the house, when critics and press wondered if Lagerfeld could ever be replaced. By then, the idea of the designer megastar was thriving – Gianni Versace, Jean Paul Gaultier, Giorgio Armani – and teamwork was not in fashion.

Come 1987, a new voice was found: the talented young designer Martine Sitbon, whose eponymous label – synonymous with youth and rock 'n' roll – was impressing the press. Sitbon's appointment would mark the start of Chloé's modern incarnation as the launchpad for fashion's brightest female stars. The choice of a French woman felt like a fitting nod to the house's Parisian roots, and yet her inspirations and icons – British street style, edgy bands and musicians – actually link her appointment to the house's eventual association with London style, formally solidified when Stella McCartney and Phoebe Philo joined the house some ten years later.

This period marked a transition for Chloé in terms of business, as well as creativity. In 1985, Gaby Aghion and Jacques Lenoir sold the house to Dunhill Holdings PLC. The following year, Aghion stepped back from her role as a director and advisor.

*

In 1992, a deal between Dunhill and Karl Lagerfeld, relating to his eponymous brand, saw Lagerfeld reinstated as creative director of Chloé – a role he maintained for five years, albeit with less critical fawning than during his first era at the house. Much of the press attention focused on Lagerfeld's extraordinary workload, and his ability to juggle four commitments – Chloé, Fendi, Chanel, and his own brand.

The shift in personnel during this period can also be related to the changes to fashion described above – including increased media attention, giant shows, and large collections full of accessories. From the 1990s onwards, it began to become much more unusual to see designers stay in their position for longer than a few years – something that is reflected in the many designers who led Chloé from this point onwards (eight across a thirty-year period). Indeed, a five-year stint as creative director at a house came to feel significant and impressive from this period onwards – and the notion of someone staying somewhere twenty years, as Lagerfeld had done originally, became almost unheard of. Three years – the typical length of a designer's contract – was often the duration of a designer's stay, before a new option was tried, or a new challenge accepted.

*

The year 1997 – when the young Stella McCartney and her then-assistant Phoebe Philo arrived at the atelier from London – feels fitting for a British takeover at Chloé. That year is, to this day, cited as a turning point in UK culture: Tony Blair of the left-of-centre Labour party won the general election; the Young British Artists, including Tracey Emin and Damien Hirst, were disrupting the art scene; and Brit Pop was booming. 'London Swings Again!' read the famous headline of *Vanity Fair*'s March 1997 cover. It's unsurprising, then, that this period in Chloé's history felt buoyant, playful, optimistic. Collections were tongue-in-cheek; sassy, even. Suzy Menkes, in the *International Herald Tribune*, spoke of a 'girlish freshness'. Indeed, the association between Chloé and young fashion and modern femininity, which had defined the house when Aghion launched it, was back, albeit with an edge of insouciance.

McCartney served as a creative director from 1997 to 2001, and when she left, to start her eponymous brand, Philo took over, helming the house from 2001 to 2006. The former embraced a romantic but streetwise mix of vintage-inspired lingerie, sharp tailoring, signature low-rise pants and printed T-shirts. Often, the look was very revealing – cropped, sliced, sprayed-on – and marked by a heady flirtatiousness that encapsulated the carefree mood of the era. To some, it read as a reclaiming of female sexuality, a cheeky nod to the growing porn industry (exemplified by the infamous debut cover of *Pop* magazine, created by stylist Katie Grand, which featured McCartney and Philo pole dancing, alongside the

photographer Liz Collins and the accessories designer Katie Hillier).
Many magazine editors enjoyed the sense of female camaraderie between
the design team, top models (Angela Lindvall, Kate Moss, Amber Valletta,
Stella Tennant) and celebrity wearers (Mary J. Blige in a skimpy boob
tube, Kylie Minogue in a banana-print T-shirt, Sadie Frost in a sequinned
cami), describing the Chloé team as a 'girl gang', and noting to their
readers that the best way for a woman to dress was not for the approval
of men, but for herself or, failing that, for her girlfriends.

Philo took over the house during a period of transition brought about by
the millennium – digitization, fast fashion, e-retail – and had impressed
CEO Ralph Toledano with her conviction and 'great business mind'.
Though widely described as a party girl in the press surrounding
her appointment, Philo was actually keen to distance herself, and by
default Chloé, from the world of celebrity. She told the *New York Times*
in 2002 that she had no interest in using the profile of the job to become
a 'B-rate celebrity', adding that 'Chloé can no longer rely on just Madonna
and Gwyneth wearing the clothes to award shows'. Given these intentions,
Philo's ascent from young star to one of fashion's most influential,
esteemed and copied designers, during her stint at Chloé, and later
Céline, makes sense. Though she certainly played a part in fuelling the
'It' girl and 'It' bag moments, with leather goods like the Paddington bag,
with its hefty padlock, her collections were clean and grown-up. Pieces
were desirable; rich in clever but discreet detail, technical prowess and
design nuance. That said, Philo was not a conceptualist, famously telling
British *Vogue* about how, when studying at Central Saint Martins, she
hated the tendency for philosophising and theorising during classes:
'I wanted to make a pair of trousers that made my arse look good,
rather than a pair that represented the Holocaust or something.'

*

As when Karl Lagerfeld left the house in the 1980s, Phoebe Philo's
departure in 2006 – after such a strong era – left a void at Chloé, and
there followed a few years of searching and uncertainty, including a short
stint with Paulo Melim Andersson in charge. This ended in 2008 with the
appointment of another Brit, Hannah MacGibbon, who, having worked
as Philo's right hand, followed the tradition of juniors stepping up into
the role after their seniors' departure. While much of MacGibbon's
tenure continued the sophisticated romanticism of Philo – capes, beige,
crisp broderie anglaise, billowing silk – true consistency was rendered
impossible due to the tempestuous nature of the times. Economic
upheaval and the financial crash led to uncertainty about how fashion,
and its increasingly popular, if often undefined, bedfellow 'luxury',
could make a case for its relevance and its role in women's lives.

These questions have continued to dominate fashion, and have been
made only more complex by significant societal turning points – whether

#MeToo, Black Lives Matter, or the global agitation around climate change. Since MacGibbon's ascension, Chloé has consistently been led by female creative directors, all of whom have sought to propose their own demands, suggestions and queries in the face of such global uncertainty and transformation. From 2011, another Brit, Claire Waight Keller, took over at Chloé, and her six years at the house were marked by experiments into what contemporary femininity could mean: how could girlishness be reclaimed, or seen as empowering? What could modern romance look like, given changing gender expectations? What image or values would the contemporary woman want to project, when dressing up?

From 2017 to 2020, the first French woman since Martine Sitbon was in charge: Natacha Ramsay-Levi, who made the feminist credentials of Chloé more explicit than ever, collaborating with various female artists and, on occasion, emblazoning her collections with feminist symbols and slogans. Ramsay-Levi spent much of her tenure considering which aspects of Chloé's history could be repurposed for the modern age, sweeping the archive for intriguing patterns, details and motifs, from Lagerfeld's graphic '70s prints to Philo and McCartney's wild galloping horses.

In 2021, the house's first non-European lead arrived – Uruguayan designer Gabriela Hearst, who extended her mission beyond branding, aesthetic and mood into the details of production, manufacturing and waste. Sustainability – alongside femininity and youth – has now become one of the key pillars at Chloé; the vital talking point, explored season on season. The quest is no longer modernity, or chicness, but circularity.

★

Writing on the occasion of Hearst's debut show, for A/W 2021–2022, Vanessa Friedman quipped, 'There's a new Chloé girl in town. Yes, that mythic fashion creature who has been through more designer reinventions than Madonna is being reinvented once again.' Friedman explained that 'the Chloé girl romped in the Provençal flower fields thanks to Karl Lagerfeld, went a little more risqué under Martine Sitbon, became Lolita-ironic under Stella McCartney, and turned baby-doll cool via Phoebe Philo. She was somewhat confused in the hands of Paulo Melim Andersson and Hannah MacGibbon, relaxed and accessible with Clare Waight Keller, and edgily bohemian under Natacha Ramsay-Levi.'

In 2013, Aghion herself referred to this multiplicity, describing Chloé as a 'living character'. 'There is no characteristic Chloé Woman. She is neither blonde nor dark haired. But she is typically Parisian,' Aghion added. Arguably, this in itself is too narrow, too modest, a vision of what the Chloé woman has been and can be. Hers is a story not just of appearances – or hair colours – but of connections and reconsiderations. Of London girls in Paris. Of global meetings and convening cultures. Of women, and of opportunities. Of reworkings, and of steps forward.

The Collections

Gaby Aghion

A Short Biography

Gaby Aghion was, according to a *New York Times* feature from 1960, 'small, energetic and bright eyed'. The daughter of a wealthy Greek cigarette factory manager and an Italian mother, she was born Gabriella Hanoka in Alexandria, Egypt, in 1921. Gaby's mother was interested in fashion, and even employed a seamstress to make dresses styled after pictures in French magazines. As was the case with most members of respectable Egyptian society of the time, the family spoke French at home. Gaby met her husband, Raymond Aghion, as a child, and the pair, who were both Jewish, married some ten years later, when they were both nineteen. In 1945, the couple moved to Paris, in order to pursue their studies, which had been interrupted by the war.

Before Gaby Aghion founded Chloé in 1952 (sadly, no pictures exist of the house's earliest collections), she and Raymond were known and liked among Paris's left-wing intellectual and creative sets: 'Her husband runs an art gallery of abstract painting. The couple are widely known in artistic Left Bank circles,' reported the *New York Times*. It was this background, and this exposure to youth, modernity and eccentric spirit, that shaped Aghion's vision for Chloé – a house that would offer contemporary women stylish clothing, free from the constrictions and fussy formalities of couture.

'One day I told my husband that I didn't want to live off his money,' Aghion told interviewers of her intentions when starting the house. 'We give it two weeks before she gives up,' she recalled her intellectual friends quipping. 'But I soundly believed ... and I held on. I enjoyed a fight.' Assisting her were seamstresses she hired from the recently closed couture house of Lucien Lelong. By 1953, Aghion had recruited business partner Jacques Lenoir, who helped grow the company season on season.

A key influence was Aghion's early life in Alexandria. 'I was inspired by what we wore in the sporting clubs in Egypt: lightweight dresses that were neither evening wear nor run-of-the-mill, but had that special something.' With her eye for fabrics, she realized that cotton poplin was supple, elegant and modern, so she used this as the basis for her early streamlined collections. She initially designed six dresses, and took them herself into boutiques – many of which knew her as a monied client – in order to sell them.

Chloé's early show venues – Left Bank cafés such as Café de Flore, Brasserie Lipp and Closerie des Lilas – nodded both to Aghion's own social life and the hang-outs and hobbies of the kinds of liberated, working women who these new, breezy clothes were catering to.

The 'smart and sophisticated' designs – when worn by models weaving in and out of the tables, while the press ate croissants and drank café au lait – acquired 'an off-beat look', the *New York Times* reported.

It is hard to convey just how radical this spirit seemed at the time, and just how refreshing the clothes of Paris's ready-to-wear champions appeared. 'Ready-to-wear aims high and goes far. Whether you live in Paris, Toulouse, Metz, Rennes or Marseille (or any other town in France) today, you can wear the fashions of 1960,' French *Elle* told its readers enthusiastically. 'Ready-to-wear designers are young, bold, full of talent,' they continued. 'Designed before the collections of the great couturiers, their [ready-to-wear] creations have a kind of (close) family resemblance in their use of shapes, colours, fabrics and style.'

Aghion's vision of women was individuals on the move, opinionated, cultured, *busy* (a 1958 story in *Elle* featured a model in a sleeveless, wide-neck Chloé dress, alongside a series of illustrations detailing exercises suitable for achieving taut arms). Aghion continued to be involved with Chloé for many years after its founding – though, ever restless, she didn't have her own office, or her own desk, but rather moved constantly from one person to the next, supervising all the steps of garment production. She also oversaw several successful creative directors who were brought in to design for the brand.

In 1985, the house was bought out by Dunhill Holdings, and Aghion retired the following year. Towards the end of her life, in her nineties, Aghion claimed her success had simply been down to teamwork and resilience: 'I was not a designer – I had taste,' she said. 'And I think really, what Chloe has become after all these years is because I worked like mad for it.' In 2013, shortly before her death, she said, 'I didn't want people to say, "Chloé – it's one of Gaby Aghion's whims." When I commit to something, I commit wholeheartedly. I was carried away as if in a tornado!'

After Aghion died in September 2014, aged 93, her son Philippe Aghion, an economics professor, said that his mother 'was already seeing [women] as they are nowadays, but this was in the '50s, where women were barely working... She had a view of women that was very different [from] the prevailing view at the time.' Aghion 'wanted women to be able to live and work in their dresses', he noted. Having succeeded in her aim, Aghion was awarded the Légion d'Honneur, France's highest honour, the year before her death.

The Studio
Late 1950s–Early 1960s

Gaby Aghion's skill in reading the tempo of youth extended to spotting new talent, and to involving the young and the opinionated within her world. She employed a steady stream of emerging designers at Chloé, including, during the earliest years of the house, Gérard Pipart, Maxime de la Falaise, Christiane Bailly and Tan Giudicelli, as well as Michèle Rosier and Graziella Fontana (see p.54) – a tradition that would cement the house as something of a factory of fashion's rising stars. Aghion herself later stated, 'I have a gift for recognizing talent in others.' These designers would produce their own sketches, then take their proposals to Aghion for sign-off. Together, their many ideas would culminate in dynamic, energetic-feeling collections. In 1968, *Contacts Franco-Italiens* referred to Chloé as having a 'veritable nursery of creators', name-checking Pipart, Rosier, Fontana and Bailly. 'Their success will be very rapid, thanks in part to the women's press, always on the lookout for new products. They will become the true "idols" of fashion in all its aspects,' the report added.

Gérard Pipart (1933–2013) was particularly prominent as a Chloé voice during these early years and was widely praised by the press as key to the strength of the collections. He joined Chloé from Patou in 1958, only a few years after completing his military service, and worked at the house for six years. 'He created collections which weren't just a copy of the couture from the previous season,' according to Claude Brouet, former editor-in-chief of *Elle* and *Marie-Claire*. *Elle* described him, in 1962, as part of a 'new wave' of couturiers, noting that he was also trained by Pierre Balmain and Jacques Fath. He went on to work at Nina Ricci for over thirty years.

Maxime de la Falaise (1922–2009) was another popular name in the press. Mother of the future Yves Saint Laurent muse Loulou de la Falaise, she herself had worked for Elsa Schiaparelli as a muse and a salesperson, and had been photographed as a model in the 1950s by various key photographers, including Cecil Beaton. Joining Chloé to assist with the autumn/winter 1960–1961 collection, she helped bring a dynamic female eye to early collections for the house. She championed the relaxed, the fluid and the playful, as encapsulated by the 'Embrun' dress (see p.38), created in collaboration with Aghion. The dress – a very modern design for its time, which Aghion would later regard as a Chloé landmark – sold out immediately.

Christiane Bailly (1924–2000) was, like Maxime de la Falaise, a former model. She was celebrated in the press for her modern minimalism and her eye for reworking details from industrial garments, whether military uniforms or raincoats, into new styles. She joined Chloé in 1961 and stayed at the house until 1972.

Tan Giudicelli, born in Indonesia in 1934 to a Vietnamese mother and Corsican father, worked at Chloé from 1964 to 1967, following stints at Christian Dior, where he worked as *première main*, and Nina Ricci. He left Chloé to design for the ready-to-wear label Mic Mac, in partnership with Brigitte Bardot's husband Gunter Sachs. In 1974, Giudicelli launched his eponymous *maison*. By the 1990s he was designing for Hermès' ready-to-wear line. Today, he is well known for his range of perfumes.

According to several reports, Gaby Aghion knew how to inspire her team, and was known to address them affectionately as 'my little kittens'. Early archive material often does not reveal who designed what, as the sketches were rarely signed by individual designers, but it is indisputable that each look was shaped by Aghion's particular spirit and her drive to create fashion that spoke to women with ambition and flair; women who were not coming apart under the weight of tradition or expectation, but who approached life with curiosity and confidence.

'ADORABLE', 'ADIEU', 'AMOUR', 'AMPHORE'

This presentation, held at Brasserie Lipp on Boulevard Saint-Germain, cemented various traditions within the house of Chloé, including the staging of fashion shows at famous Left Bank cafés, with models mingling among the tables in order to emphasize a mood of casual ease and help attendees imagine the real-life potential of the clothes. Such locations also offered a pointed and literal contrast to the Right Bank world of couture and tradition.

Another Chloé custom that debuted for A/W 1958–1959 was the titling of every garment with a name, each collection using the same letter (or consecutive letters) of the alphabet – in this case, 'A'.* These names formed a sort of dictionary, and created the sense that each garment had its own personality and character – a tradition that continued until the mid-1980s, with the alphabet restarting once all the letters had been used up: 'Adorable', 'Adieu', 'Amour', 'Amphore' (opposite, right), 'Aile', etc. The clothes on show reinforced the rejection of stuffiness that underpinned Chloé's growing reputation as a new force in French fashion.

Designed by a team including the young French talent Gérard Pipart, the collection was featured in various images in the fashion press, including a jovial story in French *Elle* titled 'Very, very cheerful little dresses', which featured a red 'two-piece dress', comprised of a skirt and a wool velours bolero: 'It's a simple, cheerful look which suits all ages', read the caption. Such praise from the press was becoming the norm for Chloé; while no catwalk pictures exist of Gaby Aghion's earliest collections from the early and mid-1950s, by the year of this show – 1958 – her pieces had already begun appearing with increasing frequency in glossy magazines, including *Vogue Paris*, where the brand was shot by William Klein and Guy Bourdin.

* For details and garment names, see p. 610.

'BABILLAGE', 'BAVARDAGE', 'BÉGUIN', 'BÊTISE'

The names of the items in Chloé's spring/
summer 1959 collection all began with a
'B': 'Babillage' (opposite, right), 'Bavardage',
'Béguin', 'Bêtise' (right), 'Bluet', 'Bon point'
(opposite, left), 'Bus', 'Bagdad', 'Banquise'.*
And yet, in response, the standout words
from critics were 'dynamic' and 'young'
(one critic even noted that the skirts were
'ultra-short'). 'And here is the fashion
of tomorrow', read a report in *La Patrie*,
which described the models as full of
'ideas' and 'charm'.

The new look was 'supple, semi-fit dresses
with wide sleeves, pleats', according to a
Women's Wear Daily headline. 'Dresses are
cut at normal waist, slightly dipping at back
in some models,' read the report. 'Collars
are short and narrow and do not accompany
entirely round necklines. Wide sleeves stop
above elbow.' Also on show were pleated skirts
in wool and tweed, shirt dresses in silk or
cotton poplin, and neat, straight jackets worn
over slim dresses or skirts. Details included
grosgrain ribbon tied in bows and attached
to the front of dresses, sometimes in rows of
two or three contrasting colours. There were
also, said *WWD*, breastplate-style shirt-fronts
'of stiff starched white cotton attached to
matching Dutch collars' on wool dresses.
These chest-plates 'have a shield appearance
with darts shaping breasts', the report added.

The collection was labelled fresh, relevant,
youthful by critics. *La Nouvelle République
du Centre Ouest* ran a report titled, 'Dresses
for any time of the day, "ready to be worn"',
thus highlighting their suitability for modern
women who no longer wished to change outfits
several times a day. *France-Soir* heralded the
'Bêtise' dress 'the emblematic dress of
spring 1959'.

* *For details and garment names, see p. 610.*

'CAMÉLÉON', 'CHARMEUSE', 'CHASSE', 'CHASSEUR'

The response to the autumn/winter 1959–1960 show, held again at Brasserie Lipp (see p.30), highlights how far excitement for Gaby Aghion's Chloé had spread. In America, the *New York Herald Tribune* told its readers that 'Chloé, one of the youthful ready-to-wear manufacturers, places all the avant-garde ideas within reach of young sophisticates', praising the fact that Aghion's 'fabrics are from all the top French fabrics manufacturers'. 'Tailored suits under coats or coat and dress ensembles call the tune for chic fall daytime wear', the *Tribune* noted of the collection.

Held in the morning – or 'at the time of "café-crème"', as *France-Soir* put it – the show included long tweed and velvet jackets, coats with wide collars, and woolen dresses with belts that subtly marked, rather than clinched, the waist. The presentation was titled 'C', and names of pieces included 'Caméléon', 'Charmeuse', 'Chasse', 'Chasseur', 'Chrysalide' and 'Clavecin'.* There was plenty of whimsy in the designs, too: *France-Soir* referred to frills 'reminiscent of chocolate wrappers' and 'large sweetheart necklines', while *WWD* drew attention to tiered skirts with 'bouffant flounces'.

That said, the story was not all lightness and femininity. The collection featured many references to military clothing and, as with the shirt-fronts of last season (see p.32), various pieces borrowed classic menswear details. The menswear-style 'Caïd' suit (opposite, left), in particular, was praised by critics for its affirmation of the new modern woman: one who embraces life on the go, and who wears make-up not to look younger but only to accentuate her features; 'the super woman', as some writers called her.

A piece on Chloé's suiting in *Vogue Paris* directed its readers to admire the loose, unsecured belts, which allowed the garment to move freely around the body. They also praised the way the jacket was cropped in line with the bottom of the arms, and the chic epaulettes, which offered a clever play on army style. Such looks marked the beginning of what would go on to become a constant at Chloé – the use of menswear vocabulary in order to create a style that is both unconventionally elegant and enjoyable to wear.

* *For details and garment names, see p.610.*

'DANGER', 'DOMINO', 'DIFFICILE', 'DARLING'

Once again (see p. 34), Chloé's show took place at Brasserie Lipp, at 9.45am (to time with 'petit déjeuner', according to the invitations). Models walked on the restaurant's signature black and white floor tiles in suits and dresses with similarly confident lines and bold details, from oversized belts to frilled cuffs. Names were equally as bold: 'Danger', 'Domino', 'Difficile', 'Darling', 'Débutante', 'Discipline', 'Devoir' (opposite, top left), 'Dictée', 'Dicton', 'Diligence', 'Dolmen', 'Don Juan'.*

'Chloé specializes in the little Parisian dress that is "easy-to-wear" in navy wool with a large white shirt-front,' said *France-Soir*, 'and in dresses whose very narrow sheath line is cut by an enormous "carpenter"-style belt' – 'a very charming idea for going out at night', the report said, especially if paired with 'a white organdy jacket that immediately gives it a festive air'. *Elle*, noting voluminous blousing bodices and puffed skirts, interpreted 'un petit air de harem'.

WWD reported that 'young designer Gérard Pipart gives his personal touch with broader and padded shoulders on suit jackets, extra wide belts on sheaths and subtle combination of colors... Among suits attracting attention is "Doute" in pale pink wool with curved out seams and pale blue tusah tucked-in blouse. "Dada" in camel-color broadcloth has double-stitched seams along sleeves and seaming under bustline. Irish hand-woven tweed was chosen in violet and white for a classical suit with violet shantung tucked-in blouse.'

The critic Anne Germain observed that 'romantic ruffled collars' and 'starched shirt-fronts' were given 'pride of place', adding that 'dresses are flimsy, sheath-like'. Germain noted enthusiastically that, 'Each season, the Chloé collection is young, dynamic, and teeming with fresh ideas.'

* For details and garment names, see p. 610.

'ENSEMBLE', 'ÉMANCIPÉE', 'ÉLÉGANTE', 'EMBRUN'

The Chloé autumn/winter 1960–1961 show was held at the Closerie des Lilas, 'a famous literary café of the Nineteen Hundreds, which is decorated in that period', according to a *New York Times* feature focused on Gérard Pipart, one of a series of bright stars contributing to Gaby Aghion's Chloé. The article noted: 'So successful are the clothes from Chloé that they hang side by side with models from Dior and Balenciaga in the closets of many an elegant Parisienne.' Aghion and her husband's artistic milieu had 'given the designs of Chloé, although very smart and sophisticated, an off-beat Left-Bank look', the article said. 'Off-beat also are her press showings, which she always gives in Left Bank cafes.'

Of the show at Closerie des Lilas, the reporter described how 'the press sits around at tables drinking café au lait and munching croissants while the models weave in and out of the tables'. The paper also noted the strength of Aghion's eclectic team of contributing design talent, commenting that '[a]dding to the allure of this unusual house is the co-designer to M. Pipart – Maxi[m]e de la Falaise, daughter of a celebrated English portraitist and wife of a French marquis [in fact, a Count]'.

One star of the collection was the 'Embrun' dress, an invention of de la Falaise and Aghion – an innovatively comfortable twist on a shirt dress, which combined the masculine (stiff collars and cuffs, lined with men's tie fabric) with the feminine (supple jersey), as was becoming a Chloé signature (see also p.44). 'It was very avant-garde to design a dress like that, almost like a T-shirt. Women would fight over it,' Aghion said later. 'This dress was tremendously successful because it says, "I am carefree."'

WWD were impressed with the range of the collection, noting that it 'met with great success both with press and buyers'. According to their report, the show featured a '[g]reat variety of dresses for day and party wear [that] is particularly welcome especially since these types have been weak in most collections shown to date... Romantic dresses in black taffeta with lace frills around neckline or hem are becoming.'*

'FRAMBOISE', 'FANTAISIE', 'FONDANT', 'FLOU-FLOU'

Writing in the *New York Herald Tribune* in December 1960, Lucie Noël equated Chloé with teen spirit, noting that the house 'expresses the new wave with charm and care'. Indeed, the spring/summer 1961 show, held at the Closerie des Lilas, featured a range of items, including dresses in bonbon hues with flippy skirts and ruffled sleeves, which suggested joy, freedom and youth. Names mimicked the mood of frivolity and fun, including the French words for raspberry, fantasy and candy: 'Framboise', 'Fantaisie', 'Fondant', alongside 'Falaise', 'Fantasio' (opposite, left), 'Farah', 'Faune', 'Faust', 'Favori', 'First', 'Flo', 'Flon-flon', 'Flou-flou', 'Fragile', 'France', 'Friandise', 'Fronde' and 'Fuschia' [*sic*].* The *Penticton Herald* explained how Chloé offered the ideal 'youthful daytime dress for both town and travel'. And yet, the *Daily News* in New York were impressed with the technical prowess of Chloé's designers and makers, referencing 'amusing, eye-deceiving effects with double layers of summery materials' (see right). These layers offered a transformative effect: the outer layer could be worn for dressiness or omitted for a simpler look.

The 'Flou-flou' shirt dress (opposite, right), knee-length with frills at the collar and cuffs, later appeared in *Vogue Paris*, in a story shot by William Klein titled 'Dresses in Motion'. The caption claimed that such summery dresses, in white or pastel tones, had 'dethroned' the eternal little black dress.

Indeed, the 'Flou-flou' dress – fluid and simple, and cut with a wrap-over top – was hugely successful and became a Chloé classic. 'Le Flou' is still a house signature, visible in the many garments Chloé has offered over the years which allow freedom of movement: adaptable day-to-night solutions for busy women who don't have time to go home to change.

* For details and garment names, see p. 610.

'GALA', 'GAZELLE', 'HAPPY', 'HAUTBOIS'

The autumn/winter 1961–1962 collection,[*] featuring various dresses cut with low backs, was, like the season before (see p.42), youthful and sensual. The 'Gala', one such gown, came decorated with graphic embroidery and finished with a dark bow at the base of the spine. Another sleeveless dress from the collection, this one form-fitting in jersey sable with a built-in scarf at the collar, was featured in an *Elle* story on 'Little Dresses', and described as ideal for those after a look that was 'discreet, secretive and dangerous'.

A key idea this season was the cape (see opposite, left): Scottish-style and worn with a gilet, it nodded to men's caped overcoats of the 19th century. The cape – another example of a 'Flou' garment (see p.42) – also became a Chloé signature over the decades.

Layering was fast becoming another important aspect of Chloé's style vocabulary. Looks such as that shown opposite, top right – encompassing a sleeveless sheath dress, in black shantung, worn over a black muslin blouse with white polka dots and a 'lavallière' (pussy-bow) tie – allowed for a play between patterns, transparencies and styles of fabric. For every deliberate mis-match or contrast, such as the collar and cuffs on an 'Embrun'-inspired dress (see right and p.38), there were moments of harmony within the layering: for example, striped blouses coordinated with the pattern used on the linings of suits, including the insides of pockets (opposite, bottom right).

The looks on the opposite page were modelled by Nicole de Lamargé, who was much photographed by *Elle* magazine, and seemed to embody the youthful spirit of ready-to-wear.

'IMAGE', 'INFANTE', 'IÉNA', 'INGRES'

This show, held at the Hôtel du Palais d'Orsay, was titled 'I' – 'Image', 'Infante', 'Intéressant', 'Ingres' were just a handful of the garment names.* *WWD* described the look of the season as 'waistlines belted ... figures revealed ... ruffled softeners'. Indeed, at Chloé some pieces came with frills and satin ribbons appliquéd onto the bottom of the skirt, while many of the designs played with opacity and transparency, creating unique effects with shine, light and volume.

Another key story was the form-fitting or skin-baring, including backless sheath dresses, which felt both sensual and, for the time, unexpected. The dresses were inspired by Gaby Aghion's distaste for the pushed-up décolletage; she preferred cuts with a more subtle, surprising approach to unveiling and seduction. Even today, the naked back is a recurring motif in the Chloé wardrobe, beloved by generations of women for its effortless glamour and nonchalant desirability.

In February 1962, a piece in the *New York Times* told readers that 'French ready-to-wear has easy-going lines'. The story featured a Chloé coat, in basket-weave tweed with a quilted silk collar, which, according to the caption, had a 'relaxed air'. These French imports with their 'semi-fitted easy lines' were, the newspaper explained, the 'star attractions' at Macy's Little Shop.

* For details and garment names, see p. 610.

'JUDITH', 'KLEBER' 'JUS', 'JAPON'

The garment names in the autumn/winter 1962–1963 collection began with 'J' and 'K'. According to a favourable review in *Le Monde*, the presentation was 'very pretty ... but much more "couture" than ready to wear'. It was notable for the plethora of long gowns, including slimline chiffon options with pleated skirts, crepe dresses with high waistlines, and dramatic layered skirts worn with shirts. One such ensemble, a ruffled purple skirt with a light pink shirt, was later pictured in *Elle* magazine against a desert backdrop, complete with camels and woven rugs. The headlines spoke of the scent of mint mixing with myrrh as adventurous women walk the sand, following the stars, clad in dresses with 'gold in their pleats'. The look (shown opposite) represents a signature example of Chloé's laidback chic, the shirt flowing over the skin, with ball-shaped buttons adding to a sense of uniqueness and intrigue.

Le Monde's coverage noted various other elegant propositions: neat overcoats with shawl collars, frock coats, and 'cosy coats with fur balaclavas or hoods'. Among many 'big successes' were 'transparent "shoulder wraps" or small scarves fringed with pearls', ideal for layering over some of the more provocative necklines – a design which reappeared across later Chloé collections (see p.52).

WWD spotted Gérard Pipart's attention to the 'fitted midriff' and were keen to draw readers' attention to the fact that the look of the season was 'longer', rendering the word in bold in their report. Overall, the journal felt the collection indicated 'a quieter and less colorful mood'. Their final analysis was concise: 'subdued with some extreme points'.*

* *For details, see p.610.*

'LEISURE', 'LIBERTINE', 'LIBRE', 'LUXE'

On viewing the S/S 1963 collection,*
the Flemish paper *Libelle* referred to
an 'irresistible Europeanized Oriental air'.
Similarly, the *Journal du Pas-de-Calais*
noticed the house's heavy use of natural silk,
which they felt had a 'Hindu colonial style'.
The report also showed the shift in hierarchy
occurring within French fashion, with
ready-to-wear increasingly staking a claim
as the place for innovation: 'Paris under a grey
sky is already thinking of summer. Before the
haute couture collections are released, it is
ready-to-wear that sets the tone.'

Garment names in this collection included
'Leisure', 'Libertine', 'Libre', 'Lilliput', 'Lilium'
(opposite, right), 'Lisbeth', 'Lolita', 'Long',
'Lucerne' and 'Luxe'. Many pieces came
teamed with large hats, or were covered
with delicate prints. *L'Est Éclair* were
particularly taken with 'Luxe', a neat evening
suit, commenting that the cut 'irresistibly
evokes Chanel' (an irony, given that soon
the Chloé design team would be joined by
the designer Karl Lagerfeld, who would,
some twenty years later, leave the house for
an infamous run as the mastermind of Chanel).

Like the other press, *Le Méridional Marseille*
noted nods to the East, praising a suit
rendered in natural Tussar-style silk
('ninghai', as they called it), 'with a long, fitted
jacket, worn with a hat of the same fabric'.
Another report in *Collections* commented
that 'the shirt dresses are numerous and
treated in a hundred different ways', cut both
from shantung and fibranne. Of the ensemble
shown opposite left, *Jardin des Modes* wrote:
'For those who like to live dangerously, take
risks and leave a big impression, here's an
evening dress in natural shantung, with
slightly sporty tailoring... It can be happily
and triumphantly worn with or without its
jacket. It's a mark-making dress: she who
wears it, therefore, must be remarkable
in every way.'

According to *Le Télégramme*, this was
an 'avant-garde collection', with 'a racy
silhouette'. *Racing* quipped that the house
of Chloé had 'created more than two hundred
lovely models to spoil Parisians with'.

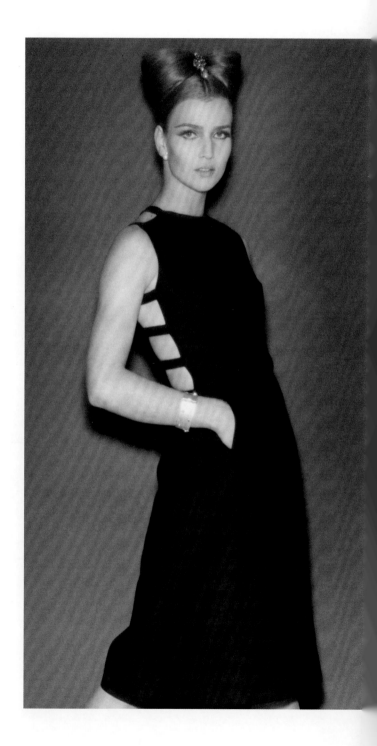

For details and garment names, see p. 610.

'MAINTENANT', 'MONZA', 'MISTRAL', 'MANDRIN'

'Maintenant', meaning 'now', was one of the garment names within this collection – a fitting title, given Chloé's association with the contemporary, the young, the new. Held at Brasserie Lipp, a regular venue for Chloé, this show also featured looks titled 'Monza', 'Mistral', 'Mandrin', 'Mathilde', 'Mildred', 'Monsieur', 'Mongol', 'Mutin' and 'Myrtille'.*

A key story was 'jewel-ornamentation', the brainchild of designer Christiane Bailly, who made innovative use of ring chainmail and rhinestones on straps and borders. One particularly eye-catching look comprised a sheath dress with straps adorned with rows of beads that fell into a cascade of long necklaces over the bust and shoulders.

Also important were easy, supple suits rendered in light and fluid material – a key interest for Gaby Aghion. Indeed, in 2017, Tan Giudicelli, then one of the designers in the Chloé studio, would recall Aghion demanding crepe suits, 'at a moment when all the suits were stiff'. 'We worked in suppleness, not stiffness like couturiers', Giudicelli noted. Such looks proved popular in the press, appearing in numerous editorials in titles such as *Vogue Paris*, where David Bailey, for August 1963, captured pieces from this collection for a story on matching coats and dresses. 'Still seductive, but more youthful, more dynamic, more daring', read the accompanying headline.

* For details and garment names, see p. 610.

The Studio
The Mid-1960s–Early 1970s

Gaby Aghion's Chloé was known, in its early days, for employing a stable of designers who worked together as a team. Indeed, it was Aghion's eye for spotting youthful talent that contributed to the company's early success and – although she likely could not have predicted it – the house's reputation thereafter, as exemplified by the later appointments of then up-and-comers like Martine Sitbon, Stella McCartney and Phoebe Philo. Indeed, in 2018, the *New York Times* commented, 'Chloé has mostly been a house where young designers, like Peter O'Brien, Guy Paulin and Martine Sitbon, were allowed to flourish on their way to becoming stars.'

In 1964, the press noted that Aghion had four young talents on the go: Christiane Bailly and Tan Giudicelli, who had worked at the house for a while (see pp. 28–9), and two new, female voices, Michèle Rosier and Graziella Fontana. They both joined the Chloé team for the spring/summer 1964 collection, one season ahead of another dynamic new voice, Karl Lagerfeld (see also p. 110).

Michèle Rosier (1930–2017) was a former journalist who turned to design in the late 1950s, founding her sportswear line V de V (Vêtements de Vacances) before joining Chloé. She worked at the house on three collections (S/S 1964, A/W 1964–1965 and S/S 1965). Rosier was fashion royalty: her grandmother was Alice Raudnitz, the owner of one of the biggest couture houses of the Belle Époque, and her mother was Hélène Gordon-Lazareff, founder of *Elle* magazine. According to the *International Herald Tribune*, Rosier was 'doing for prêt-à-porter what Courrèges did for Haute Couture', by creating new styles of clothing, 'without reference, without nostalgia'. 'The very movements of women have changed, they are larger than before,' Rosier told the press. 'It's a way of life, a way of being. We need, then, clothes that move.' After leaving Chloé, she went on to have a successful career as a film director.

Graziella Fontana worked for a number of manufacturers and design houses in France, Britain and her native Italy during the 1960s and early 1970s. In Britain, she was particularly associated with the mod scene, and became known for her sharply tailored coats and suits. As well as designing for Chloé, she worked for the Italian fashion house Max Mara, the Scottish knitwear brand Lyle & Scott, and the English designer Judith Hornby (her dress and hot pants look for Hornby, in check Liberty cotton, was selected as the Dress of the Year for 1971). Fontana left Chloé in 1972.

The Chloé Archive reveals that various eventual fashion greats began
their journeys with the house, including Paco Rabanne, who provided
freelance embroideries and embellishments for Chloé in the mid-1960s,
before he started his own label. Aghion later explained, 'I am very
fond of designers and I admire them. I never thought I was a designer.'
As she wrote in 2013: 'I respected [them]... I didn't want to crush their
personalities. When we were working on the collections, when they
would present these pieces of paper that were to become designs,
I knew there was soul in those drawings. One had to be delicate.'

Just ahead of the A/W 1964–1965 show, another young talent was added
to the Chloé roster: the German designer Karl Lagerfeld, who was quickly
singled out by critics as a star. Together with his peers, he offered new
takes on contemporary womenswear that would help define the style
and reputation both of Chloé and of youthful Parisian fashion.

'OPIUM', 'OTTOMANE', 'PETROUCHKA', 'PÉTUNIA'

By A/W 1964–1965, the fashion press was
already taking note of a new designer within
the Chloé team – a young German named Karl
Lagerfeld, who had cut his teeth at Jean Patou
and Balmain before arriving at Gaby Aghion's
studio. Writing on this show, *Le Figaro* noted
that Lagerfeld, alongside Michèle Rosier and
Graziella Fontana, had developed a 'brilliant'
collection, full of 'diversity' and '"couture"
details'.*

Held once again at Brasserie Lipp, this
presentation – of which sadly no photographs
exist (there are no known images either of the
S/S 1964 collection) – took 'O' and 'P' as the
starting letters of its garment names. These
were expectantly playful and flamboyant,
and included 'Opium', 'Ottomane', 'Paméla',
'Parade', 'Patchwork', 'Play Boy', 'Petit Prince',
'Petrouchka', 'Pétunia', 'Pinocchio', 'Piquant',
'Popof', 'Porsche', 'Pouchkine', 'Prestige',
'Promenade' and 'Pyromane'.

Les Nouvelles de Paris would interpret a mood
that was to become a Lagerfeld signature –
a taste for looking back, to the retro glamour
of the 1930s. The publication wrote that the
influence of these years gave the models a
languid silhouette that recalled the '"beauties"
of Modigliani'.

L'Indépendant Franc-Parleur would notice yet
another developing classic – the Chloé blouse.
The report praised a 'very varied and classy
collection', which was 'at the forefront of
fashion with its new ideas, its rigour in sporty
lines, and its discreet refinement particularly
reserved for blouses'.

Michèle Rosier's evening look (see right) also
attracted attention. The silver lace raglan coat
was worn over a long-sleeved black silk satin
organdy sheath dress. Of the 'chromatic
Cellophane' effect, *Elle* noted: 'The dazzle
of meteors. Flashing in the night.'

The collection was widely photographed,
appearing in various international editions of
Vogue, shot by the likes of Helmut Newton and
Marc Hispard (who captured the bell-sleeved
lace dress shown opposite, right, for *Vogue
Paris*). In September of 1964, the *New York
Times* ran a story celebrating a 'New Wave
in French Design', with a 'herb green' jersey
dress by Chloé used as one of the illustrations:
'A new breed of designer, young, unpompous
and usually uncommitted to a single house,
is revolutionizing France's fashion industry
with ebullient ready-made clothes', wrote
the reporter Patricia Peterson.

* For details, see p. 610.

'RAPALLO', 'RAQUETTE', 'SABLE', 'SALADE'

For S/S 1965, Chloé garments came titled with the letter 'R': 'Rapallo', 'Raquette', 'Riquet', 'Rivoli'. 'Radar', the long gown with striped detailing shown to the right, was a particular hit from the collection; it appeared in an editorial for *Jardin des Modes*, photographed by René Falke, which showed two glamorous women, and a pet goat, wandering amid Roman ruins, the long architectural columns echoing the lithe silhouettes of the dresses. The headline read: 'Bright Nights'.

For A/W 1965–1966, the mood at Chloé was sensual: dresses were cut close to the body, and Lagerfeld had begun the 'trompe-l'œil games', to quote a review in *L'Officiel du Prêt à Porter*, that would become his signature over the coming decades at the house. *Collections* praised the way the show managed to combine nods to the 1930s with modern, 'avant-garde' elements. A bright yellow Rhodia crepe jumpsuit (opposite) proved to be an original look for evening. As *Le Populaire du Centre* noted, 'It simultaneously suggests a sari and a pair of trousers: the bottom of the tunic is tightened at the ankles. Fun detail: the bodice is embellished with big white plastic sequins.' The letter this season was 'S', and name choices showed the usual taste for puns and quips: 'Sable', 'Salade', 'Salomé', 'Saint-Germain', 'School', 'S.N.C.F', 'Sortie', 'Sportive', 'Spot', 'Sprint', 'Stéréo', 'Studio' and 'Sweepstake'.*

'TERTULIA', 'VALENTIN', 'WEDGWOOD'

By 1966, just two years after joining the house, Karl Lagerfeld was already winning acclaim for the items that would eventually become his signatures at Chloé: eye-catching, graphic, patterned dresses and elegant, fluid blouses. For S/S 1966 (see opposite), he was still working alongside Graziella Fontana, and the designers showed, according to a report in the *Sunday Bulletin in Philadelphia*, 'doll-like camisole dresses, Pop art baby shoes designed by Charles Jourdan [Lagerfeld, in fact, designed the shoes for the French shoe company], and sleeveless surah tunics with low-slung black patent cowboy belts'. Garment names began with a 'T': 'Temps Modernes', 'Tate-Gallery', 'Tonic', 'Tiffany'.*

In the UK, *The Sunday Times* said that Chloé offered 'immaculate clothes in beautiful fabrics', adding that, for Spring, there were 'party dresses ... handpainted with blue and red mystic symbols: triangles, crescents, dots and stripes (it looks rather as though Merlin had been doodling on the dresses with a Japanese Pentel pen)'. The dresses, which seem to encapsulate the experimental spirit of the Sixties' imagination, were also a hit with photographers, appearing across various editorials, usually under the credit 'Karl Lagerfeld for Chloé'. Two short versions of 'Tertulia' (see opposite) appeared in *Elle* on models with tanned limbs and swinging hair, shot by Louis Faurer, while the long-line version shown opposite was shot for *Vogue Paris* by Norman Parkinson, with the model surrounded by a haze of paper Mexican flowers: a vision of positivity and freedom.

Critics agreed that, in terms of setting the template for how stylish young women should dress, Chloé was the show to watch. The *New York Daily News* said, 'The knack of knowing which simple ideas will dictate Paris chic next Spring depends on watching closely a handful of pace-setting innovators. The top ready-to-wear house of Chloé offers a rich crop of clues.'

For A/W 1966–1967 (see right) the house continued to embrace the punchy and the groovy, with looks including 'Valentin', 'Vapeur', 'Vendetta', 'Vermeil', 'Virulente', 'Wedgwood', 'Whipcord' and 'Whisky'. *Le Figaro* told its readers that while most of the clothes on show were serious propositions, there were three 'unwearable' mini-skirts, and some evening looks that saw models wrapped in silver and gold foil. And yet, they concluded that the collection was, overall, 'thought out, balanced and researched, which is not commonplace'.

* For details and garment names, see p. 611.

'ACACIA', 'AFRIQUE', 'BAGDAD', 'BANG'

The mood and colours of Chloé's S/S 1967 show encapsulated the spirit of the 1960s – a touch hippie, a touch spacey, a tribute to innovation, freedom and fun. The look was 'cheerful, sassy', with 'a lot of personality', according to *Silhouettes*. From S/S 1966, Karl Lagerfeld had experimented with painting on silk (notably with 'Tertulia', see p. 60). After an initial collaboration with Le Besnerais, he teamed up with Nicole Lefort (whose Parisian atelier worked exclusively for Chloé) until 1977, enjoying the spontaneity of the artisanal technique, and the possibility of creating large motifs with diverse patterns and ideas (see right; this dress was notably photographed by Helmut Newton for British *Vogue*, as well as by Henry Clarke for *Vogue Paris*). A particular source of inspiration was the work of artist Aubrey Beardsley: one Chloé sketch was explicitly titled 'Aubrey', and these looks were photographed by David Montgomery over four pages in British *Vogue*.

Chloé's signature blouses were a hit that year. In August 1967, British *Vogue* referred to them as the 'most flattering evening blouses. Marvellously elegant with ruffles, bows and pleats.' They noted that, when worn with 'high, white cummerbunds and straight silk trousers, they are the essence of the dandy'.

By S/S 1967, Chloé, once a newbie on the Paris scene, had worked its way through the alphabet, so the collection went back to the beginning, with names including 'Acacia', 'Afrique', 'Afternoon', 'Antibes', 'Arabella', 'Au bal', 'Aurélien', 'Austin' and 'Automatique'.

For A/W 1967–1968 (see opposite), Lagerfeld's bold, painted dresses remained the talk of the fashion pack. *Toulouse Informations* noted 'shiny, scintillating or hand-painted dresses, black or white, one deliciously romantic, the next stylized by a reproduction of Toulouse-Lautrec'. The furs, they added, were 'lovely, very stylish, very young'. *La Dépêche du Midi* agreed that Chloé was succeeding at the 'fur game': 'to "capitalize" on this new activity, the famous ready-to-wear brand presents coats that can be worn from morning to night, always practical, warm, elegant'.

L'Orient mentioned shirt dresses, and – due to patch pockets and buttoning – the 'presence here and there of "military" fashion, so boldly launched by Yves Saint Laurent'.

'B' was the letter of the season for A/W: 'Bagdad', 'Bang', 'Barbarella', 'Baromètre', 'Big Ben', 'Bermuda', 'Bing', 'Blabla', 'Box-office', 'Brooklyn', 'Bugatti'.*

For details and garment names, see p. 611.

'CAMELOT', 'CASCADE', 'DANAÉ', 'DIVA'

Chloé had always catered to the young, the modern; those excited for change and keen to shrug off stuffy norms or formality. And by now, the house's catwalk shows were staged against a dynamic backdrop of youthful rebellion, with widespread student protests across France and Europe, and an air of upheaval and liberation: the pill, feminism, sexual experimentation, LSD. Writing on the S/S 1968 show, *Drapery & Fashion Weekly* noted how, in response to changing social moods, 'Some high-style houses such as Chloé seem to have shortened their hemlines at the last moment.'

For S/S 1968, the title letter was 'C'. Garment names included 'Camelot', 'Cascade', 'Caviar', 'Coco', 'Condé', 'Continental' and 'Couture'. The printed white silk dresses, such as 'Catherine' and 'Calcomanie', featured heavily in editorials. Indeed, this whole collection was widely photographed, appearing in various international editions of *Vogue*, shot by buzzy photographers like David Bailey, Jeanloup Sieff and André Carrara on models including Veruschka, Marisa Berenson, Anna Karina and the painter Comtesse Jean de Rohan-Chabot (opposite).

For A/W 1968–1969 (see right), *La Dépêche Mode* congratulated Karl Lagerfeld and Graziella Fontana on producing a 'very complete' collection – full of dresses, suits and coats. The show was obviously inspired by the 1930s, the report noted, something that, by now, had become a Lagerfeld signature. *La Lanterne* was struck by the daring sensuality of the designs: 'A deceptive innocence. A seemingly demure dress, but the sumptuous "cover" of a navy blue voile embroidered with silver Lurex leaves the shoulders and arms largely visible.' The letter of the season was 'D': 'Danaé', 'Dauphin', 'Débat', 'Deborah', 'Delphine', 'Derby', 'Détail', 'Dictée', 'Douvres', 'Dragon', 'Druse', 'Dunes', and – appropriately, given the sense of autonomy, panache and confidence that surrounded Lagerfeld's ideal Chloé woman – 'Diva'.*

* For details, see p. 611.

'ÉVOLUTION', 'ÉGALITÉ', 'FASCINATION', 'FABERGÉ'

1969 was the year of Woodstock: in August, over 400,000 music fans, mostly youths, headed to Bethel, New York, to dance, revel and feel free. By now, Chloé collections were known for capturing a spirit of youthful revelry and freedom, which Lagerfeld cleverly combined with nods to the aesthetics of the past. For S/S 1969, the mood was sensuality and ease (see right). 'Karl Lagerfeld at Chloé likes silk jersey. He sees it as "a soft, supple skin that moves on the body" and does it in a collection of classical Greek tunics. In brown silk jersey, he takes the halter-neck, plunges it deeply ... then blouses it', wrote *WWD*. Several dresses from this collection – including one embellished with a sparkling silver serpent (the garment was humorously titled 'Eve') – were shot for *Vogue* by Guy Bourdin. The season's names, fittingly, included 'Évolution', 'Égalité', 'Entertainer', 'Été', 'Éclat', 'Étoile', 'Extase' and 'Effervescente'.

For A/W 1969–1970, the historical references were more contemporary: 'Karl Lagerfeld of Paris loves the spirit of art deco', noted *Harper's Bazaar*. 'From his collection for Chloé, silk crepe pajamas ... with geometric patterns that look super as you move.' Lagerfeld's motifs (see opposite) were strongly inspired by Paul Poiret's dresses of the 1910s, and Lagerfeld was even photographed for *Vogue Paris* alongside Poiret's great-niece, who was clad in a swirling design. Among the A/W season's names were 'Fascination', 'Fabergé', 'Facettes', 'Favorite', 'Fétiche', 'Folie', 'Fraternité', 'For Night' and 'Forever'.*

* For details and garment names, see p. 611.

'GRAPHISME', 'HARMONIE', 'INTRIGUE', 'JUNON', 'KANGOUROU'

By 1970, with the spirit of Woodstock and bohemia still in the air (see p.66), the Chloé signature of a long, patterned dress had come to epitomize youthful, unstuffy, ready-to-wear fashion. Lagerfeld's work complemented the zeitgeist – Peter Blake, Pop Art, the hippie freedom of festivals. And yet, he also found a way of looking backwards that felt exciting. 'Art Deco never had a more faithful fan than Karl Lagerfeld', wrote *WWD* of the spring/ summer 1970 collection. 'Karl's prints are geometric, but that's about the only hard line he takes at Chloé this summer. Everything moves and the head, shoulders and waist are Karl's stopping points... Lengths go from mini-mini to the floor but some of Karl's best looks are ankle length.'

The report also praised the details: 'He swathes heads in drifts of veiling or binds them with ring-looped scarfs... He uses fringed shawls throughout the collection and they look newest when he does them in hand-painted silks in patterns that look like 20s Cartier cigaret [*sic*] cases.' In her autobiography, the former *Vogue* stylist Grace Coddington, who regularly shot Chloé in her stories, styling Lagerfeld's Deco motifs with brightly coloured make-up and face-paint, recalls the cult nature of Lagerfeld's scarves, and the delight of attending early 1970s Chloé shows. Backstage, 'he would pick out one of the must-have accessories for the next season and insist you wear it straightaway, six months before it was available'. One such gift was a slinky lamé scarf, which became the focus of 'everlasting envy' among friends and colleagues. 'It epitomised the Art Deco-mad seventies', she wrote.

Both the S/S 1970 (see right) and the similarly pattern-heavy A/W 1970–1971 (see opposite) collections* were featured widely in the press, shot by Helmut Newton, Roland Bianchini, and Guy Bourdin, who captured Lagerfeld's autumn/winter astrology-themed dresses, hand-painted with stars and moons, for *Vogue Paris*. A Lagerfeld for Chloé scarf appeared in a feature on turbans in *Jardin des Modes*, in which two white models showed off the trend for patterned scarves, under the headline 'The new summer sultans'. 'Don't say, a turban, yes, but not on me', read the caption, which encouraged readers to create their own take on the look, with fabric and draping, and 'an idea'.

* For details and garment names, see p.611.

'LINÉAIRE', 'LABYRINTHE', 'LIBERTÉ', 'LAHORE'

Chloé's spring/summer 1971 collection continued to show off Lagerfeld's flair for patterns and playful trompe l'œil.* Stripes and checks were used heavily, alongside swirling spirals, florals, and even amusing illustrations of cats, crossword puzzles and limbs. Lagerfeld also continued to play with length, making midi and maxi silhouettes the key look. '[H]e gives "long" a whole new dimension,' said *WWD*. 'The word Karl keeps using over and over again to describe the collection is "flagada" ... which means just what it sounds like ... light-hearted relaxed things on the move. And it's the perfect description for his layering.' Emerging from his 'flou' technique (see also p.42) came fluid ensembles of silk crepe wrap skirts and semi-circular capes.

Photographers embraced the trippy, carefree nature of the designs, shooting the dresses in various hippie-ish or vaguely futuristic settings. One editorial in *L'Officiel*, shot by Patrick Bertrand, accentuated the bohemian, bold spirit of the collection, showing a model posing at night amid a backdrop of cacti, wearing 'a shirt in Taco[sa] silk muslin, hand-painted especially for Chloé [also pictured opposite, top right], and crêpe de Chine bloomers, also painted. The shirt is completely transparent, with a low-cut back meaning a bra is not an option.' The caption continued: 'If you're a fan of Pop Art and you don't mind being noticed, don't think twice about wearing this head-turning look.'

The collection also highlighted Lagerfeld's penchant for the 1940s. '[I]t was all there, from the curled hair and heavily madeup faces, right down to the platform shoes with five-inch heels,' said *WWD*. 'He even had Donna Jordan, Andy Warhol's latest discovery, modelling some of the clothes – and she looked like she stepped right out of a Betty Grable movie in those wide-leg shorts and soft print blouses.' Indeed, the show preceded Yves Saint Laurent's famous '40s-themed 'Liberation' collection by a few months. 'Keep your eye on what Karl Lagerfeld designs for Chloé – often it becomes world-wide fashion shortly thereafter', wrote US *Vogue* that year.

While the American press had been excited by Parisian ready-to-wear since the mid-1960s, it was in the early 1970s that the fashion buyers really started to take note: during these years, Neiman Marcus, Charles Gallay and Bonwit Teller all bought Chloé.

* For details and garment names, see p.611.

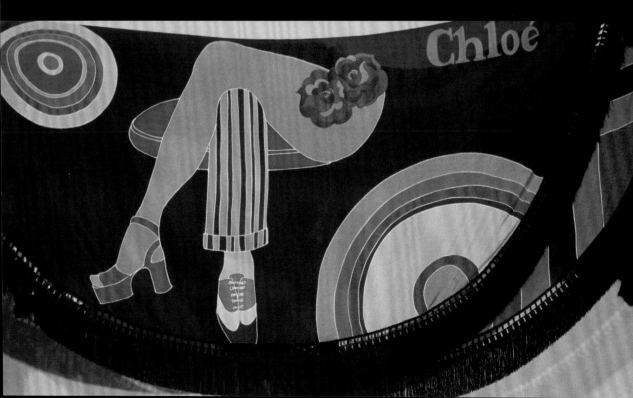

'MAJOR', 'MÉTÉORE',
'MAJESTIC', 'MODERNE'

Karl Lagerfeld's taste for the theatrical underpinned the autumn/winter 1971–1972 collection, which not only featured graphic motifs but also mini-skirts with marabou trims, sheer skirts, embellished bralettes, and Tintin-red androgynous wigs that gave models the air of being in costume (see p.74, left). Fittingly, garment names included 'Major' (a long jacket belted over jodhpurs) and 'Météore' (a leg-revealing dress that played with opacity and transparency; see p.75, right). Other names included 'Majestic', 'Miklos', 'Meeting', 'Montsouris' and 'Minotaure'.* Among the 195 looks on show, hand-painted dresses – a Chloé signature – were plentiful. One long crêpe de Chine dress (see opposite, left) was painted with a motif inspired by Albert Gleizes's 1916–17 painting *Danseuse espagnole*.

The collection's eye-catching prints were a joy to photograph. Numerous garments appeared in magazines such as *Vogue, Elle* and *L'Officiel*. The short blue marabou-trimmed halter dress (opposite, right) was modelled by a dancing blonde – her beau's face just cropped from frame – in an editorial for *Vogue Paris* by Jeanloup Sieff, titled 'Short is the Night'. A Chloé blouse with a playing card print (p.74, left) also appeared in the magazine that season, shot by Guy Bourdin. The wearer, a lithe model with a net head-piece, appeared sat atop a white block on an empty beach, an array of sandcastles before her – a vision that complimented the repeating, vaguely surrealist motifs that decorated Lagerfeld's collection.

'NAVY', 'NEGRESCO', 'ODÉON', 'OISEAU'

The spring/summer 1972 collection was
interpreted as a turning point by some critics.*
WWD noted that 'Lagerfeld really poured on
the glamor'. The journal welcomed the change
from seasons past: 'it was a new kind of glamor
for Karl – sophisticated, feminine, elegantly
Sportive [*sic*]. For the past few seasons,
Lagerfeld was hung up on the '40s bit and,
often, his clothes looked more like costumes
than real fashion. But this season, the big
exponent of kitsch showed he also has a
refined side.'

The report praised Lagerfeld's skill for
trousers – an unexpected hit, given his existing
reputation for blouses and patterned dresses
– and was particularly taken with the cuffed
Oxford bags and fluid evening pyjamas.
Jumpsuits were also big news, while dresses
were skimpy, yet elegant: delicate halter necks
emphasized shoulders and backs, and came
styled with the simplest of accessories,
such as a single flower, pinned at the waist.

By the early 1970s, Chloé was synonymous not
only with a certain style of fashion, but also a
certain type of woman: adventurous, youthful,
plucky. This woman was as comfortable in
Chloé's take on tailoring – wide on the bottom,
with sculpted jackets and waistcoats – as
she was in a slinky evening look. Indeed, the
broad wardrobe of the Chloé girl was neatly
summarized by US *Vogue*, which, in March
1972, featured the journalist Lally Weymouth
in a Chloé dress: 'though she's a sweater-and-
pants girl by day, at night she dares to wear
the daringest, barest-back dresses in town'.
The month before, the magazine featured two
suits from the collection, alongside a wisp of
a halter-neck dress, in a story shot by Helmut
Newton: 'From designer Karl Lagerfeld, the
clearest picture you can see of the feminine –
and yes, sexy – mood permeating French
fashion today', read the headline. The dress,
they said, was 'a spectacularly cut snippet
of black silk mousseline', while the suits were
'the most feminine way you can look in a pants
turnout'. 'Add a camellia corsage and no one
can stop you', they added.

* For details and garment names, see p. 611.

'PUMA', 'PANTHÉON', 'PÉLICAN', 'PUBLICITÉ'

Numerous Lagerfeld signatures were on show for autumn/winter 1972–1973: shoulder-baring evening dresses, belted coats, floral corsages.* The tones of the season were sombre, refined: brown, black and teal, with flashes of gold. US *Vogue* were particularly taken with the way Lagerfeld styled shirt dresses over skirts and trousers: 'This is very important!' they said.

The letter of the season was 'P': 'Porcelaine' (right), 'Play-Boy' (opposite, top left), 'Puma', 'Panthéon', 'Prune', 'Pink', 'Petunia' and, given Lagerfeld's success among editors and critics, the aptly named black wool pleated dress, 'Publicité' (opposite, bottom right, modelled by Donna Jordan).

US *Vogue* also praised 'silk blousons for late day, to wear over black silk pants or long slinky skirts'. *WWD* lauded the gowns: 'Karl is certainly one of the biggest dress fans in Paris and he has some great looking ones in black wool voile with tucked shaped shoulders.' Lagerfeld was, as usual, on top of the trends: 'A detail of the collection – one that's turning up elsewhere in Paris and could be significant – is crystal pleating,' said *WWD*.

Lagerfeld's seductive eveningwear was, again, popular with photographers, whose images of slinky black and white gowns frequently ran alongside captions encouraging readers to 'seduce' or embrace the 'vamp' look. For *Vogue Paris*, Helmut Newton photographed 'Pélican' (opposite, top right) and 'Porcelaine' together; in another editorial, he also managed to encapsulate the modern, liberated feel of these slight, simple gowns by photographing a model in a skimpy low-backed black Chloé dress in a sparse room, leaning backwards out of a window, her arms spread, her face confidently nonplussed.

For details and garment names, see p. 611.

'ROSCOFF', 'RÉCAMIER', 'RED', 'REINE-CLAUDE'

This collection again featured the graphic
Art Deco patterns that defined many of
Karl Lagerfeld's earlier collections for the
house (see pp. 66 and 68), alongside nature-
themed motifs, such as shells and doves.*
The shapes suggested travel, hot nights,
dancing, movement; there were halter bra
tops, full skirts, long gowns, and Lagerfeld's
signature headscarves (see also p. 68). Editors
at British *Vogue* took the dresses to Morocco,
contrasting the graphic angular motifs
against the country's signature tiles, pillars
and trellises. A separate editorial, by Barry
Lategan, made heavy use of this season's
wide-brimmed black hats: 'Chloé Out and
Out Glamour...' read the headline, noting,
'Great halo brims, brilliant silks out to slink.'

'Skirts are often full and flounced', wrote
WWD. The *New York Times* noticed that
such skirts were rarely worn with jackets,
with French designers opting instead for
sweaters or shirts or, in the case of Lagerfeld
at Chloé, bras. *Le Monde* described the
collection as 'a return to lingerie'. By now,
Lagerfeld was already demonstrating his
tendency for droll, controversial quips to
the press: 'What if bras are hard to wear?
If people took their own figures into
consideration, they would all wear
tents,' he told the *New York Times*.

Faye Dunaway posed for US *Vogue* in one of
the collection's bra and skirt combinations,
noting of the pieces, 'I like the easy things in
life... I like clothes that feel good. If it moves,
I wear it. Silks, jerseys, anything fluid.'

Capturing the breezy, spirited mood of
French fashion, the *New York Times* piece
ran under the headline 'French Designers
Favor the Casual Look'. *Vogue Italia* noted:
'The ultrachic woman who goes through life
with a cocktail glass in her hand is Karl
Lagerfeld's new love.' The classic Chloé
woman, they continued, would be 'a sensation
next summer, going to a party in a long crêpe
de Chine skirt and black draped bra, her bare
shoulders skimmed by an over-blouse, on her
head a straw hat for a parasol'.

* For details and garment names, see p. 612.

'STROMBOLI', 'SPECTACLE', 'SEPTEMBRE', 'SUMATRA'

Held at Restaurant Laurent, the autumn/ winter 1973–1974 show was, according to *Vogue Paris*, 'vigorously applauded'. Indeed, their report said 'bravo' on the new co-ords, tweed knits, layered lengths, glamorous dresses and corset-waisted skirts, which came in various shades of brown, beige, taupe and sierra. Lagerfeld, *Vogue Paris* said, met reporters backstage, 'monocle in eye'. *WWD* noted that, 'Lorgnettes and monocles on chains have been selling briskly the past few months... Seems Karl Lagerfeld started the fad when he took to wearing a monocle. At Chloé ... many of the mannequins either carried monocles or had them strung around their necks.'

The backdrop to the show was one of conflict: 'BigSkirt [*sic*] Debate Raging in Paris', read the *WWD* headline. Chloé gave wearers the option: long, mid, or even, as Lagerfeld noted to *Vogue Paris*, trousers that were flippy enough to resemble a skirt. 'I'm seeing all lengths,' Bloomingdale's then V-P, Dick Hauser, told *WWD* of the controversy. 'After all, that's the way people are dressing.'

Much praise went toward Lagerfeld's new take on the shirt dress, which could be unbuttoned down to the waist, or up to the thigh, to reveal a matching slip dress underneath. 'The underwear becomes clothing,' Lagerfeld told *Vogue Paris*. 'This fashion is a game of construction. All the elements fit together... We make dresses that are inspired by lingerie slips, so we might as well make lingerie slips that look like dresses.' The look was bound to be copied, noted *WWD*. 'He leaves a few buttons undone to give a seductive glimpse of lace and the print of the slip. The result – dynamite', agreed US *Vogue*.

Again, the collection* was a hit with photographers. A long, prune-coloured dress, featuring rhinestone detailing (see right), appeared in British *Vogue* on a blonde model sitting by a swimming pool at night – a young Grace Coddington in the water beneath her – in what would become one of Helmut Newton's most beloved editorials.

* *For details and garment names, see p. 612.*

'TOURMALINE', 'TOUS LES JOURS', 'TAHITI', 'TABAC'

Many critics found much to admire about Karl Lagerfeld's spring/summer 1974 collection for Chloé.* *Drapery & Fashion Weekly* noted that it was 'packed full of beautiful, sophisticated, elegant clothes with plenty of ideas', adding that Lagerfeld, '[o]riginator of the lingerie look, ... continues his silk shirtwaist lace trimmed dress over bra top slips'. US *Vogue* called the collection 'marvelous ... delicate, gentle, feminine', and featured a striped blouse from the collection (see opposite, left), photographed by Helmut Newton, alongside a caption referring to '[t]he float of double blouses, double scarves ... like petal upon petal of crêpe de Chine, striped and dotted in anemone colors'. They also praised a coat 'as simple as the most perfect *robe de chambre* flowing loose over a matching slip of a dress'.

'The hyper-supple is what's fashionable', Lagerfeld told reporters backstage. 'Super-suppleness, fluid *flou*, clothes that flow over the body.' *Vogue Paris* quoted the designer: 'The body must give shape to weightless clothes ... barely sewn together, which could fit in one hand, and which won't overfill luggage. What's in fashion is non-gravity, non-constraint, softness. It's a moving geometry, a game of construction based on un-constructed elements that one will assemble depending on the days and on one's mood.'

Emphasizing the mood of femininity and floatiness were fans, rendered in crêpe de Chine, 'to match [the] handkerchief-thin floats of the prettiest dresses', according to US *Vogue*, as well as parasols, also in crêpe de Chine. 'At Chloé: the delicate flowers of the 1940s ... the "bathing beauties"', noted *Vogue Italia*. 'Everything opens onto a slip. The slip, a symbol of femininity.' This season, the magazine added, the Chloé woman 'opens a silk coat to reveal a handkerchief bra'. Many critics praised the delicacy of the silks, some of which came hand-painted with Art Deco motifs in black, white and water-green.

In a British *Vogue* editorial, titled 'The Discreet Charm of...', Helmut Newton embraced the vintage-style floral dresses, using Lagerfeld's own apartment, then fittingly decorated as an ode to Art Deco, to stage a tea-party, with Chloé-clad models tended to by maids.

* For details and garment names, see p. 612.

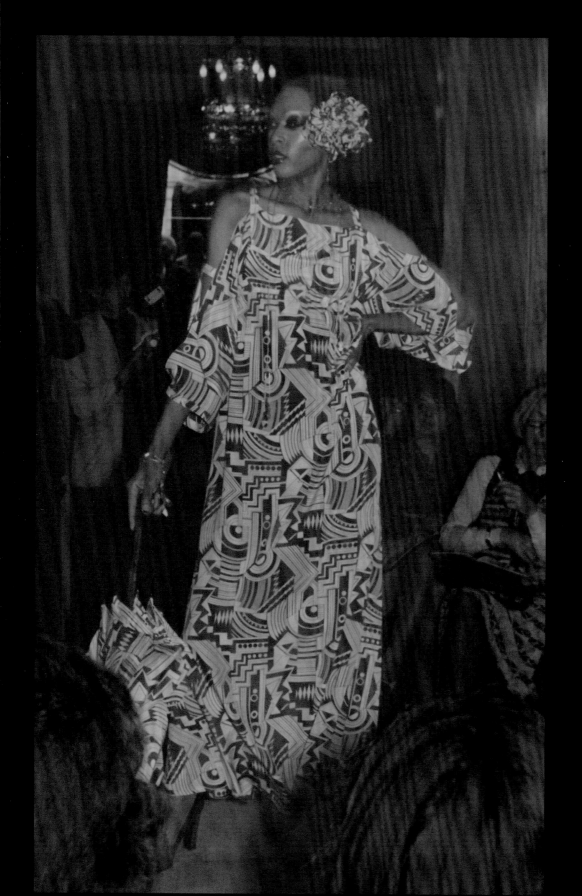

'VOYAGE', 'WEEK-END', 'XÉRÈS', 'ZERMATT'

As with the spring/summer 1974 collection (see p. 90), this show highlighted how the fashion show was changing. Here, rather than mingling among guests at a café, as had been the Chloé signature when Gaby Aghion founded the house (see p. 30), models walked above attendees on a raised runway at the Palais de Chaillot. Fashion week had become hectic: a packed schedule of packed shows. 'After five grueling days, the most important collection to come out of Paris so far is the one designed by Karl Lagerfeld for Chloé', wrote Hebe Dorsey in the *Herald Tribune*.[*] 'Lagerfeld, who has had slow but steady recognition, has now made it to the top... The look was so easy and effortless that it made all the other collections seem contrived.' The report included a comment from Norman Wechsler, president of Saks, who muttered as more and more clothes appeared on the Chloé runway: 'It gets to the point that there are so many good ones that you don't know what to buy.'

'There already is one collection that will change the look of clothes over the next few years,' agreed Bernadine Morris of the *New York Times*, noting a shift in the aesthetic and identity of Lagerfeld's Chloé. 'He has suddenly propelled himself out of his long-term obsession with the nineteen-thirties and is looking ahead.' Volume was the story: 'The difference with Lagerfeld's things is that all inner construction, and practically all seams, have been eliminated. That means no linings, no interfacing, not even any turned-under hems – the fabric has simply been cut off at the bottom. As a result, the clothes can be piled up on top of each other, layer upon layer, without making the wearer look like a moving mountain.' And yet the *Christian Science Monitor* drew attention to Chloé's signature fluidity, which remained despite the layering. 'Lagerfeld has picked fabrics – mostly flannels and gabardines – that are paper-thin, light as puff pastry.'

'Lagerfeld is playing the biggie game – including two coats at a time,' said the *Chicago Daily News*, noting reports that Jacqueline Kennedy had been spotted shopping at the Chloé headquarters. Indeed, business was booming: '[T]he year [Lagerfeld] joined them, 1965 [*sic*], the firm did a $1 million volume. This year the company is expected to gross $6 million,' said the *Christian Science Monitor*.

* For details and garment names, see p. 612.

'ACCOLADE', 'ARC', 'ARISTOCRATE', 'À LA FRANÇAISE'

This collection 'rocked the fashion professionals', according to a front-page story in *WWD*, which enthused over how 'Karl Lagerfeld's 200 trend-setting models ... do for unconstructed shapes [w]hat Balenciaga once did for constructed clothes'.* Indeed, Lagerfeld was attuned to a coming shift in mood: a taste for fitness and an awareness of form (later dubbed 'body consciousness' by magazines), which ran in tandem with the sensual mood of disco. His streamlined clothes – slinky shirt dresses and crepe blouses fastened with scarves, alongside 'filmy' dresses, to quote *WWD* – rejected any stiffness or formality.

Writing in the *Herald Tribune*, Hebe Dorsey commented that: 'There is nothing cheap about Karl Lagerfeld. Never has been. He works on a high, expensive plateau...' Dorsey noted that 'while everybody is still reminiscing and digging into the '50s, Lagerfeld jumps back a couple of hundred years into the 18th century ... he has tracked Marie-Antoinette to the Trianon rather than to the gilded splendor of Versailles. Hence the deluxe milkmaid look with ruffled and pointed shawls, ruffled aprons, ruffled double skirts, straw hats tilted forward with bouquets pinned at the back and even strings of roses around the neck.' Lagerfeld's critical and commercial success had attracted copy-cats: 'With a good sense of timing, Lagerfeld has dropped his famous big shirt, which everybody else is now making a fortune on... But Lagerfeld's biggest talent lies in his unconstructed approach to fashion which rests on a deep understanding of fabric. With a minimum of seams, it looks as if his clothes have been put together by sheer magic. As of last season, he developed a new way of finishing his hems which are cut clean instead of doubled over... As a result, everything floats.'

WWD gushed, 'Lagerfeld's clothes are so new that when the mannequins saw them for the first time Monday morning just before the show some of them didn't know how to put them on.'

By now, Lagerfeld was a fully fledged design star. In the March issue of British *Vogue*, he appeared, lounging at home, in the 'Great Designers World Series'. The model Marie Helvin was photographed by her husband, David Bailey, draped across Lagerfeld, clad in the S/S 1975 Chloé collection, complete with an eye-patch.

* *For details and garment names, see p. 612.*

Karl Lagerfeld

A Short Biography: Part I

Karl Lagerfeld became one of fashion's most successful and celebrated designers, applauded for his indefatigable approach to work and culture. And yet, when he joined Chloé as a freelancer in 1964 he was just another new face behind founder Gaby Aghion, working among a team of other bright young things. Still, it did not take long for his star to shine: as early as 1965, his first 'Karl Lagerfeld pour Chloé' credit had already appeared in *Vogue Paris*. Aghion later told interviewers that it was her business partner, Jacques Lenoir, who first spotted Lagerfeld's unique talent and force within the group.

Lagerfeld was born in Hamburg in 1933 (he later altered his date of birth). His love of fashion was cemented when he attended a Christian Dior show in Hamburg in 1949. He moved to Paris three years later. In 1954, at the age of 21 (though he later claimed to have been 16), he won first prize in the coat category of the International Wool Secretariat competition (Yves Saint Laurent won first prize in the dress category).

By the time he joined Chloé, Lagerfeld was already technically adept, having previously worked for Pierre Balmain and Jean Patou. A particular skill was knowing how to make his visions a reality; how to help a seamstress translate a look from a sketch to a toile to a workable, desirable garment. Chloé, with its modern spirit, was a better fit for him than his past posts: he had felt bored at Balmain and stifled at Patou, wearied by the weight of tradition and formality. At Chloé, he could dream, not just of clothing, but of a new vision for women, and for society.

When the other designers within the Chloé team eventually left the house, he remained alone in the studio with Aghion, whose quest for youthful spirit – for the new – appealed to him. 'Madame Aghion is a charming person,' he told *International Textiles* magazine in 1974. 'She sparks off the kind of atmosphere which has a very stimulating effect on me.' From the autumn/winter 1975–1976 collection onwards, Lagerfeld was the company's sole designer. Like Aghion, back in the 1950s when founding Chloé, Lagerfeld looked to the Paris streets for inspiration, and in particular to students. 'He would take the students' ideas and then transform them into something beautiful,' Aghion later recalled. It is significant to remember that Lagerfeld was living through a time of youth revolution, of student protests and morphing societal norms.

However, Lagerfeld's skill was his ability to look forwards and backwards simultaneously. He is remarkable for being one of the first designers to really recognize the power of nostalgia: he championed retro fashion, embracing the mood of the 1920s and 1930s, and combining it with a spirit of 1970s freedom, decadence and elegance. It was Lagerfeld who made crêpe de Chine feel fresh and new again, getting women back into the kind of fluid bias-cut dresses that hadn't been seen since the 1930s.

As much as Lagerfeld had an eye for the simple (a plain, elegantly cut blouse; a clean low-backed gown in black) he also favoured the playful and the bizarre (off-beat prints of ice skaters, Roman numerals, tango dancers and chickens), which highlighted his sense of humour. He also pre-empted the current vogue for art-fashion collaborations: many of his designs for Chloé from this period feature eye-catching motifs inspired by art movements. Many of these were hand-painted in collaboration with Nicole Lefort, a relationship that lasted years and produced an array of couture-level, bright garments that continue to hold their colour and spirit within the Chloé Archive today.

The fashion critic Sarah Mower has argued that Lagerfeld's clothes were 'a medium for the freedoms and fantasies of a generation'. 'His Chloé girls twirled, lounged, and smouldered across magazine layouts, hand in hand with the wildly creative photographers who were on the loose in Paris.' Indeed, as Mower indicates, Lagerfeld's time at Chloé coincided with a burst of creativity within fashion photography, when magazines were booming thanks to the talent, wit and nuance of photographers such as Jeanloup Sieff, Deborah Turbeville, Chris von Wangenheim and Sarah Moon. Lagerfeld himself moved in creative circles, dining out with the models Pat Cleveland and Jerry Hall, the illustrator Antonio Lopez and the fashion writer Anna Piaggi.

'Nothing is romantic forever, not even a dress. That is why I believe I should constantly try new things,' Lagerfeld told the *Houston Chronicle* in 1981. 'I like surprises. I enjoy doing what I'm not expected to do. I think that classic is often a tasteful excuse for boredom.' Indeed, the common thread throughout Lagerfeld's twenty-year stretch at Chloé was no fixed style – a nimble approach that gave the house a sense of freedom and dynamism. *Vogue Paris* captured Lagerfeld laughing in the street as he crossed a road with a couple of models in 1971: 'Karl Lagerfeld: every season a new woman.' And yet, the Chloé signatures we know today – exceptional blouses, floating gowns, intriguing layering, and 'flou' – all find their roots in Lagerfeld's tenure at the house.

By 1983, Lagerfeld had been approached by Chanel, so ended his vastly productive decades-long stint at Chloé (he returned in 1992). Gaby Aghion would later comment that what Lagerfeld had done for her house had 'made a big contribution to fashion history'.

'BAROMÈTRE', 'BAS-RELIEF', 'BOLDINI', 'BUGATTI'

This show was Karl Lagerfeld's first as the sole designer for Chloé (though, for many seasons before, impressed critics had publicized his name widely, often referring to previous collections as 'Chloé by Karl Lagerfeld').

The lightness of Lagerfeld's clothes continued to attract plaudits. 'Lagerfeld a year ago hit upon something that is probably as significant in the history of fashion as Vionnet's discovery of the bias cut 50 years ago: the elimination of all the linings, stiffening and even seams that have cluttered up clothes since the Middle Ages', wrote Bernadine Morris of this collection for the *Herald Tribune*. 'A masterful technician, Lagerfeld gets excited about such things as bypassing the seam that usually extends across the shoulders. He has found a way to do without it by inserting sleeves, so they look glued in, he explained gleefully before the show.'

It was not all praise, however. Morris noted: 'The thousand or so people who fought for places at his show in the Palais des Congrès ... were a bit taken aback by the men's oxfords, loafers and saddle shoes the models wore over heavy wool stockings with day clothes.' Such a view was common across the press. 'A school-girl look, prim and proper with woolly tights and flat shoes, very un-typical of Chloé', wrote *Drapers Record*. 'Will those elegant, well-bred, well-heeled ladies who buy Karl Lagerfeld's Chloé clothes really step out in crepe soled shoes and woolly stockings?' asked Suzy Menkes in London's *Evening Standard*.

It was Lagerfeld's skill for construction that saved the day. 'The cut is superb; the seven-eighth tubular tunic over slim straight skirt is an important new line for day and evening,' said Menkes. 'Trousers gathered into ankle boots (we are seeing these bicycling trousers everywhere). Colours flow in silken rivers – raspberry with peach and brick, lilac and china blue, a shocking pink pocket lining flares in the skirt of a fluid black dress. The new layers are a waistcoat in mohair or fur on top of a straight coat. Shawls wrapped like rose petals across the body. Sleeves that grow from the shoulder without a seam. Noel Coward dressing gowns in gold flowers on black [see right] are the ultimate unisexual chic.'*

For the last exit, the model showed off a bottle of Lagerfeld's new perfume, Chloé – the first to be released by a ready-to-wear fashion house.

* For details and garment names, see p. 612.

'CAMOMILLE', 'CANNES', 'CAPUCINE', 'CARNATION'

'Who's for tennis?' asked *Tatler* of the spring/ summer 1976 collection.* The ever-nimble Karl Lagerfeld had shifted mood again. 'I was tired of being cast as an expensive and definitely adult designer,' he told Hebe Dorsey of the *Herald Tribune* after this show, held at the Palais des Congrès. 'I felt stuck – as if I could only do pastiches of myself. I felt like branching into sportswear and using fabrics I never touched before, such as cotton.' Attendees were aghast at the vision of lithe models in sports socks, shorts and sneakers. Dorsey described the opening section as 'rowdy', with girls 'sauntering along the runway, brandishing huge, colorful parasols' (see p.124). More surprises were to come: 'He then showed a long line of beach and cruise wear with maillots cut so skimpily that the *Figaro* photographer confessed he was so shaken he could not work.'

The message was change, and – as had always been Lagerfeld's signature at Chloé, in different incarnations – freedom. Dorsey appreciated the new look: '[W]hat Lagerfeld was trying to say is that too much caviar can be too much caviar.' The 'outlandish ideas' on show included cotton eveningwear, worn with sneakers, and crêpe de Chine T-shirts. ('Why not? It's so sexy, especially when it's wet,' quipped Lagerfeld.) The new mood was 'important', said Dorsey: 'it has taken quite a few years off the Chloé look and added a crisp ring it did not have before'.

In the *Los Angeles Times*, Marylou Luther was also buoyed by the freshness of the collection. 'Lagerfeld opens with a beach-cum-tennis line-up Visconti should use if he ever updates "Death in Venice". Only he'd have to call it "Life in Venice" because these all-white clothes have a sense of happiness about them.' Luther favourably pitted Lagerfeld against the couture houses. '[H]is clothes are as expensive as those by Dior, Givenchy and Saint Laurent, and the fabrics he uses are every bit as costly. But while the couturiers seem content to recall classic fabrics and classic prints season after season, Lagerfeld continues to break new ground in both fabric and print direction... The fabric range is a remarkable commitment to the designer's continuing search for the new.'

Dorsey agreed: 'The sexy, clinging silk tubes breaking out at the knees and the embroidered-to-death dresses are more couture than what couture has produced lately.'

* *For details and garment names, see p. 613.*

'DEMOCRATE', 'DIALOGUE', 'DANDY', 'DASH'

This season,* it was Karl Lagerfeld's jackets that got critics talking. 'The evening jacket everyone craved: Lagerfeld's hand-painted crêpe de Chine flowers outlined in gold – you'd never stop wearing it!' wrote US *Vogue*. Such jackets (see p.130) were, the magazine said, 'soft as the softest lingerie'. They were featured twice in the magazine, first in July, and later in September, when *Vogue* advised, 'You could slip it over a black halter dress, over anything black – if you owned it, you could plan your whole evening life around it!'

Vogue Paris reminded its readers of Lagerfeld's ethos: it's not what you wear, but how you wear it. 'Everything must be mobile and alive,' they said, noting that, in this show, 'the coats are draped over the shoulders and pulled around the hips by always contrasting sash-belts passing through giant buttonhole slits to tie at the front'.

Not all attendees were so impressed. Hebe Dorsey of the *Herald Tribune*, usually a Lagerfeld fan, felt the show lacked cohesion. 'A few days before his Chloé collection was shown to the press, Karl Lagerfeld said: "I didn't think about anything while I was designing. I just let go and did what I felt like doing." That was just his trouble. He had enough ideas in fact for 10 collections.' Still, some messages were clear. The coat was the item of the season, and the onion-like layers Chloé had become known for recently were old news: 'he built his collection like a Barbie doll wardrobe, with basic garments that he tricks up with bits and pieces'.

And yet, Dorsey had more positive words for the eveningwear – 'a hit and again a riot of ideas'. 'For this incredibly talented man who started the whole hand-printed fabric phenomenon now sweeping the U.S. the new fall fabric medium is taffeta,' said Marylou Luther in the *Los Angeles Times*: 'Hand-painted taffetas in distinct floral designs using as many as 24 colors in one garment... They're collector's items, pure art in fashion... Just when you think Lagerfeld cannot possibly top that act, he introduces a series of sheer lamé dresses hand-painted with big Japanese figures and houses much in the tradition of coromandel screens.'

Yet again, the progression of the catwalk presentation from trade show to high spectacle was visible. With increasing regularity, attendees would begin to recognize star models on the catwalk, such as Jerry Hall, who appeared on the runway in a shining gold tunic (see p.129, right).

* *For details and garment names, see p.613.*

'EIFFEL', 'ÉTOILE', 'EN JEU', 'ECHO'

Yet again, this collection* highlighted Karl Lagerfeld's skill for celebrating the body, using adjustable clothes to envelop the form. 'Lagerfeld did it with a "waist-maker"', wrote US *Vogue* in January. '[I]t's one of the most charming devices ever to change the shape of clothes … you slip it on like a little gilet, and the ends get wrapped and wrapped – instant waistline!' The *New York Times* reported that this garment, which they compared to an Obi belt, was used 'on everything, from creamy silk dresses to bathing suits, where it forms the top for minimal bikini trunks'.

The paper also noted 'quaint 18th-century Marie-Antoinette-playing-milkmaid styles', and referenced 'an 18th- or 19th-century bucolic mood with petticoats, midriff wrappings, delicate flower prints, ruffles and even a hint of a bustle'. The shift in mood was likely inspired by changes in Lagerfeld's own life; by the time of the show, he had sold his Art Deco collection and moved into the 18th-century *hôtel particulier* Pozzo di Borgo.

Le Monde focused on the pastoral aspects of the collection, referring to 'the theme of life in the garden' and 'large apron skirts in rustic or precious fabrics, and in soft shades of pink, plum, lavender or light brown'. 'Are you one of Chloé's recherché gardeners?' British *Vogue* asked its readers. For the first time, the house used a catwalk backdrop that extended the season's theme. Biographer and close friend Patrick Hourcade noted that after trellises had been installed the previous year at Lagerfeld's château in Grand-Champ, he then designed a trellis décor to present his S/S collection; over time, the décor would become an inseparable element of Lagerfeld's fashion design concepts.

The sense of movement and femininity within the S/S collection appealed to image-makers. Guy Bourdin shot various floral and white gowns for *Vogue Paris*, including a flowing pleated dress worn by a windswept model. For US *Vogue*, Richard Avedon shot a young Janice Dickinson with a scarf piece around her waist (for similar, see right) under the headline 'Tie it...'

Among all the adaptable pieces and sinuous gowns, *Midi Libre* noticed Lagerfeld's familiar 'nostalgia for the refined fashion of the 1930s'. Indeed, some of the graphic prints on show, such as the black and white spots and stripes (see p.135, right), recalled Lagerfeld's celebrated Art Deco dresses earlier in the decade (see p.68).

* For details and garment names, see p.613.

'FRAGONARD', 'FIGARO', 'FAUVE', 'FORTISSIMO'

'Romantic fashion isn't dead: it has just been sleeping for longer than I care to remember,' said the *Daily Telegraph*. 'It took Karl Lagerfeld of Chloé to wave the magic wand and wake up this Sleeping Beauty in a mouth-watering collection awash with embroidered crêpe de chine, swashbuckling fur-lined black capes, dresses of tissue-fine wool voile flower-printed like old wallpapers in French 18th-century houses.'* The publication saw an unlikely figure within all of Lagerfeld's billowing sleeves and frills: 'His girl is a dashing, feminine version of Tom Jones.'

The paper interpreted quite the backstory for this season's Chloé woman: 'When our 18th-century beauty isn't dashing about, she is sauntering round the cobblestones of Versailles in her double-caped black coat with intriguing arm slits – the most practical way of coping with a cape I've ever seen, for from under those arm-slits come long sleeves in the same wool so that you're not frozen.'

British *Vogue* were also taken by the collection's many historical references and cultural nods, noting that the pieces suggested 'gallantry and Fragonard, Congreve and Sheridan, court intrigue and Watteau, masked balls in Venice and Don Juan'. The catwalk décor included stone benches, like those found in 18th-century French gardens, enabling the models to take up a variety of seated poses.

Lagerfeld told reporters that he had drawn inspiration from Fellini's *Casanova*, hence the capes, flouncing ruffles, black velvet hair ribbons, musketeer boots and plethoras of lace. 'To get the essence of the Chloé collection, think of Mozart as a child in a blue silk long jacket, white hose. Think of his quartets – irrepressible, gay, perfect,' British *Vogue* continued. Other press reviews referenced androgynes such as the Chevalier d'Éon and Octavian in *Der Rosenkavalier*.

'At Chloé, Karl Lagerfeld likes cotton and silk lace, lace appliques, lace-type embroidery and big romantic blooms – for day as well as evening,' said *WWD*, noting 'soft white blouses with at least a yard of lace trim on the cuffs, jabots and high collars'. 'Black, beige, cream and pale rose with gold metallic details are the important colors here,' the report added.

For critics, the collection signalled a shift: 'Karl Lagerfeld at Chloé has fed on nostalgia more than any; and it is no accident that he has by now replaced his seminal Art Deco collection with 18th-century French furniture and a Brittany château,' concluded the British *Vogue* report.

* *For details and garment names, see p. 613.*

'GARDEN', 'GARDENIA', 'GABRIEL', 'GAULOISE'

With this collection,* Karl Lagerfeld pushed against the 'Casanova craze', to quote the *Daily Telegraph*, which he had ignited in fashion with his autumn/winter 1977–1978 collection (see p.138). It was farewell to frothing blouses, velvet breeches and thigh-high boots. 'Couldn't possibly produce these today – my feeling for elaboration has now died,' said Lagerfeld. Instead, he favoured a more subdued, less romantic look, one that nodded to the uncertainty of the late 1970s, in the aftermath of Watergate and economic depressions in the Western world. 'It's wrong – and as well it's démodé – to look too chic, too beautiful in the street. Designing now is harder than ever before because of these strange times we live in. I read the newspaper between my home and the studio, and I wish I hadn't – the news makes fashion rather irrelevant,' Lagerfeld told the *Telegraph*.

'Karl Lagerfeld's collection for Chloé – now synonymous with luxury, romantic, frou frou looks – has toned down,' said *Fashion Weekly*. 'Apart from the huge theatrical picture hats covered in scarves [see p.146, right], there were plenty of interesting closer-to-the-body shapes (which look like being the next fashion direction), some good sportswear looks and still lots of pretty printed soft dresses as well as a group of white silks.'

WWD were particularly impressed by one 'terrific new skirt idea – easy crepe de chine skirts with diagonally pleated pockets and fullness falling at both sides from the pockets' (see p.146, bottom left). One element had carried over from last season: lace. 'Chloé is loaded with those extra touches that American retailers know and love him for. Lagerfeld's on to lace insets, embroidered patches at the elbows, tiny beading and a garden full of the most romantic prints in Paris. Reaction: a sure seller no matter what the price,' said *WWD*.

'No reference this time around,' Lagerfeld told *Vogue Paris*, after the show. 'What do you want me to be inspired by? *Star Wars*?' Instead, the designer made fabrics his focus, pushing forward with the material research and explorations that had first won him acclaim for the construction and form of his Chloé pieces. 'Material, just now, matters more to Lagerfeld than any other aspect of fashion,' confirmed the *Telegraph*.

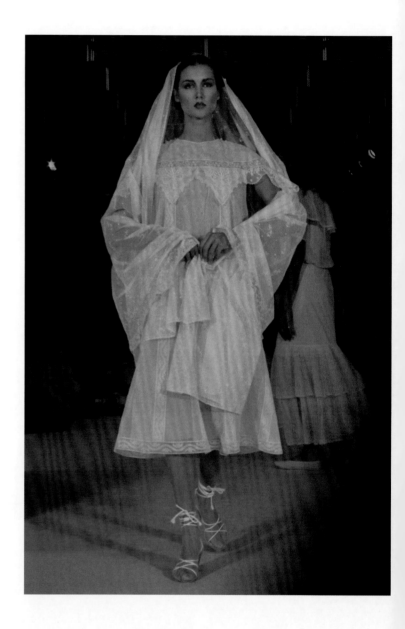

* For details and garment names, see p.613.

'HARMONIE', 'HARVARD', 'ICARE', 'ILION'

With this show, Karl Lagerfeld embraced dualities and opposites, seeking to create a collection that captured the many facets of late 1970s femininity.* The result was 'full of ambiguities, with round lines, often closely hugging the body and highlighting curves, but also with angles (strong-shouldered silhouettes, pointed necklines),' said *Journal du Textile*. The publication noted that such contrasts reflected 'the mood and psychology of today's woman, who wants to be both feminine and energetic, tender but also active and determined'.

'Karl Lagerfeld's collection … was odd. But it's significant,' said *WWD*, which ran with the headline 'Lagerfeld: "His best yet"'. The collection highlighted Lagerfeld's desire to continue to evolve Chloé, and to question the tastes and social norms of the age. 'I am tired of layering and bulky unconstructed clothes. My feeling is to create abstract but soft curves and angles and shapes.' This was, as *Vogue Paris* put it, 'Graphic fashion, with rounder hips, slimmer waist, squarer shoulders than in real life.' 'Chloé redefines glamour!' gushed US *Vogue*.

The jewelry and accessories caused much critical intrigue. Models wore 'elevator boy' caps (designed by Jeannine Montel), as well as oversized necklaces and enormous sculpture-brooches. The latter (and some corresponding prints) were inspired by the German artist Oskar Schlemmer and his Bauhaus peers, and the abstract painter Kazimir Malevich (who was, at that moment, the subject of a retrospective at the Centre Pompidou). Lagerfeld called his creations 'theatre jewels', and had them manufactured by makers of accessories for the opera. 'Accessories should be funny. Humor is vital, and I always make accessories that amuse me. They also aid in playing down the bourgeois aspect of the dresses,' he told *WWD*. 'Women can't wear real jewelry anywhere these days. The funniest thing to do is to make a joke out of the whole concept of wearing jewels.'

Politics and the news continued to shape Lagerfeld's thinking, influencing the many dualisms present in the collection. 'These oppositions reflect, according to Karl Lagerfeld, the climate of our time, where violence is concealed under an exterior of gentleness,' added *Journal du Textile*. But, Lagerfeld noted, 'People who make clothes should avoid at all cost the idea that because Paris is in a difficult mood, fashion must be severe and serious.'

* For details and garment names, see p. 614.

'LUSTRE', 'LOGIQUE', 'LEADER', 'L'ÉTÉ'

This season, Karl Lagerfeld moved away from his signature 1940s to embrace the sex appeal of the 1950s.* *Journal du Textile* noted that the tight hourglass silhouettes 'evoke that of Marilyn', and the bustier fits recall Rita Hayworth. 'We even detect nods to Jacques Fath in some beachwear.' And yet, the collection felt forward-thinking, thanks to 'the mixture of humour and seriousness which characterizes the style of the creator'. Indeed, prints, including a robot pattern on a long gown (see p.156, bottom), were playful and whimsical. Lagerfeld's signature wit and his ability to toy with references, embracing high and low culture, would go on to define his career as a designer.

Against a postmodern backdrop of columns evoking ruins, this show marked a shift from the pieces Lagerfeld had offered only shortly before. He told *WWD* that he'd used 'whalebones and polyurethane foam inside [the clothes] to give a more shaped, architectural form'. He also referred to ruffles 'like fish scales at the hips' and peplums to give 'more shapely proportions'.

Some onlookers struggled with the change in direction. The *New York Times* noted that Lagerfeld had switched to a style 'that shows off bosoms and waistlines and inspired the models to adopt a hip-swinging, twitchy gait'. One attendee, Jane Maynard, clad in a high-necked brown blouse and a wool skirt (the Chloé look of yore), quipped, 'They should have asked my husband. He would have enjoyed the show.' Another attendee, Glady [*sic*] Solomon, put it more bluntly: 'I never saw anything like it. It looked like clothes for call girls.'

'Frivolity is important,' Lagerfeld told reporters. 'I want shape and sensuousness. I'm tired of anything sloppy. And this collection is like a game.' His taste for amusing accessories, prevalent also last season (see p.148), was on show. The *New York Times* referred to 'mad hats the size of phonograph records' and 'big plastic roosters or flowers where circle pins once dwelt'. *WWD* called the accessories 'bizarre, but always innovative'; 'Junk Jewels have been pushed into their real domain – molded plastic'. Particularly notable were a disc hat by Jeannine Montel and the rooster brooch, designed by Ugo Correani; 'he sometimes pins two or three on a suit or a dress', added *WWD*.

'The odd and extreme look he started in his last ready-to-wear collection for Chloé has become more dramatic, highly structured in concept and completely amusing,' the journal concluded, noting that Lagerfeld 'continues to change the shape of fashion'.

* *For details and garment names, see p.614.*

'MAZURKA', 'MÉRIGNAC', 'MAGICIEN', 'MAGNÉTIQUE'

'Fashion without wit', Lagerfeld told US *Vogue* in 1979, 'is disastrous.' This collection* – with its bold headwear, jazzy prints and cartoonish heart-shaped fans – had plenty of whimsy. 'The clothes that Karl Lagerfeld designs for Chloé are the natural results of the world he creates; and if they sometimes seem to be from other times, it is because those other times have as much reality for him as rain and taxes have for the rest of us,' said *Vogue*. 'You can love Karl Lagerfeld's clothes, you can hate them. See them once, and you can't forget them.'

This was, the *Japan Times* argued, 'a trend-setting collection'. They noted 'big melon sleeves, nipped waists on peplum jackets, enormous brooches or plaques of beaded embroidery, and narrow skirts – on models who wear ... large off-the-face hats'.

The *Glasgow Herald* were similarly taken by the headwear: 'Designer Karl Lagerfeld, the monocled, occasionally pig-tailed king of Paris chic, takes the Edwardian Gibson Girl as his inspiration: hour-glass shapes – curved bosom, tiny waist, swelling hips and peplum jackets, legs of mutton sleeves with long slim cuffs, pearl ruffs ... [with a] saucer – if not plate – hat.' US *Vogue* enjoyed the designer's Venetian inspirations (around the time of this show, Lagerfeld threw his now-legendary Venetian Ball at Le Palace in Paris, attended by the likes of Paloma Picasso and Loulou de la Falaise): 'he's at it again, making coat-dresses with rounded shoulders and sleeves – to wear as a coat or a dress, "the 'eighties version of a suit," says Lagerfeld. He's showed them with huge Venetian "fan" hats, pearl "wing" pins, "vacuum-cleaner" coils (to wear as separate knit collars, cuffs or waist-wraps).'

Le Figaro referred to Chloé as an 'outsider' that season, noting Lagerfeld's desire to push against norms, and expectations around suitable cuts for the female form. 'I want to get the eye used to straying from too classic a view', they quoted him as saying.

Still, the committed Chloé woman would not be put off or distracted by new ideas, US *Vogue* claimed, illustrating their article with the 'lightbulb' dress modelled by Pat Cleveland on p. 165. '[W]omen will go out and buy what they've always loved from Lagerfeld: his romantic blouses, seductive dinner dresses, super sweaters. Women collect Lagerfelds by the piece, not by the wardrobe.'

* For details and garment names, see p. 614.

'NANTUA', 'NEXT', 'NETWORK', 'NARCISSE'

The British press, notorious for its tabloids, were overcome with excitement at the short cut of the skirts in Chloé's spring/summer 1980 collection. 'Karl Lagerfeld for Chloé is a high-fiver for the next decade,' gushed the *Daily Express*. '[His] minis are geometric and mobile – and they run rings round the rest I've seen in Paris and London...'

The Times read the collection as a comment on a new age: '[T]o make sure we know we're coming into the eighties, the girls carry "transistor" handbags' (see Jerry Hall on p.168, top left). Lagerfeld told the *Washington Post* that on a recent trip to the US he'd noticed youths walking around with tape recorders blasting disco music. 'So in his show one model was carrying a black patent shoulder bag marked like a tape recorder, and of course, as she went along, she held it to her ear.' The *Daily Express* noted: 'Karl's accessories are stylised and supersonic, designed to complement his clever clothes.'

Another nod to modernity came in the standout material of the collection. 'He is a man infatuated with plastic,' Bernadine Morris said in the *New York Times*. '[H]e puts the bags over his models' heads and you worry about them breathing... He crumples it up and stuffs the balls into the folds of sleeves. He ties a bag over one shoe, like a boot. He pushes it between the wings of stiff mesh he uses as headdresses. And, as they say in fashion, he "completes the look" by decking his mannequins in necklaces that look as if they were made of iridescent plastic balls, like soap bubbles.' This insinuation was hammered home by the addition of shower curtains at the entrance to the podium.

Lagerfeld told *WWD* that short lengths were part of the Sixties revival dominating Paris that season. 'But one must be careful to take only bits of the Sixties, only the mood. Literal translations of that decade – Courrèges, those stiff minis and stiff shapes – look completely wrong.' US *Vogue*, impressed with the punchy hemlines and fun take on retro-futurism, reported: 'Karl Lagerfeld of Chloé, always an innovator, came up with a top collection with ideas galore: bicolored tunics, the best little dinner dresses in Paris – one-shouldered with pleated tiered skirts, and knockout coats – all designed to make a woman look sexy and slim.'*

* For details and garment names, see p.614.

'PHILADELPHIE', 'POPPÉE', 'PNEUMATIQUE', 'PLATINE'

Referring to the A/W 1980–1981 show as 'full of ideas', and quoting both Macy's and Bendel, *WWD* claimed: 'The retailers are ready to buy.' 'It was a beautiful, neo-classic collection. I particularly like the proportion of the tunics and bermudas,' said a buyer from Bendel.

The collection* offered a shift from the forward-thinking, plastic-heavy ode to modernity from last season (see p.166). Instead, there were flashes of historicism, and costume, through the show – an ode to the Tudors, with Anne Boleyn headpieces and Medici collars on metallic lamé jackets.

A profile of Lagerfeld, published in *Le Matin* in March 1980, a couple of weeks before the show, noted that 'American newspapers all recognize that he is one of the greatest forces in fashion'. The interview, which mentioned Lagerfeld's 'Socratic smile', showed the designer in the playful, bombastic mood that would become his signature. 'Everything in this business is temporal. You can never look back, only keep running forward – fast. I don't remember what my dresses were like from the last collection and I don't know how they will be in the next one... Physically and mentally, I change over the years and my inspiration changes with me. I hate the past and I hate routine. When I sit down to work, there is no premeditation, but rather professional improvisation, influenced by my surroundings.' When asked if he felt each collection would be a success, he replied, 'I always expect the worst ... like that I am always pleasantly surprised. We must all be our own Joan of Arc.'

Despite the press buzz for each show, *Le Matin* noted that the terms of Lagerfeld's licence agreement with the owners of Chloé meant that the ready-to-wear line still did not 'bear his name'. Still, by now, fashion was well into the reign of the high-glamour catwalk show as we know it today: a pack of photographers in a pit jostling for space, celebrity models on the catwalk, and fans rushing backstage to praise Lagerfeld as soon as the music cut. As if to emphasize the modernity – and to provide a clash with the more historical elements within the collection – models emerged from a giant TV set at the top of the runway, branded with 'Chloé'.

*For details and garment names, see p.615.

'RENOIR', 'RIMINI', 'RENOUVEAU', 'RÉVEIL'

'If a single image could project Paris fashions for spring and summer next year, it would be Venus de Milo clad in a pair of Bermuda shorts or a mini-skirt,' said Tokyo's *Asahi Evening News*. A reproduction of the famous Ancient Greek statue appeared at the mouth of the Chloé runway, in a postmodern aesthetic complete with fake ruins (columns were painted in a colour gradient). The statue's nude curves seemed to encapsulate the sensual mood that defined both the Paris season as a whole and this Chloé collection.

US *Vogue* gave the look their seal of approval: 'Lagerfeld of Chloé does the newest pants – a "Bermuda kilt" – that ends a little above the knee. He says, "It's part pants, part skirt. Actually, one leg is a short Bermuda pant, then the fabric wraps over into a side-buttoned, side-slit skirt." … It promises to be a big influence on the pants scene.'

'Though Lagerfeld dwells in the 18th century, he designs for modern times,' said *WWD* approvingly. They were especially intrigued by the unique necklines – 'particularly the off-the-shoulder rolled band (sometimes padded) neckline which frames the shoulder' – and the fabrications, many of which were designed by Lagerfeld himself in collaboration with Italian experts such as Bini and Overdrive. Some of the best, according to *WWD*, included: 'A new synthetic blend called Albene that looks like crisp sharkskin but drapes like silk jersey. Huge, sumptuous tropical flowers and leaves teamed with free-form stripes in silk and cotton. Delicate squiggle and refined new wave patterns, and fragile paper-thin silk cloques.'

Also on show were bold printed dresses, worn with patterned leggings or waistcoats. Some came with cheerful flower prints, which went on to feature in a Saks promotional advertisement for Chloé, running with the strapline: 'Here, exotica. Orchids and stripes in grand contrast.' Other gowns came with embroidered lightning strikes across the front, while sundresses came in monotones with a white cuff at the top, exposing the clavicle and shoulders. 'Everything looks pared down, simple,' said the *New York Times*. 'Bravo, Karl Lagerfeld of Chloé, for making clothes people can wear.'*

*For details and garment names, see p. 615.

'SALZBOURG', 'SCIENCE', 'SCYLLA', 'SOIR'

By the time of this show (200 looks, shown in 49 minutes),* Karl Lagerfeld was also creating furs for Fendi and teaching fashion at Vienna's University of Applied Arts – a busy schedule, but one that provided ample sources of inspiration. *WWD* noted that the runway came with gold and black tiles, and was 'styled after the turn-of-the-century Viennese secessionist art movement' (this movement also inspired jewelry by Ugo Correani). According to Hebe Dorsey at the *Herald Tribune*, 'Lagerfeld ... did a tongue-in-cheek interpretation of Vienna's riding school uniforms – long, double-breasted coats with epaulets, military collars, gold buttons, everything except riding crops... Cossack-inspired embroidery was lavished on terribly ornate, costumey coats.'

'It is not the old layering,' Lagerfeld told reporters of the look for this season. 'It is weightless volume. Volume for movement, not for weight.' He was particularly intrigued by the idea of 'confusing' layers. 'Lagerfeld showed what he called his "two-step" – a skirt or dress over pants – throughout the collection,' said the *Washington Post*. *WWD* referred to 'long – very long – dresscoats over cuffed trousers, funny microshort knit dresses, longer versions of his side-slit bermuda kilt from last season [see p.178], and off-the-shoulder fox fur-trimmed evening dresses. And even these are shown over pants.'

The *New York Times* was impressed: 'Full-flowing skirts over narrow trousers and corset-belted waistlines are the key to clothes that are graceful, attractive and new-looking. Lagerfeld is back in the mainstream of fashion, leading the pack.'

Not everyone agreed. 'Karl Lagerfeld clearly expects the wife to wear his mid-calf full-skirted coat dresses ... and the mistress to step out in short leather minis topped by cape-collared knits. This schizophrenic collection produced some delicious clothes... But the dual message will leave many women confused,' wrote Suzy Menkes in *The Times*.

Even Lagerfeld himself had some grumblings – but about the setting, rather than the clothes. By this season, the Chambre Syndicale de la Haute Couture, the organizational body of French fashion, had offered houses the opportunity to show in specially designed tents in Les Halles, 'a renovated restaurant section of Paris that is bordered by sex shops and porn cinemas', according to the *Houston Chronicle*. But Lagerfeld, YSL, Marc Bohan at Dior and Sonia Rykiel were all demanding a new location. The publication noted that Lagerfeld had called the backstage area 'a pigsty (for which he paid $50,000)', dubbing the situation 'a disgrace to France'.

* For details and garment names, see p. 615.

'TALC', 'TROCADÉRO', 'TRIC-TRAC', 'TABLEAU'

'The only length that's not important is the bourgeois knee-length,' Karl Lagerfeld told the *Daily Telegraph*. Alongside micro minis, he offered full skirts and dresses, and, 'just to confuse things further ... skirts that look like trousers, trousers that look like skirts'.*

But it was actually the waist that Lagerfeld was particularly intrigued by this season. 'Hemlines don't make news anymore,' he reportedly told the *Glasgow Herald*. 'The waist, in Lagerfeld's view, is due for reclamation,' Anne Simpson explained, noting the wide array of corsetry in his collection.

Lagerfeld offered the 'wildest widest waist-whittlers in town', according to the *Daily Express*. 'His "corset" is like a wasp-like belt that encases the body from just below the ribcage to the top of the hip-bone.' The corsets, were, Lagerfeld said, inspired by *Nana*, an 1877 painting by Manet.

The team at *WWD* had their eyes on the jewelry: 'The Chloé accessories made a suitably hysterical arrival a few hours before the show – by train from Brussels – and, as usual, they were a mix of the witty and the downright bizarre,' read their report. 'There were huge bulges of bent metal hanging from the neck ("my Madame Grès draped necklaces," explained Lagerfeld), beaded metal hairnets, metal bow ties, huge rainbow-striped plastic bracelets and the daintiest double-layered straw hats.'

Already, Lagerfeld was displaying the taste for catwalk theatrics that would become his signature at Chanel. 'As usual, he started with a gimmick. This season it was a bubbling fountain at one end of the runway and cardboard treetops at the other,' added *WWD*, picking up on the playful joie de vivre of the décor (models such as Pat Cleveland dancing and playing with the water), and noting that this was the 'weekend's star collection'. '[T]he early Sunday morning audience, perked up with blaring tunes by Soft Cell (what Lagerfeld calls his "alarm clock"), loved it.' ('The blast of quadrophonic rock was so ferocious that you staggered two hours later from the place feeling like a victim of a brain surgery without the benefit of anaesthetic,' bemoaned Simpson.)

* *For details and garment names, see p.615.*

'ULTIMATUM',
'VARIÉTÉ', 'WHISKY'

'Karl Lagerfeld for Chloé has slightly relaxed his tight hold on the waistline (remember the corselet belts in his summer collection [see p.190]), and guides us toward accepting very narrow and long wrapover or split skirts,' wrote Anne Price in *Country Life*. And yet, there were still plenty of belts on offer, including wide leather straps and soft ties in rhinestone-studded suede. 'The waistline stays where nature put it, but takes short trips up and down, playing with shapes, form and colours,' read the Chloé press release.

The *Observer* was full of praise, calling the collection 'superbly sophisticated'.* They were particularly enamoured with a new long skirt shape that 'fell to low calf, wrapped and split up the back'. Other skirts came long and 'tight as a pair of pants', according to the press release, which also noted that embroidered evening dresses had a 'constructivist' mood. Lyubov Popova's 1922 stage design for Fernand Crommelynck's play *The Magnificent Cuckold* might have inspired the runway décor. This season, the theatricality of the show was enhanced with dry ice.

In the *Washington Post*, Nina Hyde called this Lagerfeld's 'biggest and most elaborate collection for Chloé'. The look, she said, was 'lots of black, and black with splashes of bright color'. Hyde was particularly taken with the 'elaborately beaded and embroidered black dresses produced by French artisans'.

Accessories stood out, from plexiglass earrings by Ugo Correani for Chloé, to colourful gloves. 'If there is one accessory MUST for fall 1982 it will be a pair of gloves,' said US *Vogue*, noting that 'Karl Lagerfeld at Chloé showed the most glove imagination by doing them in bright colors, sometimes a different color on each hand!' The other big news was brimmed felt hats. 'Men's hats were shown for every time of day,' reported US *Vogue*. 'They topped city and country clothes, even night-time looks at Karl Lagerfeld's collection for Chloé. Many of the runway models could be seen wearing these hats after the collections. The greatest accolade any designer could have, as these girls are usually a step or two ahead of the rest of the fashion crowd.'

Both the belts and hats were widely photographed in the press, including by Arthur Elgort for French *Elle* under the headline 'A Renaissance for Traditional Shapes'. Elgort shot four more of the hats for US *Vogue*. 'At Chloé: another direction, another proportion. Long. Narrow. Soft, soft, soft!' read the headline.

* For details and garment names, see p.616.

'ADAGIO', 'ARPÈGE', 'ACCORD', 'ARGENT'

This season,* the show décor took the shape of a sparkling fan (relating to the launch of a new Chloé perfume, whose bottle used the same shape). Featuring an equally sparkling array of dresses, decorated with musical instruments, this was a collection for those with a sense of humour. One cocktail dress came with a midsection that traced the shape of a violin (see p.200, bottom). A silver guitar shone on the back of a gown (p.200, top), while a clutch bag came decorated with piano keys (opposite, bottom left). The collection kicked off the mood of surrealism and trompe l'œil that dominated Karl Lagerfeld's final few seasons for Chloé during his first tenure at the house.

The collection was an early insight into his later much-publicized love for music (in the mid-2000s, he claimed to own hundreds of iPods for storing his music). Chloé's press release noted that: 'Music is the base of the collection. Embroideries, the jewellery, the prints and many other details are inspired by music, even the cut and the guitar-like form of the body.'

Bernadine Morris for the *New York Times* noted that: 'Under all that jazz were some pretty good clothes.' She praised supple suits, blouses with 'wide, flaring wing collars', and waist-cinchers 'about a foot wide, made of suede or velvet with elastic side panels'. She had less praise for Lagerfeld's 'over-elaborate' evening look (see p.203, top): 'Some of the fancy dresses looked like the one the Good Fairy wore when she told Sleeping Beauty's mother her daughter would awaken when her prince came by.'

Behind the scenes, Lagerfeld was busier than ever. His contract with Chloé was coming to an end and reporters noted that he was having 'battles' with owners Gaby Aghion and Jacques Lenoir (though he initially told reporters he planned to stay on at the house). And he had a new job: at the S/S 1983 couture shows, held in January, Lagerfeld debuted his vision for Chanel (a 'long-stagnant name and legend', according to a *New York Times* report on the appointment), a job he briefly balanced with his duties at Chloé with the help of teams of assistants. 'He sees no conflict in designing for Chloé, Fendi, Chanel, Alma and who knows who else,' reported the *Washington Post*. 'It is like playing another instrument,' Lagerfeld told the reporter. 'You don't throw away the first instrument when you learn to play another. I like to play them all.'

*For details and garment names, see p.616.

'BAIN', 'BRIO', 'BAGAGE', 'BADGE'

Karl Lagerfeld again opted for glittering trompe-l'œil embroideries for this season's Chloé show.* A blue dress came with two taps pouring water down the back (see p.208, left), while a beaded showerhead sprayed sparkling water down a halter-neck gown (p.210). The press note informed attendees that the collection was 'largely based on contradictions' – hence, an elongated look was proposed for daytime, while 'the night reveals the legs'. 'The humour of the "hydraulic" and "useless tool" themes is found in the accessories and also among the embroideries,' it stated. Models emerged from a runway backdrop that resembled a road, complete with white-painted markings.

By this season, change was afoot on the fashion landscape. Lagerfeld was balancing Chloé with Chanel, and a new wave of designers had arrived on the scene. In March 1983, the *New York Times* ran a headline announcing 'The Japanese Challenge to French Fashion', citing the deconstructed looks pioneered recently by Yohji Yamamoto and Rei Kawakubo of Comme des Garçons. 'These clothes from the East represent a different attitude,' said reporter Bernadine Morris, noting that they often attempted to conceal, rather than reveal, the body. And yet, the report declared, the Chloé show was still the highlight of Paris, and Lagerfeld 'managed to stand firm in the face of the Japanese attack on the basic tenets of Western fashion'. Morris explained: 'His basic shape was long and lean, and his clothes had considerable ease. The humor took the form of jewelry shaped like plumbers' tools and hardware. Wrenches, hammers and pliers set with jewels decorated collars and shoulders. Faucets dripped pearls... It was all stylish fun.'

Meanwhile, Lagerfeld was putting on his second Chanel couture show. 'Both collections are quintessentially French... But, while the Chanel and Chloé collections resemble one another in no other way, both are proof of the remarkable talents of Karl Lagerfeld,' read a piece in the *New York Times Magazine*. The story concluded that 'the Chloé collection was judged to be one of its best'.

For details and garment names, see p.616.

'CISEAUX', 'CACHE-CACHE', 'CANDEUR', 'CARACTÈRE'

'Will Karl Lagerfeld leave Chloé? This agonizing question, which obsesses everyone while we wait for the next presidential elections in 1988, defines this spring/summer collection,' read a report in the French publication *Femme* after this show, which was staged in October 1983.*

In the end, François Mitterrand would be re-elected President, and Lagerfeld did indeed depart Chloé, with this collection marking the end of a nearly twenty-year stint at the house (he would return for a second run in 1992; see p. 296). The process of him leaving was protracted and led to much gossiping in the press. By November 1983, *WWD* reported that Lagerfeld had moved his belongings from the Chloé offices. Come December, they announced that Guy Paulin was his likely successor – an appointment that would be confirmed by January 1984.

Still, the S/S 1984 show was well received. One theme, among several, was Classical dress, including new takes on togas. These appeared alongside striped pieces with a nautical feel. Critics, such as Bernadine Morris in the *New York Times*, praised the 'inventive prints', 'some with a childlike quality and something suggesting computer printouts'.

Femme noted the surrealist mood of the collection. One dress came furnished with embroidered sequins in the form of a Chloé top on a hanger (see p. 218). Sewing motifs, such as scissors on collars, spools of thread on belts and pincushion bangles, showed Lagerfeld's wit, and nodded to his skill as an expert of cut and construction. Bernadine Morris called it a 'homage to the craft of dressmaking', noting, 'Mr. Lagerfeld did for people who sew what he did for plumbers last time [see p. 204]; He eulogized the tools of their trade.'

'I love trompe l'œil: it's not pretentious, it's a new touch for Chloé's little black dress, of which the client already owns several versions,' Lagerfeld told *Vogue Paris*. 'The motif of embroidered scissors forms part of my silent tableaux, which do away with any of the boredom of the traditional black dress. The world turned upside down is a concept for our age, an inversion of concepts.'

The show décor included giant tailors' dummies, as well as a background painted with a little plane, its pilot sporting a ponytail. Chloé seamstress Anita Briey recalls that, as soon as the seamstresses saw the décor, they understood that Lagerfeld would soon be departing.

* *For details and garment names, see p. 616.*

The Studio
The Mid-1980s

Immediately after Karl Lagerfeld's departure from Chloé, press speculation was rife that his colleague Guy Paulin would be named the house's next creative director. Paulin (1946–1990) had a rich background as a freelance designer. His journey in fashion began aged 17, when he arrived in Paris from Champagne and took a job as an elevator boy at the Printemps department store. He soon transitioned into working with the buying team, where he learned about design and created illustrations for the store's press releases. Later, he worked as a designer for the raincoat brand Jimper and as an assistant at Dorothée Bis. In the late 1960s, he moved to New York, working for the boutique chain Paraphernalia, as well as Mary Quant, Emmanuelle Khanh and Lison Bonfils. On returning to Paris, he worked as a designer and stylist for various brands, including Georges Edelmann, P. Plume, Bercher, Olivier de Verlon, Mic Mac, Max Mara and Byblos. In 1980, he founded a ready-to-wear collection under his own name, which he would suspend upon confirmation of his appointment to the top job at Chloé, in January 1984, aged 38. Sadly, Paulin's work for Chloé was widely critiqued, and he left the house the following year. He returned to his own label, and also worked for a number of other brands, including Charles Jourdan and the French company Heaston (footwear) and the Japanese company Kanematsu Gosho (knitwear). He died in 1990 from an AIDS-related illness, aged just 44.

While Paulin was at Chloé, the house hired former Chanel designer Philippe Guibourgé to work on the collections alongside him (a somewhat ironic switch-around, given that Chloé's former star Karl Lagerfeld had just left for Chanel). Guibourgé (1931–1986) had got his start in fashion at 24, when he showed his sketches to Jacques Fath. After three years at Fath, and a short period at Lanvin-Castillo, he joined Christian Dior, where he worked on the couture and accessories collections as an assistant to Marc Bohan. In 1967, he took a role working on the diffusion line and helped create Miss Dior. At the age of 34, Guibourgé became the creative director of the Miss Dior ready-to-wear collections. Eight years later, in 1975, he moved to Chanel, where he launched the house's first ready-to-wear line, named Création Chanel. In 1982, he left to establish his own label. He joined Chloé in 1984 but left in 1985, after which he aimed to resume his own label. However, he died of chronic hepatitis in 1986, at the age of 54.

For the autumn/winter 1985–1986 season, Guy Paulin was joined by the London-born Irish designer Peter O'Brien (b. 1951), an existing Chloé staffer, as well as the Milanese designer Luciano Soprani (1946–1999), who also created the ready-to-wear for Basile and ran his own line. Teamwork – and collaboration between different talents – had been a key component to Gaby Aghion's early vision for Chloé. So, in one manner, the involvement of various voices in establishing what Chloé could look like, post-Lagerfeld, was natural. And yet, unsurprisingly, the lack of direction, or clear vision, confused and frustrated both press and buyers, who were consistently unimpressed with Chloé in the first few years following Lagerfeld's departure.

By S/S 1986, the house had decided that a single, strong voice was essential, and settled on Peter O'Brien as the leading man. He was a Central Saint Martins graduate, who had worked at Christian Dior under Marc Bohan, and at Givenchy. His reign was, like Paulin's, short-lived. Come August 1986, O'Brien was replaced by 38-year-old Carlos Rodriguez (b. 1948), who had previously worked at the Italian ready-to-wear firm Maska. However, he left Chloé the following year.

This period marked a time of transition and disruption for Chloé, where, beyond the design studio, various changes were afoot: business staff came and went, and, in 1985, the house was sold to Dunhill Holdings PLC, leading to the departure of Chloé's founder and long-term guide, Gaby Aghion.

'DAMAS', 'DIAGHILEV', 'DAIMLER', 'DANIELI'

'This is a dream to me,' Guy Paulin told *WWD* of his appointment at Chloé. The 38-year-old French designer temporarily closed his own ready-to-wear line in order to focus his attentions solely on Chloé, but immediately things did not run smoothly. 'The first collection this house has tried with designer Guy Paulin* fell, to put it mildly, flat,' wrote Hebe Dorsey in the *International Herald Tribune*. 'After a deadly silent show, some buyers were running away from reporters, refusing to talk, or if they did, insisting that they not be quoted by name.'

Paulin told *WWD* that he had been seeking to capture the elegance and independence of women like Katharine Hepburn: 'Someone who is free-spirited, who follows fashion with a maturity and assimilates it perfectly.' Suzy Menkes in *The Times* noted that Paulin 'wants, he told me in his gentle voice, to bring femininity to sportswear, to produce tender colours and gentle fabrics to counter the aggressive trend of tough leather and hard-edged man-tailoring'. Paulin, she said, 'had all the right ideas but used them wrongly'.

'The long-awaited Chloé show for next winter's ready-to-wear proved a lackluster affair,' wrote Suzy Patterson in *News-Free Press*. '[T]here was nowhere near the excitement and pizazz as when Karl Lagerfeld was the fashion guru at Chloé... Paulin – who has designed under his own name – produced clothes that neither excited nor tempted one to go out and buy. They ranged from an uninspired pyjamas look with cardigans a la '30s to rather tightly fitted jackets or loose-pleated boleros over long-pleated skirts or culottes.'

WWD were similarly dismissive: 'Chloé, with Guy Paulin designing, is unfocused and undirected, notable only in its penchant for Fifties bargain-basement looks and a muddy color palette that appeals to Middle Europe, but not to Middle America.'

Such was the distress of buyers, Gaby Aghion made an emergency hire to pad out the collection. 'When American retailers – who comprise 60 per cent of Chloé's export business – were not sated by the eveningwear in Guy Paulin's fall collection ... the house recruited former Chanel designer Philippe Guibourgé to whip up a capsule collection of sparkling evening looks in record time – about a month,' read a report in *WWD*. The new set was displayed at New York's Pierre Hotel in June 1984.

* *For details and garment names, see p. 617.*

'ÉLYSÉE', 'EASY', 'ENERGIE', 'EXTASE'

Reviews of this collection* – while less barbed than for Guy Paulin's debut for the house (see p.222) – were still negative. To balance Paulin, Gaby Aghion had again hired Philippe Guibourgé to create eveningwear. The dynamic in the Chloé studio now recalled the earliest years of the house, when various designers contributed to each collection. And yet, the results of teamwork, this time, were not a success.

'Just as a camel is a horse designed by a committee, so the Chloé collection was this uneasy marriage, only this time it was a marriage à trois for the shade of Lagerfeld hung very visibly over many outfits,' said Serena Sinclair in the *Daily Telegraph*.

WWD explained, 'It began with Philippe Guibourgé's evening wear, a ho-hum procession of well-made, matronly dresses masquerading as sweet young things. Paulin followed with clothes that did, in moments of schoolgirlish joie de vivre, rekindle the Chloé image.' But a faulty runway set, which required a handyman with a hammer and nails as models walked, did not help create a sense of optimism: 'cruel fate intervened to pronounce [Paulin's] design signature as yet inchoate, with the letter C in the Chloé logo repeatedly dropping to the floor of the runway during the show. This house is in need of repair.'

Others were more positive. 'The collection was excellent, proving again that no one is indispensable. Lagerfeld, however, has the satisfaction of knowing it took two men to replace him,' said the *Palm Beach Daily News*, noting that the designs were 'perfect for the woman who spends the summer lunching in a big city or the winter in a sophisticated small town like Palm Beach'.

'Paulin does not have the sparkle of Lagerfeld, but his admirers praise his low-key sense of elegance,' wrote Hebe Dorsey in the *International Herald Tribune*, singling out a group of beige knits 'which looked as if they had just escaped from some stylish convent'. Evening dress, however, 'was still a problem... Aghion, realizing that Paulin, who is essentially a sportswear designer, could not cope, kept looking for somebody else and finally hired Guibourgé... All one can say is that Aghion should keep looking.'

For details and garment names, see p.617.

'FIDÈLE', 'FAÏENCE', 'FRANCHE', 'FRISSON'

Perhaps unsurprisingly, given reviews of his collections (see pp. 222 and 224), Guy Paulin had, ahead of this show, announced that he would be departing Chloé. 'This season will be the last. It is not in my interest to continue. It was a casting error,' he told *WWD*.

To bulk out the team, Gaby Aghion added two more designers to help create the autumn/winter 1985–1986 collection:* Peter O'Brien, an existing Chloé staffer, and Milanese designer Luciano Soprani, who helmed his own line and created the ready-to-wear for Basile. Referencing the possible additional contribution of Philippe Guibourgé, the *Philadelphia Inquirer* quipped: 'The Chloé fall collection was reportedly whipped up by four designers ... which is three too many. There were lots of hors-d'oeuvres but no main course. Name the style and it came trotting down the runway, and though most of the clothes were quite attractive and wearable, they were also quite forgettable.'

'The house of Chloé has been having a particularly rough year since Karl Lagerfeld left them to set up his own label,' said the *Observer*, adding, 'There were some garments in the Chloé show which would ... have looked far better hidden in the back of a very dark wardrobe.'

There was change going on in the boardroom, as well as the studio. In 1985, a few days before the show, the sale of Chloé to Dunhill Holdings PLC was announced in the press.

* For details and garment names, see p. 617.

'GIRASOL', 'GRANDIOSE', 'GEORGIE', 'GRAVURE'

'We decided that one strong designer would make a better impression than a group effort,' Gaby Aghion told reporters ahead of her S/S 1986 collection.* The chosen man was Peter O'Brien, the London-born Irish designer and Central Saint Martins graduate, who had been part of the team behind Chloé's poorly received A/W 1985–1986 show (see p.226). His solo effort went down far better with critics.

'The House of Chloé made a long-awaited comeback Friday with a vibrant collection that was well balanced with short and long alternatives,' said the *San Francisco Chronicle*. O'Brien 'dipped into children's playrooms for ideas', they noted, of the toy prints featuring yo-yos and balloons in primary colours on black and white backgrounds. 'These were clothes to be seen in once and remembered,' the *Chronicle* concluded.

'Designer Peter O'Brien comes up with the best Chloé collection since Lagerfeld's departure and gives the buyers plenty to rave over,' agreed the *Washington Post*. He 'brings to Chloé a sense of wit and humour it is hoped will assert a new, young contemporary image for the house, which has sadly missed the talent of Karl Lagerfeld,' added the *Daily Telegraph*.

Aghion – who briefly stayed on, despite the sale of her house – told reporters, defiantly: 'People said that when Karl leaves, the house will crumble. But when an orchestra leader leaves, the orchestra is still there. People think Chloé is Lagerfeld, they are mistaken.'

Chloé

'HISTOIRE', 'HARMONIUM', 'HALLUCINANT', 'HALTE'

The reception for Peter O'Brien's second collection for Chloé was mixed. Some reporters were intrigued by the 'dandy' air of the looks, and the play on contrasts. *Le Figaro* praised the combination of cuts and fits: 'by combining extremes – the very short and the very long, the very wide and the very narrow – Chloé offers us a collection for the well-to-do who like to change their silhouette and style according to their mood'.*

And yet, other critics felt the collection still lacked punch. 'Chloé ... with Karl Lagerfeld, put deluxe ready-to-wear on the map. Lagerfeld left long ago and the house was sold to Dunhill. One cannot expect the same kind of fireworks now, but the collection Friday made it clear that the house still needs a good designer,' said Hebe Dorsey in the *International Herald Tribune*. 'The opening was a sad rendition of WWI, with gray flannel coats over long pleated dresses. The headmistress glasses, long amber necklaces and unbecoming hats did not help.' 'Just OK from Peter O'Brien. Evening, just bad,' said *WWD*, curtly.

By June 1986, Chloé had opened new offices in New York. 'We'll certainly open a boutique in New York and it will be on Madison,' new managing director Gaël de Kertanguy told *WWD*. 'Chloé will be in Tokyo in a year's time,' added another official. O'Brien also had (short-lived) plans for expansion, with a new, accessible look and more affordable price structure. 'We're aiming for a younger image,' he told *WWD*. 'A lot of younger women – from about 25 to 35 – buy designer clothes. They know the Chloé name from perfume.' Kertanguy added, somewhat awkwardly, 'Even if sales disappeared after Karl's ... departure, the name remains strong.' Perhaps predictably, by August 1986, O'Brien had departed the house.

'ICI', 'INDÉNIABLE', 'ICEBERG', 'IMAGE'

Chloé's new creative director – the latest
in a revolving door of designers, who had
all received almost entirely negative reviews –
was 38-year-old Carlos Rodriguez, formerly
of the Italian ready-to-wear firm Maska. He
was appointed in August 1986, and by October
the reviews for his debut spring/summer 1987
collection* were in. 'Buyers were left confused
by an undisciplined collection that desperately
needed editing,' said *WWD* of the show, which
featured a predominantly black-and-white
colour palette and some unusual styling,
including round sunglasses and caps.
Chloé, they concluded, 'continues to
search for a new identity'.

The press, however, did offer some support.
Jardins des Modes featured Chloé's 'culotte
de petit marquis' (opposite left), fastened at
the sides with satin bows, noting: 'Strong
point: the use of classic lace for pirate pants.'
Peter Lindbergh photographed a Chloé bustier
and trouser combination on the model Yasmin
Le Bon for *Vogue Italia*, under the headline
'Ruffles and Puffs', while Patrick Demarchelier
featured a nautical ensemble on Christy
Turlington for US *Vogue*. The season's
advertising campaign, carried in *Vogue*,
included a vivacious line drawing of
a Chloé look, signed 'Rodriguez'.

* *For details and garment names, see p. 618.*

PLEATING AND PLAYS WITH ASYMMETRY

Shortly before the A/W 1987–1988 show, Chloé had yet another departure. In January 1987, recently appointed managing director Gaël de Kertanguy announced his resignation. 'Business in fashion is very difficult,' he told *WWD*. 'It is taking a long time to reorganize and get results. That is the challenge of Chloé today.' The house announced that designer Carlos Rodriguez, who had debuted his vision for Chloé the previous season to little fanfare (see p.232), would remain.

The look this season featured pleating and plays with asymmetry. For evening, there were fitted velvet tops paired with draped taffeta skirts.

The reviewers were pointed in their lack of praise and excitement. 'Carlos Rodriguez showed a collection' was all *WWD* could bring themselves to say in their 'Paris Now' round-up of the season. (Compare that to the Agnès B review – 'democratic fashion for all ages' – or Martine Sitbon's 'good collection of ladylike clothes, styled with a modern and often humorous touch'.) At least one of Rodriguez's peers got the same treatment. 'He showed a collection, too,' said *WWD* of Bernard Perris.

Unsurprisingly, by May, Rodriguez had departed, with a Chloé spokesperson citing 'difficulties' as the explanation.

Martine Sitbon

A Short Biography

French, young, daring: Martine Sitbon had showed only three collections of her eponymous brand before being headhunted as a design consultant at Chloé. She was a rarity on the Paris scene: a young, female designer, doing her own thing. 'It was very new to take a young designer to rethink a house – it's normal now, but not then,' Sitbon later told the journalist Sarah Mower. 'My own collection was much younger, more fun and extravagant. But it was great for me to be able to work on something more couture and grown-up.'

Born in 1952 in Casablanca, Morocco, Sitbon first became interested in fashion as a teenager, attending music concerts and putting together going-out outfits from flea markets. She enjoyed drawing and illustrating, and, encouraged by her sister, she applied to the Parisian fashion school Studio Berçot. She graduated in 1974, at the moment Karl Lagerfeld's Chloé was dominating fashion press.

Sitbon later told *AnOther Magazine* that it was her visits to London that formed her voice as a fashion designer (interesting, given Chloé's later preference for cool young London creatives, such as Stella McCartney and Phoebe Philo). 'There was a lot of freedom, it opened my imagination. Music, fashion, art – culture. They were all thrown together, and it all came to life on the street. London was very different from Paris – when I was in London, I would dress up and no one would look twice... When I started my first collection, in 1986 or '87, the journalists were saying that I was the most English of the French designers.'

Music – and, specifically, the music of the 1970s with which Sitbon came of age – provided an enduring point of reference. She also had a strong interest in costume design. In 1989, Sitbon created studded leather waistcoats with Hells Angels motifs. At Chloé she incorporated these kitschier elements – leather, studs, sequins – with the luxury materials and delicate textures more typical of Chloé's ready-to-wear, such as fine organzas made to look like petals.

Where Sitbon's eponymous collection was youth-focused – taking inspiration from the street, where cutting-edge styles toyed with ideas of gender and beauty – in her vision for Chloé, she focused on the notion of the Chloé girl as an emblem of strong femininity. She added to this an interest in 'ethnic' influences, as they were called by the press, including elaborate beading and rich, earthy hues.

Unsurprisingly, given that Sitbon's partner was the acclaimed art director Marc Ascoli, her tenure also saw a shift in the vision of Chloé within photography, with bold advertising campaigns featuring supermodels such as Tatjana Patitz and Linda Evangelista, shot by the likes of Max Vadukul and Philip Dixon.

Like Lagerfeld before her, Sitbon made clever use of nostalgia and wistfulness – 'sometimes old Hollywood, sometimes more Victorian', as she put it – all while pushing forward ideas of what a 'feminine' wardrobe could be. Her epoch at the house is particularly defined by a move towards androgyny, visible in the many tuxedos and trouser suits that appeared on her runway, punctuating the more expected gowns and embroidered dresses. As had been the case during Lagerfeld's reign, Sitbon's Chloé was the era of the glamazon – Naomi Campbell, Christy Turlington, Helena Christensen et al all walked for Sitbon – but she also cast quirkier, more androgynous models of the day, such as Kirsten Owen and Kristen McMenamy.

Sitbon later categorized her time as part of a tradition at Chloé for hiring young, often female talents. 'Chloé had this thing where they began to pick up young designers and they carried on,' she told Sarah Mower in 2012. 'I think it's really become part of the Chloé heritage... I was the first young girl to be a named [sole] designer for the house. And for me, it was an incredible experience.'

After nine seasons, Sitbon left Chloé when her contract ended in Spring 1992 and Lagerfeld was reported as poised to rejoin the company. It was time to focus exclusively on her own label, whose brand identity she had been developing with Ascoli, photographer Nick Knight and graphic designers M/M, among other fashion luminaries. She remained on the Left Bank, inaugurating her rue de Grenelle flagship store in 1996. In 2006 she launched a new brand, Rue du Mail, which ran until 2013. By then, she had been made Chevalier des Arts et des Lettres by the French government.

SINGLE-TONE TAFFETA AND GIANT STRAW HATS

In May 1987, Chloé announced their new design partnership with the buzzy young French designer Martine Sitbon, who, they confirmed, would work as part of a team. Sitbon, then 35, already had an up-and-coming eponymous line (see p.234), which she declared plans to continue, alongside Chloé.

Sitbon's 'signature collection was launched in 1984, and she has gained a reputation as a designer to watch for young, trendy looks', noted *WWD*, who referred to her, in a separate piece, as 'French fashion's *femme totale*'. 'A Parisian touch – always a Parisian touch. That's me, I guess,' Sitbon said of her look and inspiration. 'Her eccentric style has generated a lot of noise from the press and spawned a fanatic following that swoons for the psychic quality of her baby doll and empire dresses, madcap trims and feisty hats,' continued *WWD*. Sitbon herself noted, 'Maybe you can't wear everything I design to the supermarket, but I still try to create something that would be beautiful, not foolish.' Her debut collection for Chloé included various single-tone taffeta gowns – in olive, lilac and rose – and giant straw hats.

WWD noted that, since Karl Lagerfeld's departure in 1984, Chloé had suffered from lagging sales and a lack of vision. 'I think it will be an interesting experience to recreate the Chloé woman,' Sitbon told the reporter.

FROCK COATS, SCARVES AND STOLES

Despite the appointment of the talented Martine Sitbon (see p.240), Chloé was still struggling to drum up attention in the press. A brief reference to Sitbon's A/W 1988–1989 collection could be found in *WWD*, in a piece titled 'The Pants of Paris'. At Chloé, 'pants get a touch of the exotic', the article said. 'Designer Martine Sitbon pairs gathered, billowy sarong [s]kirtpants with tailored jackets and vests.'

Still, Sitbon was starting to fine-tune her look for Chloé: the heavily embroidered jackets and waistcoats shown here would foreshadow the Eastern-inspired, ornate yet breezily bohemian pieces that would define her tenure at the house. Indeed, many of her looks were inspired by her time spent living and working in India and Mexico.

The *Washington Post* felt that this season's frock coats, which had shades of the 17th and 18th centuries, were on the money and part of an interesting trend that season: 'Romeo Gigli likes them. So do Jean Paul Gaultier, Lagerfeld and Chloé. Think of a man's swallowtail jacket worn for white tie occasions (or high school proms) and you get the silhouette perfectly.' *L'Officiel* praised the scarves and stoles, and the way Sitbon had turned her attention to 'sculpting and draping giant collars for an extremely glittering and sophisticated silhouette'. Sitbon, they said, was 'reinvigorating the sense of luxury at Chloé'.

SARONG SKIRTS
AND SAILOR PANTS

This was a 'well-made collection that hasn't found its voice yet', said *WWD* of Chloé's S/S 1989 offer. 'Martine Sitbon, now the sole designer at Chloé, has put some consistency into the collection,' they noted. 'Most successful were the sarong skirts with long men's wear jackets which echoed the Indian trend that's sweeping Paris. The sailor pants or culottes paired with cropped jackets also worked.' (A separate article in *WWD* commented that the look fitted with the season's trend for '[n]autical, seaside looks', thanks to the gold button-trimmed trousers.) And yet, there was room for improvement: 'Evening, which featured heavily embroidered saris, was ... a faux pas.'

British *Vogue* felt that Sitbon was on the money. In their 'Collections '89' guide, they highlighted how Chloé's '[g]ilded buttons shine' in a trend piece on the vogue for navy, white and black ensembles. An intricately embroidered red waistcoat (see p.252) was also featured in a piece on fine detail: 'Close scrutiny of summer shapes and fabrics reveals connecting themes,' read the article's introduction. 'Sarongs continue as a summer staple, gold and silver embroidery shines at night...' *Le Monde* agreed that the collection fitted with the strong mood for 'Orientalism', thanks to glittering jackets and waistcoats embroidered with gold and precious stones.

Writing in the March issue of British *Vogue* on the trend for nostalgia, the critic Sarah Mower noted, 'seventies references are turning up all over the place in "young" London and Paris fashion', citing Katharine Hamnett, John Galliano and Jean Paul Gaultier. 'Most exaggerated of all were Martine Sitbon's collections, for Chloé and under her own name, which have been drifting through the late sixties for some seasons, and have now arrived firmly in the early seventies for summer '89.'

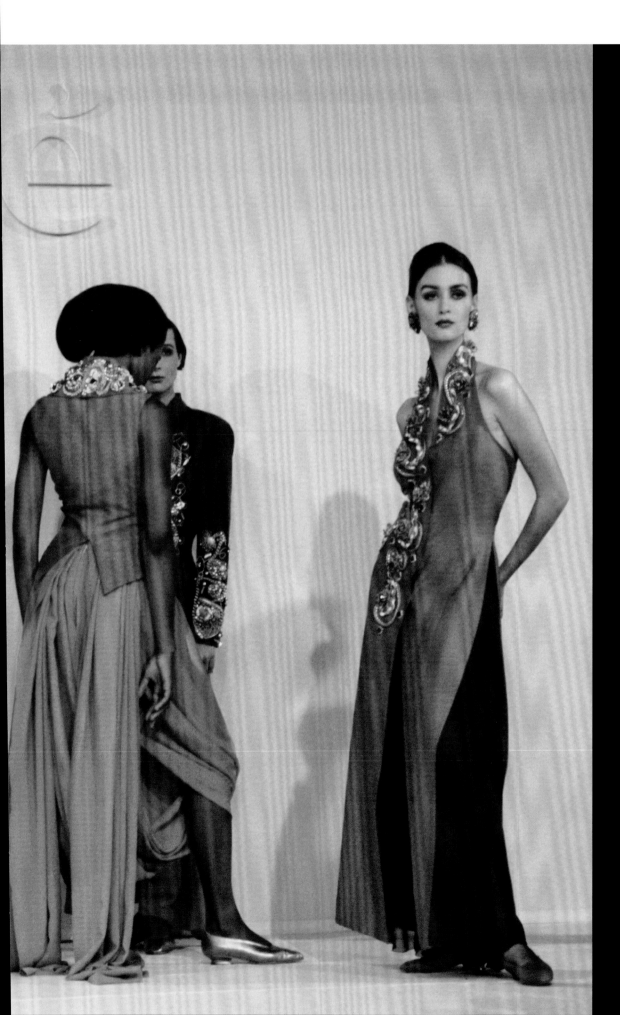

DANDIES AND EMBROIDERIES

By now, Martine Sitbon's collections had started to attract more attention. 'Sitbon is the doyenne of massive lapels and floppy collars, hipster bell-bottoms, maxi coats, hippy embroideries,' wrote Sarah Mower in British *Vogue*. Sitbon told Mower, 'With Chloé, particularly, I am not joking so much. I like real clothes, perfect cuts – I don't like bad taste, even if I play with it. I'm always walking on the edge.'

An Early Fall collection, staged in New York in February 1989 was well-received. 'The emphasis is on softly tailored sportswear looks,' said *WWD*. 'That's where Sitbon excels.' The main Fall collection was met with a more muted response: 'Faltered,' said *WWD*, curtly.

However, after a quiet few years, Chloé garments were once again appearing in editorials, including a story on the 'dandy' look, shot for French *Elle* by Friedmann Hauss and featuring Chloé embroideries – a Sitbon signature that often drew inspiration from Indian and Mexican garments (she had spent time in both countries).

Sales were also up. A report in *WWD* titled 'Who's Selling and Who's Not' in March 1989 noted that Chloé garments were moving again. 'Chloé was good for fall and this spring looked very good,' said one American buyer. 'It looks new, young and elegant with a luxe feeling.' (Claude Montana was also doing well; Christian Lacroix and Paul Louis Orrier were not.) By June, Dunhill announced that Chloé was profitable for the first time since they had acquired the house in 1985. 'Everyone knows Chloé has had a difficult time,' said Sior Pendle, the group's managing director. 'But a lot of work has been put into it and it looks like it is on the way to making good profits. We are very pleased with it and look in the future to its being a significant worldwide business.'

KNOTS AND DRAPES

'Paris: Moving and Shaking', reported *WWD*
in September, of the S/S 1990 season. 'This
was Martine Sitbon's fourth season at Chloé,
and she's proving she can go the distance,'
read their review the following month.
'While she plays wild child in her own
collection, Martine tames her savagery here.
The result this time was some pretty clothes.'
WWD were particularly impressed with the
mini-jumpsuits in dotted silk, which were
styled under long 'bathrobe coats', and the
chiffon T-shirts covered with mosaic-style
beading on the chest. One such embellished
piece – a dress with sequins over the bust and
hips, revealing the midriff behind a delicate
layer of sheer fabric (see p.265) – was shot
by Irving Penn for US *Vogue*. 'Front & Center',
read the headline: 'This season's midriff-
baring fashions demand a well-toned torso.'

'Sitbon has dreamed up Deauville in the
Thirties in a mix of checks, stripes and
polkadots of all sizes,' continued *WWD*'s
September report. 'Evening is inspired
by Isadora Duncan's dancing costumes …
with knotted and draped shapes.'

British *Vogue* were fans of Sitbon's knotted
shirts, worn with coordinating trousers.
'Martine Sitbon at Chloé opted for the
gypsy-cum-rumba musician, [teaming] hot
orange tie-blouses with skintight trousers –
only the maracas are missing,' they said.
That season's advertising campaign echoed
the sensual, vibrant mood of the collection,
featuring Linda Evangelista shot by
Max Vadukul.

A financial report in *WWD* noted that the
Chloé business was continuing to recover,
and that its licence business was growing
(that season, for example, a new deal for
women's golf clothing in Japan, under
the Chloé name, had been confirmed). An
executive from Dunhill, Chloé's owner, noted
plans for the house to push into accessories.

CLEAN SHAPES
AND SLINKY GOWNS

Reviews for Martine Sitbon's autumn/winter
1990–1991 show for Chloé continued to
highlight how the designer cleaved distinct
identities for her eponymous label and for
her Chloé collections. 'Martine Sitbon must be
schizophrenic,' said a review in *WWD*. 'In her
own collection, she has a wild side, but in her
fifth collection at Chloé, Sitbon is schoolmarm
tame.'

The review noted her continued taste for
the retro: 'Her Seventies-style showed in
unfortunate plaid jackets over striped flared
pants, but Sitbon toned it down with clean
jacket shapes in mixed bright and muted
tones.' Historical influences were present
elsewhere in the collection: from 19th-century
dandies in double-breasted two-piece suits
(see right – a recurring reference in Sitbon's
collections; see also p.254) to 1940s Hollywood
vamps with *femme fatale* tight sequinned
dresses, gothic hoods and show-stopping
cape-style sleeves.

Slinky silk gowns, in block colours, were
popular with photographers. For US *Vogue*,
Peter Lindbergh shot Linda Evangelista, in
character as Ava Gardner, in a silver dress
from the collection. The supermodel Yasmeen
Ghauri, who modelled in this season's runway
show (see p.271), wore the same dress in a
shoot for *Elle*, photographed by Walter Chin.

Three months after the show, an obituary
announced the death on 13 June 1990 of
Guy Paulin, who had helmed Chloé shortly
before Sitbon (see pp.222–7), from AIDS-
related complications.

CHIC, FRENCH FEMININITY

'With this collection, Chloé begins to rediscover the charm it had been missing,' said *WWD* of this show. 'Martine Sitbon's collection for Chloé was chic, feminine and utterly French, and it was a refreshing breath of air on Friday. Her organza blouses, in white under a gabardine jumpsuit for day [see opposite, right] or in lovely colours for night [see p.275], were a knockout, as were some of her short cocktail dresses.' These evening looks also included bejewelled pieces – a Sitbon signature – and gowns with origami-style rose motifs (see right and p.276).

And yet, despite this press acclaim, consensus among Chloé bosses was that the correct vision had still not been found. 'Chloé Reshapes Its Identity', read a headline in *WWD*, three months after the show. The article included an interview with Chloé's new president, Mounir Moufarrige, who stated that the house would be pivoting towards a 'more feminine, fresh and younger' look, and would be padding out its spring/summer offer with newly introduced accessories, including leather handbags with a gold-plated fastening shaped like a lily. 'We'd gone a bit too much toward tailoring,' Moufarrige said of Sitbon's spring/summer creations. 'Martine is a tailor. That's her forte. We've redirected her to go more toward femininity, sensuality and a flow in dresses. It's the essence of what Chloé stands for.'

BRIGHT HUES AND OPULENT EMBELLISHMENT

Shown just two months after Chloé's new president declared that he wanted a new look from Martine Sitbon for the house – less tailoring, more youthful femininity (see p.272) – this collection, unsurprisingly, included many bright hues and much opulent embellishment.

'Martine Sitbon celebrated color in her Chloé collection,' said *WWD*. 'Bold splashes of turquoise, coral, lipstick red and apple green livened up simple ribbed knit catsuits and oversized sweater dresses.' The look was a hit with photographers. The ensemble worn by Helena Christensen on the catwalk (opposite, top) was later shot by Ellen von Unwerth for *Vogue Italia*, while an outfit with a jewelled bra held up by a choker necklace, modelled at the show by Carla Bruni (p.280, bottom), was shot for *L'Officiel* (a caption dubbed the look 'an evening treasure'). Similarly, a floral-printed dress coat, which came with a long train and a fuchsia lining (see p.283), was worn by Juliette Binoche in an editorial in *Elle* to promote the release of her new film, Leos Carax's *Les Amants du Pont-Neuf*.

WWD praised Sitbon's fresh take on uniforms: 'Sitbon blended British and military style in short, double-breasted brass-buttoned wool coats and suits with shirt collars. But she went off-duty at night, with her glistening gold and silver embroidered satin suits and dresses that had a whiff of Eastern incense.' The report was less impressed with Sitbon's inclusion of marabou, and Paris's wider trend for plumage: 'Like other members of the fashion flock, Sitbon declared open season on birds – there were just too many feathers, on cuffs, hats, collars, boas and even some very ticklish short jackets that looked like down parkas with their shells stripped off [see opposite, top].'

SOPHISTICATED AND SASSY

This collection continued Chloé's migration towards the young, the feminine, the frilly, flippy and slinky. 'At Chloé, Martine Sitbon went from sexy sophistication in navy on black to bold and sassy with her bright printed separates. When it came to the season's trends, her fringed dresses, transparent blouses and high-slit skirts were right on the mark,' said *WWD*.

On show were silk organdy blouses in block colours, a reworking of those shown for S/S 1991 (see p. 272). A lilac version, adorned with flowers (see p. 286, top), was featured in *Elle* alongside the caption 'Imperial peonies'. The magazine called the blouse 'splendidly low-cut and ruffled'. Indeed, the many floral prints, including more origami-style flower shapes, also offered a nod to past seasons. Similarly, jewelled bodysuits and corsets, for evening, recalled Sitbon's taste for glitter and cabaret show costumes adorned with embellishments (see also pp. 272 and 278).

Creating fresh excitement were Chloé's accessories – part of the new strategy for boosting sales at the house. A report in British *Vogue* announced the opening of Selfridges' accessories department with an exclusive launch of Chloé's accessories line: 'perfectly Parisian silk scarves, signature jewellery and colourful leather bags'.

HOLLYWOOD GLAMOUR

'Martine Sitbon, a great favorite with the French, designs two collections, one under her own name and one for Chloé. Both are rather theatrical, but in different ways,' read a report in the *New York Times* on the season. After the departure of Karl Lagerfeld, whose collections had been met with clamouring attention from reporters, Chloé had struggled to drum up significant international press attention, but, with the growing success of Sitbon's work and rumours of coming changes at the house, this was starting to shift. The *New York Times* said that Chloé's models resembled 'Hollywood movie stars of the 1940's, with bright red lipstick and softly waved shoulder-skimming hair'. The house offered 'fur scarves with classic daytime suits for the lunching ladies' and 'went glamorous for evening with pouffed dresses that were short in front and long in back, and with a series of black dresses loaded with enough jet beads, ruffles, lace and fringe to qualify for the Ziegfeld Follies'. The equestrian garments – such as jodhpurs, veiled top hats, and silk riding gloves teamed with a slinky dress (see right and opposite) – added another element of kink and theatricality to the collection.

And yet, it was the drama off the catwalk that enthralled many attendees. In November 1991, *WWD* first reported rumours that Lagerfeld had plans to return to Chloé, and in March 1992, during the A/W 1992–1993 shows, they followed up again: 'You have to pity poor Martine Sitbon. The day she showed her Chloé collection was also the day rumors resurfaced that Karl Lagerfeld was coming back... There may be an announcement in a few days. Does this mean Karl would actually design three Paris collections, in addition to Fendi in Rome? Apparently so. Only recently, Karl's fortune teller told him he would return to Chloé 10 years after he left. Thus, it seems, it was preordained that Mounir Moufarrige, president of Chloé, attend the KL collection Friday morning...'

Karl Lagerfeld

A Short Biography: Part II

Chloé 'will be the soft side of my personality, while KL [the Karl Lagerfeld brand] is more the hard side. It'll be like Dr. Jekyll and Mr. Hyde,' Karl Lagerfeld told *WWD* of his return to Chloé, the house that had launched his career back in the mid-1960s. Since leaving almost ten years before, in 1984, he had achieved acclaim as the creative director at Chanel and had started his own eponymous label, all while continuing his work with Fendi. The fashion press was aghast at the workload, even for the notoriously indefatigable Lagerfeld. 'Why not?' retorted the designer. 'I'm very organized in my head and in my studio and I have great people. You have to remember that I do nothing else. That's how I manage. Twenty-four hours a day. I don't go on holiday. I have a very quiet life. I spend my time reading, sketching and designing.'

'Karl, Chloé Reunited by Dunhill Deal', read the 2 June 1992 *WWD* headline, which explained to readers that – after six months of negotiations – Chloé's owners had acquired a stake in Lagerfeld's eponymous line, and had used the deal as a means to re-position their former golden boy at Chloé once again.

'Chloé is a language I already know,' Lagerfeld told *WWD*. Indeed, not only had he led the house through its 1970s heyday, he had also maintained a relationship with the company through his Chloé fragrance deals – shrewdly negotiated during his original tenure at the house, during which time the scents were created – which saw him receive a 60% royalty each year from Elizabeth Arden. When asked if he earned more than $10 million a year, Lagerfeld replied, 'Oh, it's much more than that!'

In October 1992, *WWD* would call Lagerfeld's first collection for the house since his return, 'What everybody's been waiting for.'

ROMANTICISM AND LACE

This show – the most anticipated on the Paris schedule, according to *WWD* – marked Karl Lagerfeld's triumphant return to Chloé, the house he had helped to build. The tone was set with an invitation decorated with images of cherubs and a press release promising 'the freshness of Monet's gardens, the lightness of a poem or a sonnet'.

'The backdrop was sky blue with fluffy clouds and cupids. A white trellis enclosed the runway. Then out came a parade of the world's top models, beautiful creatures who are used to being tricked up in everything from heavy metal to the most beautiful (or dreariest) clothes. They had, however, never looked like this,' said Carrie Donovan in the *New York Times*, noting 'startlingly sheer' outfits, soft tones, blocks of pastel hues, and prints which recalled the trellis that climbed the show venue (a nod to the Impressionists and the beauty of sun through leaves, according to the press release; the *mise-en-scène* also referenced Lagerfeld's own S/S 1977 collection [see p.132] – his first to include themed décor – which saw models enter the catwalk through white garden trellising). On the pastoral theme, entire dresses came crafted from lace, while rickrack lace also appeared on the edging of many pieces. 'Everything fluttered with femininity,' said Donovan.

The show seemed emblematic of a shift: 'In those few minutes, fashion took a new turn.' This collection was 'the most extreme example of a wave of softer, feminine fashion now emanating from Paris' (a mood Donovan also accredited to Christian Lacroix, Issey Miyake, Hermès and Jean Paul Gaultier, among others).

'It's lingerie, but not for the boudoir,' Lagerfeld told reporters before the show. '[I]t was hard not to wonder what mere mortals would wear under these very fine, if flimsy, clothes,' noted Cathy Horyn in the *Washington Post*. She was also concerned by some of the beauty looks on show, which 'seemed to be in a '70s holding pattern, such as Naomi Campbell's long flower-and-butterfly-flecked Afro'.

'I have a sudden flashback to 1970, or thereabouts,' agreed Suzy Menkes in US *Vogue*, concluding, 'Lagerfeld's Chloé dresses are a hippie revival that expresses a new freedom, softness, and tenderness for women in the 1990s.'

BELLE ÉPOQUE VELVET

'Karlie's Angels,' quipped *WWD*, noting that
Lagerfeld's three Paris collections – for his
eponymous label, Chanel and Chloé – offered
an ideal uniform for the stars of the hit 1970s
TV show. 'Chloé is perfect for Farrah Fawcett –
although her hairdresser would have to think
more poodle than afghan,' read the report.

'Is Karl Lagerfeld getting laid-back? He's
sporting a suntan, letting his hair grow
longer and, if the clothes he showed for Chloé
Saturday afternoon are anything to go by, his
uncontrollable urge to do manic fashion shows
is subsiding,' continued *WWD*. The show, they
said, was full of romantic loose silhouettes,
sexy knit dresses and louche velvet: 'Lots of
designers have been flirting with velvet, but
Lagerfeld is having a full-fledged love affair
with it. He loves it for day dresses, evening
dresses, even pants.' US *Vogue* noted that the
sweeping velvet capes 'exuded an ambiguous
sexuality'. The romantic, wide-sleeved, highly
ornamented coats of guipure lace and muslin
(see p.309) were inspired by the fashions of the
Belle Époque, recalling the ornate garments
worn by figures such as Sarah Bernhardt
and the Comtesse Greffulhe.

WWD called the show 'one of the best' of the
European season, though they were somewhat
unsure of the 'frizzy hair' and the flowers
pasted onto models' faces. Lagerfeld himself
seemed to agree. 'Maybe I tried too many new
girls,' he told *WWD* after the show. 'I thought
it was a mess.'

Cathy Horyn in the *Washington Post* was,
at first, unimpressed: 'Viewing the penitent
frocks at Chloé, it was hard not to think that
Lagerfeld had designed a collection solely for
fashion nuns,' she said. Of the mohair dress
modelled by Linda Evangelista (opposite,
right), she commented that its 'loose lines ...
articulated the current mood for plainness,
but one wonders how many women are
prepared to accept condolences for their
clothes'. And yet, Horyn had a more positive
take on the collection a few months later,
after seeing it close up: 'On the runway, the
fall clothes designed by Karl Lagerfeld for
Chloé looked almost drab, but up close they
are simply elegant.' Indeed, for those able
to see the collection at close range, there
were plenty of surprising details, including
prints of paintings by the Belgian artist
James Ensor – a key influence on
Expressionism and Surrealism – such
as those on a look modelled by Helena
Christensen (see opposite, bottom left).

PRETTY NEOCLASSICISM

The consensus among the fashion press this season was that some designers – Lagerfeld at Chloé and newbie John Galliano – were making the case for femininity and softness. 'Going Gentle Toward 2000' read a headline in the *New York Times*. The word 'pretty' is 'so far out of the fashion vocabulary that it has inevitably become hip'. Their critic, Suzy Menkes, felt that the white tunics and flowing gowns on show at Chloé were a turning point for her industry: 'In Karl Lagerfeld's collection for Chloé, women turned neo-classical. His Grecian drapes, fluttering tunics and marble-print chiffon dresses played much the same counterpoint to stiff 1980's suits that Marie Antoinette's switch to muslin chemise did to pouf dresses two centuries ago.'

'Karl's Toga Party', read the headline in *WWD*. After the show, Manolo Blahnik quipped to guests: 'Nijinsky on the beach.' '[H]e was not far off,' agreed *WWD*. '[T]here wasn't a hard edge to be seen here. The dresses – and there were a lot of dresses – were soft and fluid, almost always short, and in Empire shapes that swept away from the body.' Also on show were striped pyjamas with matching robes, thigh-high stockings, golden sandals, and twisted streamers woven through models' hair. '[S]quiggly prints on sheer chiffon dresses that reminded some in the audience of Zandra Rhodes in her heyday' were inspired by Minoan Crete – and, specifically, the Akrotiri frescoes of Santorini, which Lagerfeld replicated complete with cracks and gaps. The dresses came in pale hues, complemented by the show's faux-Antique cracked-fresco décor, and were hand-painted – a technique used extensively by Lagerfeld in his early Chloé collections.

WWD noted that the show was a strong contrast to the strict mood Lagerfeld was showing at his other houses. Cathy Horyn in the *Washington Post* agreed: 'Freud himself could not have found a better subject for analysis than Karl Lagerfeld, whose Chloé collection today was a vision of modern beauty... Dr. Jekyll or Mr. Hyde, poet or panderer: Therein lies a conundrum to defeat a lesser mind,' she wrote. 'Not a lick of black, not a shroud of crepe, not even so much as a proletarian boot. Those traipsing out of the show onto the cobblestones of the Cour Carrée of the Louvre must have felt a little stab of dread, thinking perhaps that their own clothes, so fashionable this morning, now looked rather old and too gloppy.'

GREEK MAIDENS
AND SNOW QUEENS

The invitation for Chloé's autumn/winter
1994–1995 collection – the fourth since Karl
Lagerfeld's return to the house – featured
a painting of two blonde women, embracing
under an arch, two white doves floating just
above. Again (see p. 310) – and unsurprisingly –
this was the most romantic of Lagerfeld's three
Paris shows. The look was 'farm girl meets
sexy siren', according to Virginie Viard, then
a Chloé muse and head of the house's design
studio, but later the woman who would
succeed as creative director of Chanel after
Lagerfeld's death, having worked closely
with him for decades.

Some critics were shocked by the childishness
of the looks on offer, and many made
comparisons to figure-skaters' costumes.
Suzy Menkes quipped that 'you have to wonder
what is going on in fashion when women are
supposed to regress into little girls', adding,
'Even the statuesque Linda Evangelista was
garbed in a flurry of fake fur sparkling with
crystals like some junior high prom queen
[see p. 321].' However, Menkes noted that
'the show ended on a high note with long
draped chiffon dresses worn with ivory knits,
reflecting Lagerfeld's Ice Maiden theme in a
fine way … like the Snow Queen in a fairy tale.
Lagerfeld's stated aim for Chloé is to express
modern romance, which was easier with the
droopy long hemlines of his earlier shows than
with skirts so short you could only pray that
your posterior never hit the ice.'

Ironically, the press release – a long, rhyming
poem in French – told attendees, 'The young
girls have grown up / The baby-doll is over'.
It promised 'taffeta in Balzacian colours'
and 'plenty of eveningwear / Because, in
winter, we spend so much time in the dark'.

The stated inspirations were not only
ice-skaters, but also elements of Greek and
Nordic dress and culture, the latter both being
continuous influences for Lagerfeld. 'From
the Greek sunlight to the Norwegian snows',
read the press release.

WWD praised the collection, noting that
Lagerfeld 'still loves his Greek maidens',
but adding that this season he had abandoned
the nightgowns of past collections in favour of
'draped columns, in panne velvet printed with
forest scenes, and long layers of dreamy white
knits and chiffons'. The finale, *WWD* said, was
'a kingdom's worth of sparkling snow queens
with silver and gold dresses under fluffy
silver-dusted fake fur wraps'.

PASTEL PANOPLY

'Lingerie is not lingerie any more... It's part
of dressing,' Karl Lagerfeld told reporters
of his spring/summer 1995 presentation.
'There are zillions of dresses in this collection,
and practically no daywear,' he added. These
included short frothy party frocks, demure
ballgowns and tiered chiffon dresses in
sweet pastel hues.

Of the varied looks on offer, *WWD* wrote:
'It could only be Lagerfeld who covered the
fashion waterfront from the most exquisite
lace suits to the weirdest evening dresses
dripping with sequins, beads and all kinds
of paraphernalia. It seemed that Karl just
couldn't make up his mind. Does he want
his ladies to wear elegant slip-tunics over
layers of ombréd chiffon? Or would he prefer
them in flashy satin suits? It's all about pick
and choose, which is why Lagerfeld always
produces a large collection for Chloé.'

Émile Gallé Art Nouveau glassware was
the inspiration for the colours, which
included amber alongside pale watery
green and silvery mauve. 'The collection
was sugar sweet, with no fabric stiffer than
the consistency of whipped cream,' said Suzy
Menkes in the *International Herald Tribune*.
'It was very finely crafted.' But she gave the
clothes mixed reviews, questioning their
relevance. 'Chloé is primarily an evening wear
collection, and as an exercise in style it was
romantic... Yet even when embroidered jackets
went with flared pants or dresses opened over
underpants, the show seemed dedicated to
decorative women of a different era.'

'Karl Lagerfeld's collection for Chloé was
so thoroughly feminine – flounced hems,
ruffled knits, Creamsicle colors and wallpaper
prints – that one felt vaguely oafish just
looking at it. Here were clothes to incite
both envy and lust,' quipped Cathy Horyn in
the *Washington Post*. Horyn was impressed by
the proposed alternative to the mannish work
suit: 'A woman can, at the very least, wear a
slim skirt and a cardigan to the office.' Less
practical, though, she admitted, were the
'crinolines under princess frocks' and 'loops
of beads in a style better suited for an idle lady
nosing through a box of bonbons in her bed'.
Still, Horyn called the general mood one of
'unperturbed elegance – women looking
beautiful for themselves'.

COLLARS AND FROZEN COLOURS

'It's soft-angled modernity,' Karl Lagerfeld told reporters of his autumn/winter 1995–1996 collection, which was shown beneath various Oriental-style lanterns. Indeed, the show – held again at the Louvre – was seen as offering a more contemporary vision for Chloé than Lagerfeld had shown in recent seasons. The pastel colours which attendees had become used to had been pumped up, into brighter hues – 'frozen colours', Lagerfeld called them, like 'deep-freeze pink' – and there was more structure and tailoring. 'Last season's Chloé [see p.322] was a dreamy, romantic woman who seemed to live in an idyllic past dressed in gossamer chiffons and laces. She has made strides into the modern world for fall, wearing neat suits and coats with double rows of buttons that define her midriff,' said Anne-Marie Schiro in the *New York Times*. 'Anyone who craves color can find it at Chloé. And anyone who yearns to be swathed in mohair can get her wish.'

WWD reported that the show was defined by a 'collar fixation', noting that this interest was the collection's one consistency. 'Lagerfeld's really into doing new things with collars, so he doubled, tripled or angled them in all sorts of interesting ways for many of his coats, suits and dresses.' Some (see opposite, top and bottom right) looked to have been inspired by 19th-century carrick coats and riding coats.

'Karl Lagerfeld is the Vesuvius of fashion – he spews out ideas like red-hot lava and lets them flow all over his various runways,' read the *WWD* report. 'In the collection he showed for Chloé on Thursday, he had about a billion ideas, sending out a blinding whirl of conflicting colors, shapes and textures that came and went before you knew what had hit... If satin-trimmed mohair's not your thing, can the house of Chloé interest you in a nice wide-wale cord? Sweet-tart? Disco Mum? How about the gypsy revisited? You could call it witty eclecticism, or you could say it was all over the place. But either way, there were plenty of terrific clothes.'

'Any show starting more than 30 minutes late would provoke a walk out. No one walked from the Chloé show, designed by Karl Lagerfeld, despite a 50-minute delay,' noted the *Independent*.

LIGHTBULBS AND FLUORESCENTS

This season, Lagerfeld opted to reference himself, showing embroideries in the shape of lightbulbs, which recalled the whimsical motifs – showerheads, scissors, tools – that had decorated his final few collections for the house during his first stint at Chloé (see pp. 204 and 212; also p.160). 'You've got to hand it to Karl Lagerfeld – he's tenacious. Chloé is a troubled house, and he's sparing no effort trying to resuscitate it,' said *WWD*. 'What other designer would whip up a runway homage to Thomas Edison?'

'The Chloé woman is a lightbulb,' Lagerfeld said before the show. He added in his program notes: 'Electricity is the fairy that lights the world.' The *International Herald Tribune* felt that the embroideries were only 'a low wattage version of the witty decoration Karl Lagerfeld played with a decade ago', with 'no electricity crackling off the runway'. Some of the clothes, the paper said, 'were pretty, like dresses in black or rainbow-colored lace [see p.337, left]; or voile prints worn with Bo Peep hats. They were in the romantic turn-of-the-century vision of earlier Chloé collections.' But: 'The show, for all its occasional beautiful pieces … did not illuminate fashion.'

The *New York Times* agreed that there were some hits to be found. 'The lace here, Chloé's forte, was delicately cut out into sheer cropped jackets with black bandeaus beneath.' Lagerfeld, they noted, 'is a master of combining the sort of off-hues that are all over Paris. With models wearing floppy hippie hats, he showed his own electric Kool-Aid acid test, with lace dresses dyed in acid green, mauve, magenta and plum.'

FROM SEVENTIES DISCO
TO EXOTIC GLAM

A black velvet suit, styled with a matching
black shirt, made the cover of *WWD*'s 14
March 1996 issue. 'Chloé's Velvet People',
read the headline. The show, the publication
said, 'took Chloé on a voyage from Seventies
disco to Bombay glam'. The energy of
Studio 54 was all around, *WWD* said,
noting that former regular Liza Minnelli
was in attendance (though Bianca Jagger
was simply there in spirit).

'Lagerfeld wandered the globe – and the
decades – at Chloé,' continued *WWD*. 'The fall
collection he designed for Chloé was presented
the way Karl talks – stream-of-consciousness,
at machine-gun speed. Lagerfeld went from
the simplest little sweaters and floaty dresses
to the most ornate concoctions with an exotic
flavor.' The report noted vibrant embroidery,
sparkling lace, sheer trousers, and aqua-toned
jewelled saris embellished by embroidery
house Montex, all worn with 'metallic boots
that would send Nancy Sinatra into an
absolute tizzy'. *WWD* concluded: 'While
there is an Indian air wafting around Paris,
it's doubtful that anyone else will capture
it as Karl has.'

Lagerfeld also quoted 'Flou-flou', a dress
from Chloé's S/S 1961 collection (see right
and p. 43, right), 35 years after its release,
when it was designed by Gérard Pipart.
This reinterpretation attests to Lagerfeld's
ability to identify strong codes – such as, here,
Chloé's 'flou' (see p. 42) – and play with them.

NEON FLORAL

The invitation to Chloé's spring/summer 1997 show featured blooming flowers, in bold neon colours. 'As in many gardens, some things flourished and others wilted, but the overall effect was colorful, pretty and Lagerfeld's best shot so far at revitalizing Chloé's fluid femininity,' said Suzy Menkes in the *International Herald Tribune*.

The mood was bright, light, frivolous. 'Take a dash of Goldie Hawn in "Laugh-In" or "Cactus Flower," and add a touch of Cher from "The Sonny & Cher Show." Then put them together with Karl Lagerfeld's irreverence and wit, and you have the funny, over-the-top spring collection for Chloé that he delivered on Wednesday,' said *WWD*. 'It was loud, tacky, over-the-top – and tons of fun.'

'Pop romance,' Lagerfeld told reporters backstage. The show featured fluid chiffon dresses, scallop-edged tailoring (a key Chloé code that Lagerfeld had first used in his S/S 1972 collection), pale pink lingerie with faggoting, lace-up leathers and hot pants. It conjured the mood of Paris evenings out in the Seventies and Eighties. 'The good clothes looked great, while the tacky clothes were sometimes good and always amusing. And, as anyone who has sat through the many dull shows in the past few days knows, there's a lot to be said for that,' wrote *WWD*. 'Karl's theme for the season was anything goes. Anything, that is, except subtlety.'

SPACE ODYSSEY

'Reports are circulating that fall '97 will be Karl Lagerfeld's last season designing Chloé. His contract expires in March, and he has reportedly told friends that he's thinking of leaving. Sources said Chloé officials have been quietly looking for a successor,' said *WWD* in December 1996.

Come March 1997, the rumours were confirmed, and Lagerfeld made his final presentation for the house – a trippy ode to space. 'Earth to Karl, Earth to Karl,' quipped *WWD*. 'Everyone knows Karl Lagerfeld is a whirlwind of ideas – many brilliant, others that seem to have come from outer space. And outer space is exactly where Lagerfeld was in his last collection for Chloé… Instead of a traditional runway, Karl created a vast universe of giant floating planets and their satellites through which the models meandered, occasionally giving Jupiter or Mars a good slap to knock it out of the way.'

The show was 'all over the place', *WWD* said, fitting with Lagerfeld's recent tendency to 'send out a little of this, a little of that' at his Chloé shows. The report praised the 'sexy knits and appealing fluid dresses', but noted that these were almost lost amid a 'barrage of strong-shouldered jackets', 'heavy velvet coats' and 'a far-flung array of droopy dresses'. They concluded, 'it was a universe in chaos'.

On the front row, editors gossiped about a future successor. For a while, it looked as if an Italian designer, Luisa Beccaria, would be named, but she told *WWD* she'd lost interest due to 'continued delays and indecision' from Chloé management. Come May, the announcement was made: the 25-year-old Stella McCartney, just a few years out of Central Saint Martins, had the job. 'Her Beatles connection landed her on the front page of every British tabloid when she got Chloé,' wrote US *Vogue*. Lagerfeld was unimpressed, *Vogue* reported: 'Upon hearing about McCartney's appointment, Lagerfeld, who didn't want the job at Chloé anymore, sniped to the press, "They should have taken a big name. They did – but in music, not fashion."'

Stella McCartney

A Short Biography

Born in London in 1971 to the Beatles frontman Paul McCartney and Linda McCartney (née Eastman), the American photographer and pioneering animal rights advocate, Stella McCartney was exposed to the Chloé brand from a young age. During the 1970s, her mother regularly wore Karl Lagerfeld's first iterations for the company. 'My Mum was quite ahead of her time in the things she wore. She'd mix big boots with little argyle jumpers and old dresses,' McCartney told *The Times* of London in 1998, noting, 'She cut her own hair ... and she would throw it all together in a really unusual way and always got so much shit for it in the press.'

Linda McCartney, and by consequence Lagerfeld, would form key influences on McCartney during her tenure at Chloé, particularly visible in her retro-look dresses and embellishments. In a strange coincidence, McCartney's history with Lagerfeld began long before she worked in fashion. As a four-year-old, she had appeared in the same issue of *Vogue* (March 1975) as the then-Chloé maestro, when he was featured in the 'Great Designers World Series' (see also p.102). Shot by Norman Parkinson, McCartney was shown jumping up and down in excitement on a beach under the headline 'Now and Future Stars'.

Above her Lagerfeld inspiration, however, was an appreciation for that free-wheeling, rule-breaking dressing that would define McCartney's time at Chloé. Just 25 and two years out of Central Saint Martins when she was appointed, she brought an insolence, and a playfulness, to the house, pushing low-slung jeans, skimpy tops, humorous pop culture motifs and pretty party dresses: 'They're just lovely clothes that I and my friends want to wear', as McCartney put it to *The Times*. Many onlookers were initially aghast at her appointment, given her inexperience, but her collections swiftly attracted critical acclaim, strong sales and a new generation of Chloé fans.

'Baby, you're a star', said British *Vogue*, as the headline for a profile on McCartney in 1999 that ran shortly after her fourth show for the house. They described her look as 'Portobello Road meets Paris' (McCartney was known for having a taste for vintage, picked up while working from a studio close to the famous Portobello Market in Notting Hill). Many critics were taken with her new vision not just for Chloé and its clothes, but for womanhood. McCartney's females were sassy, sexually confident; 'ladettes', according to some press. Photographer Liz Collins, who shot the Winter 1999 advertising campaign, recalled: 'It was an intense time, when there were all these independent girls who were free, coming up together – female and free, all the same age group... The idea was to shoot joy – life's moments of joy.' McCartney was herself known for having a

young and dynamic female team – or 'girl gang', as several critics put it –
including a talented British assistant, plucked from the class below her
at Saint Martins: Phoebe Philo.

'I'm not really a fashion person,' McCartney told British *Vogue* in 1999.
'What the next millennium is about, for me, is confidence. Women
shouldn't have to worry about what they wear, they shouldn't feel they're
being told what to do – I can say that, having felt dictated to myself by
magazines or whatever when I was younger, and now being in the position
of doing the dictating myself, a bit. That whole philosophy, for example,
of having a gown with a jacket that matches is not my way of thinking.
To me, the way forward is a totally couture sequined cape with a pair
of jeans or an incredible evening gown with a denim jacket...'

Indeed, McCartney was known for her strength, as much as her tongue-
in-cheek wit and sass. A committed vegetarian, she famously made it a
condition of her contract that she didn't have to use leather or fur on her
runway. And she brought to the house the experience she had gained as
an intern on Savile Row: she could – in addition to T-shirts and jeans –
create clothes that revealed a very high degree of savoir-faire in their
fabrication and ornamentation, such as sharp jackets that featured
artisan-level embellishment and embroidery work.

McCartney's appointment and tenure in charge of a French house formed
part of a moment of dominance for London and its culture within the
international fashion scene, and a perceived moment of optimism and
opportunity for British youth culture, bolstered by the victory of Labour's
Tony Blair in 1997. Alexander McQueen was at Givenchy, John Galliano
was at Dior, and UK style magazines and Brit pop were booming. Chloé
garments began appearing on the new crop of celebrities and across this
fresh wave of magazines, whether *Dazed & Confused* or *Pop*, shot by the
likes of Juergen Teller and Liz Collins.

McCartney left Chloé in 2001 to start a label under her own name, but her
legacy was important in reaffirming the house's connection with strong
femininity and youth – and, by default, with the original mission of house
founder Gaby Aghion.

PARIS MEETS LONDON

Stella McCartney's first collection, staged at Opéra Garnier in Paris, 'confounded the cynics who said that she had been hired only for her name', wrote Suzy Menkes in the *International Herald Tribune*.

Here, Chloé's signature French ethos was merged with a young London energy. 'Sexy meets modern in a festival of tacky vivid colours, so very British, or a midnight blue or a shocking pink', said Chloé's press release.

'Anyone who's seen my work knows I'm not about shock tactics,' McCartney told *WWD* ahead of the show. 'This will be a nice, mellow, pretty collection. It's all really wearable.' Still, the press release promised a lot: '1. Innocence', in the form of white cotton; '2. Movement', with long scarves and flowing dresses; '3. Audacity', thanks to slip dresses and small tops, monogrammed with the Chloé logo, which 'barely hide the bosom'; '4. Masculine fashion "au féminin"', in the tailoring (McCartney had once interned on Savile Row); '5. Poetry', via eveningwear inspired by the lingerie of 1940s American movie stars; '6. Body geometrics', hence the many stripes and chevrons; and, finally, '7. Fireworks', in the form of short tops and long gowns in fine chinaware colours and sequinned dresses with long beaded tassels. A 'feast for the senses', the release concluded.

Other reviewers agreed with Menkes; the show was a success. 'England swings,' said *WWD*, in a report on McCartney's debut and fellow Brit Alexander McQueen's latest collection for Givenchy. '[S]imply delightful,' they wrote of the Chloé clothes, which were modelled by friends of McCartney, such as Kate Moss and Lucie de la Falaise (the latter's grandmother, Maxime de la Falaise, helped shape Chloé in the early years; see p. 28), to a soundtrack which included the Sex Pistols' 'God Save the Queen'. 'Stella showed fairly simple shapes done up with gentle flourishes – ruffled or lace edges, fagotted insets, sweeping sleeves, a drawstring hem,' noted *WWD*.

Much excitement came from the front row, the publication added: 'Here were Paul and Linda McCartney, acting like the proud mum and dad, leading the applause throughout the show, and, at the end, leaping first to their feet for a standing ovation. And, oh, they brought along Ringo Starr to punch up their cheering section.'

TIGHT SATIN AND GEOMETRIC SCALLOPS

Stella McCartney's second collection for Chloé was met with a more muted response from critics than her debut (see p.362). 'With bosoms spilling out of the necklines of tight satin dresses, with unzipped zippers and rhinestone studs on black leather, the effect was more London party girl than chic Parisienne,' said Anne-Marie Schiro in the *New York Times*.

'Stella McCartney is a child of celebrity; she must know that life in the big time can be tough. Now, McCartney is in the big time in her own right, faced with building a reputation as a designer of serious merit,' said *WWD*. '[H]ers will be a high-profile learning curve, out there for all to see. Unfortunately, the collection McCartney showed on Wednesday indicated that the curve has a long way to go.'

WWD felt that some of the clothes were overly sexy; 'cheesy', even. And: 'Things that didn't look too tight – all those shiny, slippery satin Jessica Rabbit dresses, for example – often looked droopy.' The report did, however, praise a series of dresses and skirts made from embroidered tulle, cut in geometric scallops (see p.373, left).

'The sweet musings of a schoolgirl – even a very cool English schoolgirl – do not on their own translate into a major collection, nor do they necessarily find a guaranteed market,' added the report. And yet, two months after the show, in May 1998, *WWD* would eat their words: 'Chloé's Stella Performance', read the headline above an article announcing a boom in sales. 'The label was sort of dying and she revived it completely,' Nicole Fischelis, fashion director at Saks, told the reporter.

ROCK 'N' ROLL CLUB,
RUFFLES AND BIAS CUTS

Stella McCartney opened her Chloé show with
a soundbite from Bill Clinton's January 1998
PBS interview, in which he denied having a
sexual relationship with Monica Lewinsky.
'I had to use it,' McCartney told reporters
after the show. 'The collection is about
female sexuality – and Bill Clinton, he's
about female sexuality, too.'

Unlike last season (see p. 368), reception of
the blatant sex appeal of the clothes was good.
'At Chloé, McCartney is going for a different
customer – a rock 'n' roll club vixen – but
she's courting her as eagerly as [Alexander]
McQueen is going after his ladies,' said *WWD*.
'[W]ith this collection, Stella took a huge step
toward maturing as a designer for a major
house. Rather than wallow in the reaction to
last season's effort, which many found poorly
delivered and way too trashy, Stella acted on
the criticism in a smart way. She didn't change
her message, she refined it. Her clothes are
still feminine, provocative and lots of fun,
but here she exercised a level of restraint
that made all the difference.'

The *Daily Telegraph* were also impressed:
'The show, in the Palais Brongniart of the
Bourse de Paris, was McCartney's third for
Chloé, and it was widely agreed, her best.
It was filled with her naughty-but-nice lingerie
for the street, saucy, ruffled chiffon dresses
and racy boudoir corsets... Everything was
delicate, fragile and sensual.' The paper also
praised the frilly floral petticoat-dresses,
styled with matching jackets, skimpy silk
camisoles and bias-cut skirts trimmed
with lace, noting that they 'all looked as
if they had been designed with romantic
assignations in mind'.

The *New York Times* said that McCartney
'received the first standing ovation of the
season'. Their report mentioned 'dresses
that clung to the torso through bias cuts
and floated away at the hemline', as well as
'[w]rapped tops edged with ruffles', noting
that they were 'the height of femininity with a
sweetness that was never cloying'. McCartney
had also begun to master the retro references
that were so central to her predecessor Karl
Lagerfeld's tenure at Chloé. The *New York
Times* commented that '[s]liplike evening
dresses ... achieved a high degree of 1930's
movie star glamour for a new age'.

DENIM, LACE AND SEQUINS

'If ever there was someone who didn't need to prove themselves any more, surely it's Stella McCartney,' gushed British *Vogue* after the success of this show.

US *Vogue* noted that elements of the collection were 'reminiscent of Lauren Hutton's sultry 1970s elegance'. When McCartney was young, her mother, Linda, regularly wore 1970s-era Chloé, then designed by Karl Lagerfeld, so it was natural that the designer gravitated towards this era of the house's history. 'Stayin' Alive', read *WWD*'s headline. 'The Seventies trend just won't die ... her sequined halter dress, just right for heading out to Studio 54.'

WWD explained that the collection was 'a sexy, spicy frolic that combined elements of schoolgirl, screen diva and London hipster'. McCartney's biggest message, they said, was jeans – 'the tighter, the better. She cut them in silk denim, either long and flared or cropped above the ankle. Sometimes she added red or yellow tuxedo piping down the side...' There was also plenty of lace ('she loves the stuff') – on blouses, camisoles and fluttery dresses.

McCartney's 'see-through styling is hardly for the wallflower set', *WWD* added. Indeed, British *Vogue* reported that McCartney and Chloé president Mounir Moufarrige clashed ahead of the show over the transparency of the dresses; McCartney wanted knickers on show, Moufarrige insisted on gowns being lined (McCartney eventually relented, acknowledging it was an autumn collection, 'but if this was spring, no way would I have agreed').

As was becoming signature at McCartney's shows, given her celebrity connections, the press were just as excited by the front row as the catwalk. 'Mistress de la Mode', read *WWD*'s headline: 'Forget Hollywood starlets, presidential wives or vulgar White House interns. The House of Chloé managed to snag the biggest paparazzi bait in the world on Wednesday: the Mistress of Wales herself, Camilla Parker Bowles... Nobody could quite figure out why – she's not exactly what you would call a style icon...'

'It was wonderful,' Parker Bowles told reporters of the show, backstage. McCartney, a famous vegetarian, who refused to include any fur or leather goods within her shows, had fewer kind words in return. 'Shouldn't she be supporting a designer who's pro-fox hunting?' she said to British *Vogue* after the show.

RACY TOPS AND SHORT SHORTS

'Just how sexy does a woman want to look?' asked Ginia Bellafante in the *New York Times*. 'At a basic level, fashion offers women a range of sexual poses – ravenous, assured, aloof, hesitant, indifferent.' Bellafante praised designers who managed to infer a nuanced sexuality: 'Mr. McQueen at Givenchy and Stella McCartney at Chloé put sex in the forefront, but they did so in a considered, literate way that many young American designers can't quite manage.'

Bellafante noted that McCartney's show was heavy on the 'wide-bottom trousers and delicate dresses for which she is famous', but it was the new ideas that really shone with excitement, including tops created from 'mere strings of fake diamonds'. She added that, in another designer's hands, the show could have looked vulgar, over-sexed, but 'McCartney has a keen understanding of the contemporary young woman – and a sense of humor, too. She knows that sometimes women want to be objectified… [S]he also knows that they want to *appear* as if they're above all that. So throw on some white jeans with that racy top, which is how Ms. McCartney presented it.'

'Sex in the City', read *WWD*'s headline, a nod to the television show which launched just a year before and championed the same kind of liberated, sexy, fashion-conscious girls-about-town that McCartney's Chloé seemed to speak to. *Le Monde* called the look 'glam-chic', noting 'disco shine' and plenty of long tanned limbs. Alongside skin-exposing sparkling tops, models wore tube dresses adorned with embroideries of kneeling topless women, and plenty of short shorts – a popular look on runways that season – in frayed white denim: 'Long Hot Summer, Short Hot Pants', read a headline in the *New York Times* on the trend. There were some less sensual additions: some models carried fluffy handbags in the shape of animal faces, while others wore pieces decorated with skull and Playboy Bunny motifs.

A few weeks after the show, a story in *WWD* noted rumours that Chloé were anxiously searching for a 'back-up' designer, lest McCartney leave. Word around Paris was that she was not planning on extending her contract and might jump ship to Gucci.

BEADWORK AND JEANS

In March 2000, The *Washington Post*
reassured its readers that the buzzy Stella
McCartney had squashed any rumours of a
change at Chloé by signing a fresh contract
for the house: 'She's young, she's hip, she's
good-looking... She's also a Brit designer who
gave an old French house some much-needed
CPR,' the *Post* said.

This season, the paper noted sequins for day
and denim for night, alongside maxi military
coats, parkas in distressed canvas, skirts that
were 'shorter than short' and trousers hung
'lower than low'. The clothes, they said, were
ideal for 'young women with thin legs and
thick investment portfolios'. The report
praised the lack of fur, especially within
a season where skins dominated. 'One
of McCartney's skills is to take delicate
clothes and make them look cutting edge,'
the *Post* concluded.

The *New York Times* praised McCartney's
'exquisite tops with 1920's-inspired
beadwork splaying from the collar'. Their
report lamented the plethora of denim
on show, though admitted that '[s]kinny
jeans paired with high heels are another of
Ms. McCartney's trademark looks'. 'At the risk
of repeating herself every season, the designer
goes back to her basics: "jewel" tops that move
around the body, stretch jeans that taper the
leg,' said *Le Monde*.

As usual, the many famous front-row guests –
including Jerry Seinfeld, Sean Lennon and
Farrah Fawcett – delighted the waiting
photographers.

FRUIT PRINTS
AND HORSE MOTIFS

The invitation for Stella McCartney's spring/
summer 2001 show was a vest top printed
with an illustration of a half-peeled banana –
a suitably playful motif for a designer known
for wit and sex appeal.

The show opened with drama: a two-minute
film clip of a stampeding herd of mustangs.
Horse motifs ran across the collection, in
the form of stylized silhouettes taken from
paintings by Théodore Géricault and George
Stubbs, which appeared screened, appliquéd
and embroidered onto jackets, shirts and
dresses. (The *New York Times* noted that
horse prints were, oddly, a trend that season,
appearing also at Alice Roi and Miguel
Adrover.)

As the invitation had projected, fruit prints
were also rife across McCartney's collection,
which would be one of her most memorable,
thanks in part to an advertising campaign
shot by the artist Taryn Simon that featured
a model splayed on the beach in swimwear,
surrounded by horses. Skimpy bikinis and
one-pieces came with 'cheeky pineapples
strategically strewn to suggest that something
tasty lies beneath', said US *Vogue*. 'The Lady
Vanishes', wrote the *New York Times*, in
response to the sexy, youthful mood of
the season.

This season also saw the announcement of
a forthcoming diffusion line, See by Chloé,
envisaged to meet the heavy demand for
McCartney's pieces from young consumers,
offering them a wider range at more affordable
prices. Sales of the main line were performing
better than ever, and pieces even became
collectors' items on the re-sale market:
'such is the demand for Chloé's spring 2001
collection, which featured a horse motif on
slinky one-shouldered dresses and draped
tees, that most of it is sold before it even
makes its way to the [vintage store] sales
floor,' reported US *Vogue* in 2004.

SEA GRASS AND PEARLS

Attendees at Stella McCartney's autumn/
winter 2001–2002 show for Chloé did not
know, as they took their seats, that it would
be the designer's last for the house.

The *Washington Post* called the runway
presentation 'short, and short on ideas'. While
the report praised crisp cadet coats and pretty
corsets embroidered with sea grass, alongside
garments printed with images of Chrissie
Hynde (see right), who sat in the front row,
next to Paul McCartney, it had fewer kind
words for the jeans, into which models looked
'vacuum-packed', or the pearl-encrusted
jackets: 'The effect was overpowering, like
too many salt crystals ruining a perfectly
good bagel.' Overall, the report concluded,
McCartney's collection 'lacked her usual
spirit'. A review in the *New York Times* was
similarly muted. 'Missing a Beat', read the
headline on that season's Paris shows, with
critic Ginia Bellafante particularly critical of
Chloé's 'flashy' fake fur coats and 'pencil-thin
jeans that cost as much as television sets'.

Le Monde, however, were more positive, calling
the show 'highly accomplished'. They praised
the 'energy of pronounced sensuality', and,
unlike other press, liked the jeans, which,
they said, 'created the longest legs of the
season'. The paper were also impressed
with the addition of engraved metal plates
on belts and the backs of jackets, which were,
according to McCartney, inspired by Victorian
tales. 'Embroidered with sea grass or glass
beads, the corset creates an allure which
combines the rigour of English tailoring with
the lightness of the Roaring Twenties,' added
Le Monde.

Weeks after the show, *WWD* were
reporting renewed swirling rumours that
McCartney was leaving Chloé for Gucci.
'Gucci, McCartney Close to Deal', read their
headline on 4 April. A few days later, on
10 April, her exit was confirmed, and Gucci
Group announced that they had signed a deal
with McCartney to launch her own eponymous
brand. The same day, Chloé announced
that 27-year-old Phoebe Philo, McCartney's
long-term assistant, and a fellow Brit,
would be their new creative director.

Phoebe Philo

A Short Biography

Born in Paris in 1973 but raised in London, Phoebe Philo arrived at Chloé as Stella McCartney's assistant in 1997. Philo had studied fashion at Central Saint Martins, graduating in 1996, a year after McCartney. By 2001, aged 27, Philo was herself creative director at Chloé. No other candidates were seriously considered, such was the consensus on Philo's indispensability by those behind the scenes at the house.

Philo's tenure – nine years at the company in total, and nine seasons as creative director – saw Chloé grow into a fashion mega-house, a sparker of trends copied the world over, and a titan of accessories. This period was also marked by Philo's own rise: from new voice to one of fashion's most respected and most influential designers, and a key figure in the media's new focus on 'women designing for women'. It was also a time of change in fashion, as the industry was growing from a small, tightly focused business into a pop culture juggernaut. This was the time of 'It' girls, and 'It' bags – a moment defined by the runaway success of Chloé's 'Paddington' bag, with its oversized proportions, XXL padlock and 'luggage' spirit. Scrutiny of fashion shows was becoming more intense than ever, with every image pored over on websites such as Style.com and the front rows quickly publicized on social media.

When she joined the house, Philo was – like McCartney before her – known for her youthful style, which blended the casual with the formal, the vintage with the new. 'With its signature mix of jeans with feminine pieces, pretty dresses and serious tailoring, the McCartney-Philo era at Chloé crystallized a British gift for pairing high and low,' US *Vogue* said. Philo told the magazine, 'It developed like that because Stella and I really looked at what we were wearing and how we wanted to dress.'

The look was, according to some, risqué. Such was the hullabaloo that *WWD* ran an article in October 2001, ahead of Philo's debut for Chloé, confirming that the designer 'has never had dreadlocks'. 'Several articles have mentioned the hairstyle in chronicling the supposedly "out-there" style of Philo,' continued the publication. 'I did have the gold teeth and really long fingernails, but I'm just a young girl growing up. I'm going through different trends all the time,' Philo told *WWD*.

Despite this press clamouring around her style, and her taste for parties and hip-hop, Philo was quickly credited with having made Chloé more sophisticated. 'I changed direction,' she told the *Telegraph* in December 2002. 'Chloé is feminine and sexy, and I'm trying to make it a bit more refined and less gimmicky. The older I get and the more collections I do, the more I'm driven by real style and beauty. My real aim is to reveal and not to display women.'

Indeed, Philo, like McCartney, drew praise for her female team. 'I find it really helpful working with other women and doing fittings together, because you really look at each other and say, "Would you wear it like that? Do you want that to fall on that part of your hip or a little lower?" We all try on the clothes. Sometimes late at night we are running around like mad freaks wearing the samples,' she explained.

Philo's elevated collections – and her elegant campaigns by photographer duo Inez van Lamsweerde and Vinoodh Matadin – would, without doubt, redefine Chloé in the contemporary, and shape every future designer who would lead the house after her. Philo left in 2006, having already undertaken a maternity leave, in order to focus on her family. She would return to fashion in 2008, taking over as creative director of Céline, a project which was seen by some as a way of extending questions she had already been asking herself – about how women should be viewed and seen, about what contemporary sexiness can mean – during her celebrated tenure at Chloé.

SAINT-TROPEZ STYLE

Ahead of her debut show for Chloé, Phoebe Philo told US *Vogue* that the collection would be 'elegant but very sexy'. Since being named the new creative director of Chloé a few months before, Philo had been, *Vogue* said, 'pursued all over town by the press in her native London eager for any news on where she goes and what she's wearing'. Indeed, like Stella McCartney before her, Philo was known for her effortless personal style, which combined the chic with the witty, the sexy with the casual or street – a look she mimicked in her designs.

A few weeks later, *Vogue* gave the collection a rave review. '[S]he's getting it all right,' wrote André Leon Talley. 'Phoebe's first collection for Chloé won unanimous critical acclaim.' Even Karl Lagerfeld had praise, telling Talley for his 'StyleFax' column, 'I am totally in favor of this charming Phoebe... Her show looked very refined.'

The presentation opened with a white and cream piqué trouser suit with scalloped edges (see right) – 'totally Bianca Jagger, totally Talitha Getty', wrote Talley. Indeed, the show was based on the notion of icons such as Getty and Brigitte Bardot hanging out in Saint-Tropez: 'a new take on the golden age of holiday style', as Philo put it to *WWD*. Talley called the first look 'a remix' of a Chloé suit Lagerfeld had designed for S/S 1972. The outfit was a clear nod to the history of the house: scallops were, in fact, first featured on dresses in the S/S 1960 collection (see, for example, p. 37, bottom right) – a detail which Lagerfeld later revived.

Other reviewers admired the shift in mood, which they felt was still sexy but more sophisticated and assured. 'Philo delivered the goods and then some,' said *WWD*, praising lacy pieces edged in gold, bright tight knitwear in yellow, red and green stripes ('the colours of the Rasta flag', according to *Le Monde*), and a tiny bikini embroidered with monkeys (a nod to Getty's holiday style and island hopping). Philo also created her first Chloé bag for this show. Named the 'Bracelet', it was inspired by a charm bracelet she had purchased in Ibiza, its circular clasp enlarged and transformed to become a handle (see p. 418, right).

'It's going to sell well,' *Le Monde* reported of the collection, hearing buyers gush as they left the Carreau du Temple, the show's venue. Later, Chloé CEO Ralph Toledano told reporters: 'With Phoebe, we are in a great tradition of elegance, while keeping the young and sexy side.'

MASCULINE MUSES

'Can a man be a muse?' asked *WWD*, with a now amusing incredulousness, following Philo's second collection for Chloé. 'According to Phoebe Philo in her show notes, he can,' they continued, noting that Philo had picked two guys: 'guitar god Jimi Hendrix and Ballets Russes designer Leon Bakst'. Two famed innovators, and yet, *WWD* said, 'Philo could have used a little more of their daring'. 'Astonish me', they quipped, was the famous Ballets Russes credo, but this show 'fell a little flat'.

In the *Washington Post*, Robin Givhan complained that 'an impressive collection' had been 'hamstrung by a frumpy, vintage sensibility'. She theorized that Philo was missing the raucous influence of her former boss, Stella McCartney, who leaned towards sex appeal. 'Philo still needs a devil on her shoulder,' Givhan concluded.

Ginia Bellafante in the *New York Times*, a frequent critic of Chloé, remained unimpressed, calling the mood of the show 'banality'. The distressed jeans, chiffon blouses and motorcycle pants suggested, she said, that 'Ms. Philo's idea of a woman has not evolved beyond the most obvious references to the kind of person who would write the sequel to "I'm With the Band"'. Given the high praise from critics after Philo's debut, the reviews this season were an indication of the pace of fashion; how quickly mood – and, in turn, status – can shift or dip. Fittingly, Philo's critics would come back around swiftly.

MODERN DEBUTANTES

The invitation to this show, created by the artist Richard Prince, featured a photograph of a blue plastic lilo, floating in a pool. Phoebe Philo had returned to the holiday mood of her critically praised debut (see p. 414): sun, sea, 'blue summer skies and the whitewashed houses of Mediterranean villages', according to the *Guardian*. Their report called the show 'easy and upbeat'.

And yet, others felt it continued a move towards sophistication. 'At Chloé on Sunday, the fashion temperature was at a low level, but Phoebe Philo is making a good job of taking the house back to the upscale womanly image it once had – before she worked with Stella McCartney to rev the shows up into a rock chick rave,' said Suzy Menkes in the *International Herald Tribune*. Philo's 'little black draped dresses ... reflected the fluid style that Karl Lagerfeld invented for the house 35 years ago,' Menkes noted.

'It's been a slow drift, but with her spring Chloé collection, Phoebe Philo finally slipped from the shadow of Stella McCartney's reign,' said *WWD*. 'Philo's Chloé is softer, a little younger and more subtle, though she has maintained the feminine edge that brought McCartney's fans to the house. She has also addressed a customer that most of Paris has left behind – the modern debutante.' For this shopper, *WWD* identified Philo's 'charming black minidresses, studded with pearls or trimmed with round gold beads or gold discs', which, they said, 'played it both demure and sexy'.

There was plenty of swimwear, too: 'very Bo Derek, all wrapped and tied around the body', said *Fashion Wire Daily*, adding, 'For what the show lacked in exuberance it made up in clothes that many women will want in their summer wardrobe.'

'It's Chloé sexy,' Philo told reporters backstage, 'which is not vulgar, not cheap but refined, and hot and raunchy. This collection is all about finding great things to wear.'

The show also received praise from arguably the most important critic of all, Philo's mother, Celia, who told reporters, 'I could see Phoebe wearing every single outfit. It's so her, it just looks so right.'

PARTY CLOTHES

The invitation for the A/W 2003–2004
Chloé show, also created by artist Richard
Prince (see p.426), will surely have quietened
critics who had suggested that Phoebe Philo's
vision for this house was less sexy and more
grown-up than that of her predecessor Stella
McCartney: it featured a woman's bronzed
back and bare bottom, photographed by
Helmut Teissl.

'The invitation featured the star-spangled
naked torso of a hot dancer from the carnival
of Rio, but this was a very French collection
from the house of Chloé,' said Godfrey Deeny
for *Fashion Wire Daily* of the show, which
opened with a rap version of David Bowie's
'Fame', containing the repeated line, 'It's
your birthday' – a nod to the fact that this was
Chloé's 50-year anniversary (feather necklaces
in the show – see p.434, right – were another
Bowie inspiration). Deeny praised 'curvy ra-ra
culottes, dresses with huge animal prints and
a pair of great gold sequin and chain dresses
that screamed "let's party!"'

Some Paris-based critics didn't agree with
Deeny's notion that this was a 'very French'
look. In *Le Figaro*, Virginie Mouzat said the
collection was too 'overtly sexy'. 'Phoebe Philo
at Chloé dresses girls, chicks, bimbos,' she
added.

Chloé might have been celebrating her 50th
birthday, 'but she looks about 27 with London
girl Phoebe Philo in charge', quipped Sarah
Mower in Style.com, noting that the look
was personal, rather than Parisian: 'Philo
projects her own mixed-up vintage-meets-
sexy-streetwear look onto the clothes, which
is fine as long as she polishes things up to
the Paris mark.'

'It is the girl rather than the woman that
Phoebe Philo prizes,' agreed Ginia Bellafante
in the *New York Times*. 'Her show for Chloé
this morning had an obvious muse in mind:
the girl who lives in Williamsburg, Brooklyn,
or in London's East End. She dates a guy in a
band, and when she runs out of his apartment
in the morning because she has overslept,
she throws on the biker jacket he tossed on
the floor at 3 a.m.' Bellafante noted flouncy,
many-tiered skirts and dresses 'plastered
with embroidered flowers and who knows
what else – perhaps sea creatures'. 'Ms. Philo's
looks were each a big, fun mess,' she concluded.

FRESH LOOKS AND
BANANA PRINTS

'I went through my mum's old fashion magazines – she had a garageful, from when my parents were living in Paris in the late seventies… I just thought the girls looked so gorgeous, fresh, and happy,' Phoebe Philo told Style.com of her spring/summer 2004 show. And yet, the show invitation suggested a more international, and slightly mad-cap, mood: a giant blow-up Chloé-branded banana photographed in tourist locations – in London, Tokyo, New York (riding in a yellow cab), Milan (eating pizza), and Paris (gazing at the Eiffel Tower) – and turned into a spoof of cheesy sightseer postcards.

The humour extended to the collection. 'Phoebe Philo admits that she's gone ape, so to speak, for bananas,' said US *Vogue* (it was, by now, easy to guess who in the studio was responsible for the banana motifs that Chloé had shown before, for S/S 2001, when McCartney was at the helm; see p.398). Philo 'traces the genesis of this obsession to her teenage years', said *Vogue*. 'I remembered a white cotton Fruit of the Loom T-shirt I had with the famous fruit basket,' Philo said. Now, her vision was somewhat less personal: 'the banana print is really relevant to the global spirit I wanted to show on the catwalk'.

Philo told *Vogue* she'd settled on two main moods for her collection: 'A seventies urban feeling and early-eighties freshness, inspired by Oliviero Toscani's pictures for French *Elle* from that time – outdoor life, a sporty, happy attitude.' 'During the late seventies,' she recalled, 'cotton T-shirts in bright colors with large stripes or fun characters on them were a part of every girl's wardrobe! We selected bright colors, especially green and yellow, so the banana print became obvious.' Another 1970s-inspired look that met with great success was the wide high-waisted denim with a braided belt.

WWD praised the collection, noting that Philo was gaining a dedicated market among 'slim, tan starlets' in Los Angeles and 'members of the swan set' in New York. The reporter admired slinky smocked dresses, lace shirts, and the 'popular pompons and webby macramé' that Philo had carried over from the season before. 'Sometimes,' *WWD* concluded, 'you just can't get enough of a good thing.'

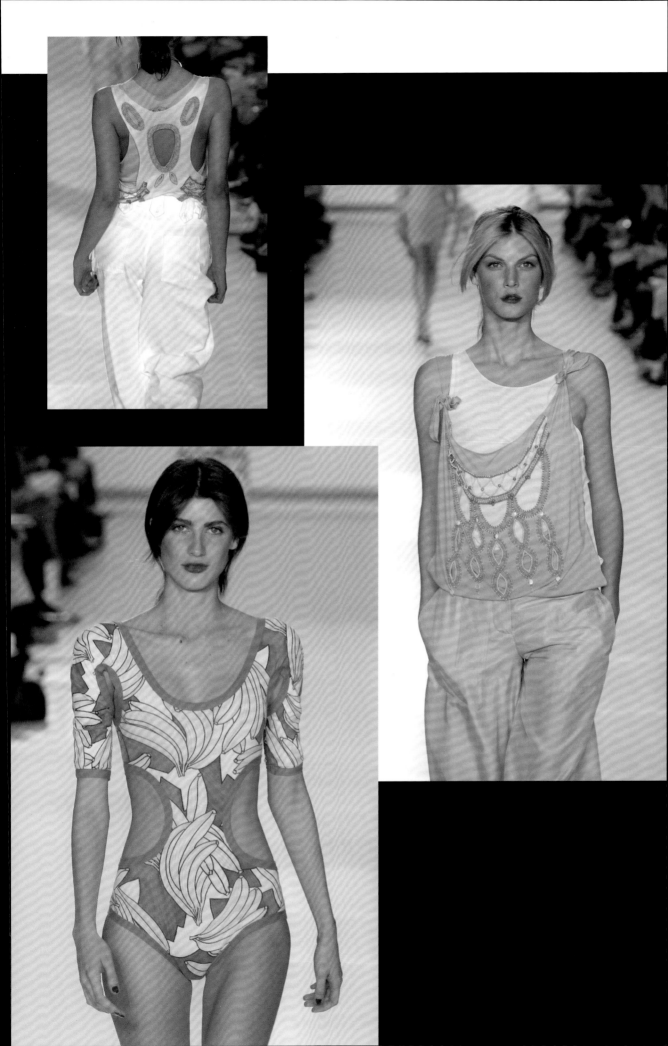

FEMININE TOPS AND MASCULINE TROUSERS

A resounding critical success, Phoebe Philo's A/W 2004–2005 collection is – like her next show, for S/S 2005 (see p. 450) – still cited today by fashion critics as an important collection in the history of fashion, and one that cemented Philo's skills in anticipating how women wanted to present themselves, and doing so with sensitivity and dignity, all while offering the unexpected, the witty, the cleverly tongue-in-cheek. '[H]er best yet,' said André Leon Talley in US *Vogue*. 'She has made Chloé soar in a way it has not soared since the seventies, when Karl Lagerfeld first made the house one of fashion's most-wanted labels.' Talley continued, 'What's special about Phoebe Philo? She is master of the imperfect perfect. Of the modern vintage. She blurs the lines between the hippie-comfortable and the hippie-sexy... Philo is a rara avis: a woman designing in a field dominated by men. Without ego, she makes clothes as clean, as crisp as the music of a Caribbean steel-drum street band.'

The spectre of the 1970s was visible to others, too. The *New York Times* noted that the run of 'bulky sweaters, some that fell to the ankles', in and among the pretty pleated dresses and tailoring, brought back 'happy memories of 1975'. Their reporter, Ginia Bellafante, called the show 'terrific'.

Philo's trousers and unstructured suiting gained much praise. 'It's strange how fashion desires seize you out of the blue sometimes,' said Sarah Mower in US *Vogue*. 'Put on your trusty habitual garment the next morning and, hello, it's wrong. Just such a thing has happened in the pants arena this season. I time the event to precisely 10:46 A.M. on March 6 in Paris, when the second model walked down Chloé's fall runway. She was wearing a pair of Phoebe Philo's glen-plaid mannish trousers with deep cuffs and a narrow leather belt... Putting it together like that – the feminine top and shoe with the man-cut bottom – was a stroke of styling brilliance that made a radical idea look not just wearable but also relaxed and pretty.'

Philo told reporters, 'I think it's incredibly sexy, an oversize man's trouser on a woman. It reverts back to that old *wearing your boyfriend's clothes*. I buy men's trousers quite often... We cut ours with a slightly shorter crotch, so that it still looks like a man's pant, but it's for a woman.' The wooden-soled platform shoes would soon become a Chloé classic, too.

SENSUAL SATIN AND
SMOOTH TAILORING

'Stepping on the Gas: Chloé Gets the Cash
To Become $1B Brand' ran a headline on the
cover of *WWD* on 6 October 2004. 'It's truly
a pregnant moment for Chloé. Not only is
creative director Phoebe Philo expecting her
first child in two months ... the high-flying
French firm is embarking on an aggressive
expansion drive that could see it become a
billion-dollar baby for parent Compagnie
Financière Richemont,' read the report.
CEO Ralph Toledano told the journal that
Chloé sales had multiplied by five in the five
years before, thanks to the success of Philo
and, before her, Stella McCartney.

Three days later, Philo's spring/summer show
was met with critical praise. *WWD* called it
'effortlessly sexy', praising the sensual tuxedo
shirts, billow blouses, 'angelic' dresses, and
easy reworking of menswear tailoring staples.
In the *Washington Post*, Robin Givhan said
Philo's pieces 'achieve the magic that allows
a woman to be effortlessly cool'.

'Chloé's show was as wickedly smooth as
French dark chocolate,' wrote André Leon
Talley, a nod to the invitation – a box of
Ladurée bonbons.

'I am feeling very dressed up for spring,'
Philo told reporters of the collection. 'I am
feeling satin.' In the *New York Times*, Cathy
Horyn quipped, 'Ms. Philo knows how to
make a dirty dress look clean.'

Philo's accessories were also booming. In
February 2005, a few months after the show,
WWD reported on a 'mounting frenzy in the
U.K. over Chloé's Paddington bag for spring/
summer [see p. 452], for which there is a
lengthy waiting list'. The report added that a
London police officer had even visited Chloé's
Sloane Street premises to plan security details,
as he was 'concerned over the possibility of
muggings or theft when the bags arrive in
store'. A month after the show, Philo was
named British Designer of the Year at
the British Fashion Awards.

KNIFE PLEATS
AND RIDING BOOTS

While Phoebe Philo had set the direction for this collection, it was her studio team who took her vision forward, working alone while Philo took maternity leave. Consequently, at the end of the show, it was the team, not Philo, who took to the stage to accept the applause. 'Phoebe Philo sat in the front row and insisted that her assistants take the bow for work they had completed during her maternity leave,' reported US *Vogue*. 'A good support system – what every new mom needs,' quipped *WWD*.

Even without Philo's physical presence in the months leading up to the show, her influence was clear. 'Lacy vintage-inspired tops, unironically pretty dresses, shrunken jackets, sexily saggy trousers: This is, was, and – even in the hands of assistants – remains pure Chloé by Phoebe,' said US *Vogue*. Not everything was a repeat, however: knife-pleated silk shirts, and styling that united black with rich navy, felt new. As did long white maxi dresses, in white lace and linen, edged in black tulle. There were also clever nods to the old: a flowing white gown with a triangle print, modelled by Isabeli Fontana (see p.460, right), was a reworking of a dress designed by Karl Lagerfeld and modelled by Naomi Campbell for S/S 1993 (p.303, right).

'Under her watch, Chloé has moved toward something prettily sexy, as well as internationally accessible,' US *Vogue* said of Philo's booming success, remarking on the worldwide popularity of Chloé bags such as the 'Paddington' and 'Bracelet' (see pp.450 and 414). 'Over time, she's co-opted Francophile influences like Brigitte Bardot and Talitha Getty, and brought her love of riding to the job, sliding riding boots and horse-blanket ponchos into the collection... Her passion for her horse, Toby, is cast into the metal horse-shaped handle you push every time you enter a Chloé boutique, as well as the horseshoe charms that dangle from some of this season's bags,' they added.

PRISTINE COTTON
AND LACE

By the time of this show, Chloé's Phoebe
Philo – once seen to be toiling under the
shadow of her predecessor, Stella McCartney –
had become one of the most acclaimed
designers working in fashion, a position
she has continued to hold to this day.

'Phoebe Philo is one of the hottest, most-
copied designers in fashion, having infused
girlish dressing with a whole new savvy,' said
WWD. Given that Philo's 'engaging signatures
are all over the contemporary market and
beyond', *WWD* felt it made sense that
Philo had often to go in a new direction,
and 'shake up her m.o. a bit for spring'.

The result was 'more structure and less fluff',
according to *WWD*. The look was pristine
white dresses, matching skirt and shirt
combos, and even pieces made out of metal
gauze. Critics were excited by the new
direction, clear vision, and innovative use of
fabrications. 'At Chloé, all the different uses
of lace come together in imaginative ways,'
said Rita Konig in US *Vogue*. 'There are doilies
stitched on organza shirts and tunics, and
loose, flowing tops that look like the sort of
thing Henry VIII might have gone to bed in...'
Konig said her favourite pieces were 'the
wonderful appliqué lawn dresses with cutwork
detailing, covered buttons, pinked edges,
and mini bobble fringes', adding, 'You can't
imagine a day going wrong while you are
wafting about in such crisp, starched
white cotton.'

By this season, however, the rumour mill
was churning. 'Philo in Talks to Leave Chloé?'
asked a *WWD* headline on 22 November 2005.
The article theorized that the designer may
well be keen for a break: 'Philo has long been
uncomfortable with the media limelight,
valuing her privacy over the lure of fashion
celebrity.' Come January 2006, the news
was confirmed. Philo had quit, for 'personal
reasons', to focus on her family, wrote *WWD*.
'Philo's reign at Chloé is over,' they mourned,
noting that she had helped 'catapult the
growth of the Parisian brand with coveted
handbag designs and feminine frocks'.

The Studio &
Paulo Melim Andersson
The Mid-2000s

After Phoebe Philo's departure from Chloé, at a point when sales were booming and scrutiny was higher than ever, the house went through a few years of insecurity in terms of leadership; a period that can be seen to mirror the uncertain years after the departure of Chloé's other great design success, Karl Lagerfeld, in the 1980s (see pp. 220–21).

Initially, the in-house Chloé team, featuring Yvan Mispelaere, Blue Farrier and Adrian Appiolaza, took charge, as they had during Philo's maternity leave. Rumours abounded about who would be named as a formal successor: some suggested team leader Mispelaere, or – to echo Philo's appointment – another young female Brit, Luella Bartley. Then, in September 2006, the 34-year-old Swede Paulo Melim Andersson, formerly design director at Marni, was appointed. *WWD* called him 'a hidden talent instead of a media star'.

'Few have heard of him and even fewer know what he looks like, but as of yesterday morning Swedish designer Paulo Melim Andersson became the most watched designer in the fashion world', read a report in the 12 October 2006 edition of the *Guardian* after the announcement. 'Chloé, the fashion label that has launched a million high street copies ... finally named its new creative director after the departure of Phoebe Philo earlier this year. With sales increasing 60% annually it is one of the most popular designer brands around.'

Andersson was noted by the press for having an edgier, less sensual look than Philo, in part due to his background with Marni, a house known for off-beat eccentricity, favoured by intellectuals. Still, he was complimentary of his predecessor. 'Phoebe was the right age. She did a fantastic job,' he told *WWD* shortly after his appointment, but noted that he intended to evolve the Chloé aesthetic. 'It's just a tweaking of the taste, and that's what I'm doing,' he said. 'For me, Chloé is a blouse – effortless blouses.'

Andersson was born on the island of Madeira and raised in Gothenberg, Sweden. As a child, he became a Lego champion – a backstory that was cited by fashion journalists as a link to his eye for structure and detail, and his use of small models of garments when working. 'I don't just sketch. I work much more 3-D,' he told *WWD*. 'I drape, and the most fun is in a fitting, when things can happen.'

Before Chloé, Andersson was an apprentice tailor for four years, then studied literature at the Sorbonne in Paris, and later studied at both Central Saint Martins and the Royal College of Art in London. He began his career in fashion in 1995, working part-time at Martin Margiela, before shifting into design at Marni. His tenure at Chloé was a difficult one: press response was muted, and many journalists mourned the easy confidence of Philo, viewing Andersson's work as tricky or clunky. In March 2008, his departure was announced. *Harper's Bazaar* noted that Andersson had 'been given his marching orders, cutting his debut short at a questionable 17 months', adding that 'his vision for Chloé has not fuelled the kind of label-mania that was seen under Philo's reign'. Andersson went on to work with Vanessa Bruno and Zadig & Voltaire, as well as lecturing in fashion at Iuav University in Venice.

OVERSIZED COOL

Following Phoebe Philo's departure, the A/W 2006–2007 collection was left to the studio team, comprised of Adrian Appiolaza, Blue Farrier and Yvan Mispelaere, who all took a united bow at the end of the show. While press response was muted – unsurprisingly, given a replacement for Philo had yet to be announced – *Le Monde* called it 'a coherent transitional collection'.

The trio 'thought big', joked *Dazed & Confused* magazine, pointing to the slouchy, oversized dresses and 'ballooning' boilersuits. Appiolaza, Farrier and Mispelaere 'gave the house's signature pretty aesthetic an injection of mannish cool by dressing the Chloé girl in her big brother's oversized coats over her favourite sheer organza shirts', commented the magazine, noting that 'low-slung pocketed skirts and sky-high heels ensured that none of the collection's sex appeal was diminished'.

Crash magazine were impressed by the 'nonchalant silhouette' and the 'unusual discretion' of the pieces; the halftones and the thick matte fabrics with 'no superfluous embellishment, no embroidery, no print'. This, they felt, signalled a new direction for Chloé – 'that of an artistic temperament, discreet but poetic, the new poor'.

SEVENTIES PATCHWORK

In August 2006, *WWD* reported that Chloé
were still holding off on naming a successor to
Phoebe Philo. The house had, however, named
Emma Hill as an accessories consultant, in
order to steer the rapid growth of the bags
and leather goods. A few weeks later, Yvan
Mispelaere, who many felt would soon be
leading the house, announced that he would
shortly leave Chloé to take a job under Frida
Giannini at Gucci. 'The move could turn up the
heat on Chloé to name a designer successor to
Phoebe Philo,' noted *WWD*. A few days later,
their front page reported rumours that Paulo
Melim Andersson, then design director at
Marni, would shortly be named head designer.
Representatives from Chloé refused to
comment.

By the day of the show, there was still no
certainty. And yet, the collection that was
presented, *WWD* said, was a hit. 'One might
have understood, if not exactly forgiven, had
Yvan Mispelaere decided to phone in his last
collection for Chloé, where he's been the
interim team leader for some time. But rather,
in his finale for the house, he turned in another
fine continuation of the Phoebe Philo tone,
which is to say one that radiates youthful
charm.' The show notes cited Gloria Vanderbilt
as a muse for the season's look, though, as
WWD noted, the inspiration seemed 'vague'.
Instead, the Seventies mood was fun and light,
with two-tone dresses, sportswear combos,
quilt motifs and decorative collages: 'good-girl-
goes-boho', said *WWD*.

Shortly after the show, on 28 September, Chloé
confirmed the rumours and named Andersson
as the house's new creative director.

EDGY BLACK AND ORANGE

'Could there be harder, more round-toed and girlish shoes to fill than those vacated by Phoebe Philo and, before her, Stella McCartney at Chloé?' asked US *Vogue* on the occasion of former Marni designer Paulo Melim Andersson's debut for the house. 'Both Philo and McCartney had the knack, in addition to designing terrifically cool and irreverent clothes, of making women desperate to look just like them. Baggy-ass trousers? If Phoebe was wearing them, so too gals from Austin to Osaka. It is unlikely that Paulo Melim Andersson will have a similar effect.'

Andersson, a 34-year-old Swede with a penchant for the avant-garde, had been appointed after a year-long search 'that had the fashion world turning red from holding its breath', according to US *Vogue*. 'What we have, in essence, is a shrewd, clever boy – instead of an alpha girl – running the house of Chloé,' they continued. However, a sharp-minded boy in the Chloé hot seat was not without precedent: 'The shrewdest, cleverest boy of them all, Karl Lagerfeld, led the brand from 1965 until 1983, and in doing so defined city-wise, lighthearted bohemianism for two decades.'

'Andersson's challenge is to maintain Chloé's dominance of the dirty-pretty-thing market without the benefit of personal iconicity,' *Vogue* added. Still, they praised his debut collection, calling it in line with Chloé's recent 'engagingly quirky sexiness'. 'It's nice when clothes just land on someone and look effortless,' Andersson told the press.

WWD called the show 'an attitude adjustment', referring to Andersson's Chloé woman as 'brooding and decidedly edgy', thanks to her black and orange wardrobe, and the many 'Marni-isms' in the silhouettes and details, including lines of mirrored embellishments and curved architectural sleeves.

Robin Givhan, writing in the *Washington Post*, was unimpressed with the change of direction. 'While every house has to evolve, Melim Andersson tossed out everything that was charming, enticing and – arguably – revenue-producing about the brand. He gutted a charming little cottage that just needed a new paint job,' she wrote. 'Part of that decision is related to a reality of the fashion industry. Designers hate being predictable, and the fashion industry's philosophy is that change is always good... But beautiful clothes, the kind that set off a melody in your head, never bore.'

ASYMMETRIC, SHEER AND ARTSY

WWD noted that Paulo Melim Andersson had toned down his vision for his second collection for Chloé, in response to many critics finding his debut (see p.474) 'too aggressive for a house better known for its charming, girlish appeal'.

For this season, he 'lightened the mood considerably', offering various sheer pieces – 'playing majorly to the current transparency trend' – alongside dresses and jumpers decorated with large brushstrokes or crafted from patchworks of bold, unusual colours. Many seams and cuts were asymmetric. The garments had 'artsy panache', *WWD* said approvingly, noting that the gentler attitude suited the house. '[T]he Chloé customer doesn't stomp all angst-like; she steps out, rather, with an alluringly cool confidence.'

Cathy Horyn, writing in the *New York Times*, agreed that Andersson's clothes looked 'light and friendly', praising the off-beat palette – 'chocolate, salmon and hot pink' – as well as the 'layered loose dresses crimped with random pleats'. She concluded, however, that Andersson 'seems to want to fit his abstract style to Chloé, but after two seasons, it's starting to feel like a square peg'.

FLORAL PRINTS
AND BEADED GOWNS

Paulo Melim Andersson continued to
veer away from his early abstraction and
conceptualism and towards the feminine, for
this, his third collection for Chloé. He showed
chiffon tea dresses in Seventies-style floral
prints, patterned blouses and beaded gowns.

The show notes referred to the Chloé woman
belonging to 'the magpie school of looking
good'. 'That amounts to throwing in the towel,'
responded Cathy Horyn, in the *New York
Times*. While conceding that '[p]aisley and
floral prints, in rose and slate-blue tones,
at least looked fresh', she complained that
Andersson 'creates pastiches from three or
four trends, like the filmy draped dress and
tweed boyfriend jacket, and then adds
splashes of embroidery and sexy pointed
footwear'. Her conclusion: 'as with any
magpie operation, most of the styles
had a half-consumed look'.

'Pretty', said *WWD*, more approvingly, noting
that Andersson's line-up of garden prints and
mannish jackets 'nodded nicely to Phoebe
Philo's sweet-miss template without losing
his edgier stance'. Overall, they found the
look 'a little bit English countryside and
a little bit rock 'n' roll'.

However, *WWD* soon reported, 'the effort
proved to be Melim Andersson's last for the
house: Two weeks later, he was pushed out,
to be replaced by longtime design team
member Hannah MacGibbon.'

Hannah MacGibbon

A Short Biography

Following the appointment of the British female designer Hannah MacGibbon as creative director of Chloé in March 2008, some critics pointed out that MacGibbon – who had served for five years at the house as second-in-command under Phoebe Philo – should have been given the top job two years before, when Philo left. In fact, MacGibbon had been offered the position but reportedly turned it down several times. She had spent some of the time in between working on the launch of a new Chloé fragrance: following her promotion to the top job, she showed a confident understanding of how to distil Chloé's history and codes into products and accessories as well as garments.

Rather than embrace trends – 'I'm "anti-trend",' she told *WWD* in 2009 – she focused on the Chloé signatures: scalloped edges, broderie anglaise, pleats, lace, crepe silk, the sandy beige adored by founder Gaby Aghion, the blouses of Karl Lagerfeld, the floaty dresses that Philo had become known for, which, in themselves, nodded to Lagerfeld. 'There's a sentiment in the house that I love. It's the house, rather than any particular period,' MacGibbon commented. That said, her favourite era in fashion was evident – the 'late-Seventies, early-Eighties period: It was very sexy,' she told *WWD*. 'I love what Karl created, and there is definitely a spirit of him left somewhere,' she told Suzy Menkes of the *International Herald Tribune* in 2009. She also admitted to being influenced by Philo. 'I do think that us Brits have a bit more of a relaxed style. But the British/Parisian mix is what I love about Chloé.' She noted, though, that Stella McCartney's playful pieces would not see a resurgence under her tenure: 'I've never thought about what Stella did. She did a great job, but I think that I have quite a different style.'

Like McCartney and Philo before her, MacGibbon had been educated at Central Saint Martins (she completed her master's degree at the college in 1996), and, further mimicking their backstory, she was a Brit, a Londoner (she was born in Camden in 1970). But the wider circumstances were different from those of her predecessors: MacGibbon's first collection was shown just days after Lehman Brothers collapsed. Fashion and luxury's place in the world was uncertain, awkward even. 'Everything's so hard at the moment,' MacGibbon told *WWD*. 'There's a lack of romanticism in the air.'

Before her appointment, MacGibbon had worked with Valentino, rising through the ranks to become his first assistant (in August 2010, *Harper's Bazaar* quoted the legendary designer as saying, 'She brought a freshness to my studio and a precise feeling for what a girl wants to wear. She knows her customers, and she's determined and strong'). However, MacGibbon joined Chloé when she still felt as green as the then-creative director Phoebe Philo. 'We were both young and didn't have any idea of what was in store,' MacGibbon told *WWD* of that time, noting, 'It's also that naïve, fresh approach that's so important.' She added: 'I would love [my designs] to be just effortless, desirable clothes that you want to wear, and I'm really starting with daywear because that's at the core of the company.'

MacGibbon did, indeed, mature the Chloé look, pushing new signatures such as capes and knee-high boots. Her look was confident and consistent, and her clothes were desirable, though they rarely surprised or shocked critics. 'It's so important to me for women to feel good,' she explained to *Harper's Bazaar*. 'Sexiness and confidence come from feeling relaxed in your clothes. It's not about wearing a piece of architecture.' Asked by Menkes, 'Are you the Chloé woman?', MacGibbon noted, 'I think everyone's got a bit of Chloé inside her. That's what I love: realness. And I think I am quite real.'

SHARP SHOULDERS
AND SCALLOPED EDGES

Ahead of her debut collection for the house,
Hannah MacGibbon dined with Chloé founder
Gaby Aghion. The latter relayed to MacGibbon,
according to a *WWD* report on the meeting,
'how she plunged into the fashion business
55 years ago with a simple impulse: to do
beautiful, cotton day dresses at a time of
highfalutin couture – and then went on
to create one of the most iconic brands
in French ready-to-wear'.

It was fitting, then, that – like Phoebe Philo
before her, for whom MacGibbon worked in
the Chloé studio – the designer opened her
first show for Chloé with an Aghion signature:
scallops. The look was a yellow coat, with
scalloped edges, worn with apricot shorts,
also trimmed in scallop, by a teenage
Karlie Kloss (see right).

MacGibbon told *WWD* that she believed a
'naïve, fresh approach' was vital for Chloé.
'I don't think there's any house that provides
clothes for the girls we design for,' she said.
And yet, she also noted that her look would
reflect 'more sophistication; maybe [be]
a little less girly' than the Philo days.

The show received mixed reviews. In the *New
York Times*, Cathy Horyn called it 'a fair start',
praising a 'sharp-shouldered jumpsuit' and
a 'cool, one-shoulder dress in nutmeg cotton
with side lacing' (see p. 486). But MacGibbon,
she said, 'will hear from plenty of critics about
her very large trousers, and look back upon
them critically herself and feed her eye
from smaller plates'.

Writing in the *Washington Post*, Robin Givhan
noted, in relation to the Parisian fashion
industry: 'This city gives its designers license
to play out their aesthetic fantasies. But with
that freedom comes responsibility. The needs
of women cannot be entirely dismissed. Their
dignity is not to be toyed with. And make
no mistake, female designers have the
same capacity as their male counterparts
to stitch up devastatingly undignified frocks.'
MacGibbon, she said, 'dressed models in
scallop-edged jackets and shirts that made
them look like a prehistoric centaur: half
woman and half brontosaurus'. (Similarly,
Horyn referred to the scalloping as 'dinosaur-
like'.) But, Givhan noted, 'the most egregious
garment on the runway, perhaps on all the
runways this season, was a pair of metallic,
high-waisted, copper balloon pants [see p. 487,
left]. They prompted one editor to note that
the answer to that paranoid question –
Do these make my bum look big? – would
be: No, they make it look enormous.'

FLAMBOYANT CAPES
AND BERMUDA SHORTS

'Two Words For Fall: Toughen Up', read a report on the season in the *New York Times*, which noted that harder, sharper fashions were in vogue. Indeed, Hannah MacGibbon's comments, on her appointment – that she intended to replace some of Philo's girlishness with clean sophistication (see p.484) – suited the mood of the moment. Robin Givhan, in the *Washington Post*, said that MacGibbon had found her footing: 'Her second collection for the house focused on outerwear with bravura capes, as well as sportswear that enticed with fuller-than-usual cuts, surprising translucence or an enthusiastic embrace of comfort.'

WWD said that MacGibbon had 'desweetened' Chloé this season, relying on 'elements borrowed from the boys'. The result, they said, was a 'less coy, more worldly look with a waft of the Seventies, if not in its cuts per se, then in its casual flamboyance, as if the designer were channeling Lauren Hutton'.

MacGibbon told Suzy Menkes, of the *New York Times*, that she had drawn inspiration from old Antonio Lopez fashion illustrations, later finding Lopez's drawings for Karl Lagerfeld in the Chloé Archive. 'I love what Karl created, and there is definitely a spirt of him left somewhere,' she said, of the retro mood.

Backstage, her look – high boots with shorts – echoed the mood of the collection. 'I like the idea in winter of still showing some flesh,' she told Menkes. 'You don't feel vulnerable in shorts – it's not the obvious sexiness of wearing a skirt. You can be active.'

Le Monde said the models resembled Calamity Jane, referring to grey blouses with gold buttons, leather Bermuda shorts rolled up on the thigh, and carrot-shaped pants and 'cape coats worthy of the wildest gauchos'. They disapproved of the evening outfits ('grandma's white lace shirts'), preferring 'the masculine confidence' and 'heroism' of the opening looks.

EASY SPORTSWEAR

'I was going for the anti-cocktail,' Hannah MacGibbon told the *New York Times*, of the look at this show, which included slouchy tailoring in beige and khaki, buttoned-up boyish shirts and easy double denim. 'Cowgirls, Get the Blues', instructed the paper. Suzy Menkes noted that a mood of the season, championed with particular gusto by MacGibbon, was 'gender-blending' fashion, with looks that seemed suitable for either men or women, or that borrowed simultaneously from both wardrobes.

MacGibbon's 'take on the roomy jacket and easy trouser and the khaki button-down shirt is more boyish than most', agreed Sarah Mower, in her review for Style.com. '[H]er girl has a refreshingly natural look – all recently washed hair and un-made-up skin,' continued Mower. 'She also dispenses with the agony of high heels, preferring the comfort of flat leather walking sandals...' Mower questioned the dominance of sporty, casual silhouettes over the 'floaty, fluttery side of Chloé', but this may have been the mood of the season.

'In a Surprise, Fashion Rediscovers Sportswear', read a headline in the *New York Times*. Indeed, this season also marked Phoebe Philo's return to fashion, and her debut at Céline, which was applauded as streamlined, clean, focused – the apex of the easy, casual mood that dominated S/S 2010. Such a sporty look was, classically, the domain of American fashion – where designers such as Claire McCardell, and later Calvin Klein and Perry Ellis, had spearheaded the look. But, as Suzy Menkes wrote in a separate piece in the *New York Times*, 'Whereas designers in Europe like Philo for Céline and Hannah MacGibbon for Chloé seem to be working in an American idiom, few leading labels in New York today – leaving aside the bright and breezy collections of Michael Kors – aspire to sportswear.' Indeed, Paris was now the place to look for the effortless and the modern; for young female designers rethinking, again and again, how contemporary women should present themselves, and how their clothes should fit around their lifestyles.

FROM CARAMEL
TO DESERT SAND

'The camel and beige love affair continues
for Hannah MacGibbon,' said *Dazed* of this
season's Chloé show. '[T]he sophistication
level was ramped up further motioning to
the 70s styles that we've been seeing a lot
of this season,' their report noted, referring
to wide-legged flared trousers, fringing,
blouses with oversized pussy-bow collars,
and sparkling evening jackets.

'It was beige all the way, or almost, in shades
ranging from caramel to desert sand,' agreed
Vogue Paris, who noted a 'very masculine
attitude in the often sporty designs'. The
magazine informed its readers of a shift in
the Chloé look, under MacGibbon's direction.
'Chloé is usually known for its easy-going
frivolity and bubbly, accessible charm, but
current artistic director Hannah MacGibbon
seems to have opted for a more militant
femininity, intent on projecting an image
of uninhibited poise and well-being.'

'Beige, beige, and more beige,' said Sarah
Mower, who summarized the stand-out look
as being 'a long-sleeved silk blouse and
high-waist flared trousers, and the bouncy,
blown-out Charlie girl hair that captures
the seventies American sportswear attitude
this trend is all about'.

Mower, like editors at *Vogue Paris*, noted the
feminist implications of the look, referring, in
her Style.com review, to an 'early-Armani-like
jacket that might have jumped out of *Vogue*'s
pages in the post-women's lib era – when
dashing to work while looking enthusiastically
businesslike was the thing'.

Mower was intrigued by the synergy
between MacGibbon's commitment to clean,
sophisticated sportswear and the similarly
refined, edited mood being proposed by former
Chloé creative directors Stella McCartney,
at her eponymous label, and Phoebe Philo,
at Céline. 'They left [Chloé] with a reputation
for girly dressing, jingly-jangly It bags, and
statement shoes, but now that they're all
into their thirties, these young professionals
are leading a different life,' Mower said of
the pair. And yet, she worried about where
MacGibbon's new look left Chloé, in terms
of positioning. 'MacGibbon's house-cleaning
instinct has thrown out ... all the frills, prints,
funny bags, and chunky clogs and platform
shoes that last made Chloé hot... In terms of
brand differentiation, though, that leaves a
conundrum for buyers. Chloé's offering for
Fall puts the label in direct competition with
what so many others are producing now.'

LIGHTNESS
AND MINIMALISM

'Hannah MacGibbon still loves beige. That hasn't changed, but there was a welcome lightness in her Spring collection,' said Nicole Phelps, for Style.com. This latest Chloé offer was indeed an ode to 'lightness', whether in terms of weightlessness, transparency or shine. Looks included gleaming black leather contrasted against matte fabric (see opposite, top left) and an opaque white cotton poplin top paired with a see-through black tulle skirt (p. 502, right). With regard to easy dressing, MacGibbon maintained the house's characteristic mix of high and low/chic and casual – expressed, for example, through a range of sophisticated clean white cotton poplin dresses.

'If last season's Chloé girl [see p. 496] was headed off to work in seventies-inflected sportswear, now she looks like she's on her way to dance rehearsal,' said Phelps, pointing to a scoop-back leotard, pleats, sheer skirts that recalled tutus, and ballet pumps. Phelps welcomed the collection for offering 'some of the girlishness that used to be this label's defining factor'.

Still, there was plenty for those looking for the strictness and sophistication that MacGibbon had made her signature at Chloé, including streamlined coats with minimal decoration, save for discreet buttons. The colour palette of the collection was also notable for its narrowness: optic white, black, chocolate, red and sand. '[M]ostly, designers have stopped trying to agitate,' was Robin Givhan's take on the season for the *Washington Post*, noting that a whole cadre of designers – including MacGibbon, alongside Céline's Phoebe Philo and Giambattista Valli (usually known for ruffles and bouncy gowns) – had 'turned to minimalism'.

PYTHON AND PATCHWORK

From beige to python. The shift in mood, from
timeless camel and sand to scales, surprised
critics at this season's Chloé show.

'Last season [see p.500] was about simple
balletic grace and from there it was amped
up to the max as Hannah MacGibbon sent
out an onslaught of python,' said *Dazed*. The
magazine noted snakeskin was used both as
a material, on shoes and accessories, and
as a print, 'effective on a pair of pleat front
wide-legged silk trousers, continuing in
the vein of the 70s, easy-breezy gal that
MacGibbon seems to always evoke with
her collections'.

'Snakeskin, and plenty of it, is Hannah
MacGibbon's obsession du jour. A year ago it
was camel. For Spring it was sheer,' said Nicole
Phelps, for Style.com. 'As preoccupations go,
this one produced one of her livelier outings,
maybe a shade too much so... In the end, it's
simply a material best applied in small doses.'
Phelps noted, 'The patchworks of python print
in different colors had a graphic impact on the
runway, but their chances off of it are slim...'

Other press reaction was muted, with
many referring to MacGibbon as part of a
considerable run of Paris-based designers
stuck on minimalism, the results of which
were pleasant, if not particularly challenging
or thought-provoking.

Shortly ahead of this catwalk presentation,
the *New York Times*'s Eric Wilson noted that
MacGibbon's contract would be up after this
season, adding that those familiar with the
goings-on at Chloé 'said the reaction to her
show on Monday could determine whether
her contract is renewed'. Wilson reported
rumours that Chloé were, apparently,
already interviewing designers.

Unsurprisingly, given the subdued reaction,
swiftly after the show, rumours spread that
MacGibbon's exit would be certain – a fact
that was confirmed in May 2011. Chloé used
its Twitter feed and website to make the
announcement that MacGibbon would be
replaced by Clare Waight Keller, formerly
of Pringle – a form of communication that
echoed the rapid digitization occurring across
the industry in this period, from e-commerce
to online show reviews. '[A] stroke of
technological savvy', was *The Cut*'s pragmatic
take on the form of the announcement.

Clare Waight Keller

A Short Biography

Unlike the three fellow Brit women who preceded her – Stella McCartney, Phoebe Philo and Hannah MacGibbon – Clare Waight Keller was not nearly new to professional design, nor fresh out of college, when she took up the role of creative director in May 2011. Before arriving at Chloé, she had already worked at Calvin Klein, designing for the women's main-line collection during an exciting time for the brand – Kate Moss was the face, and Carolyn Bessette-Kennedy was working on the same floor. Next she went to Ralph Lauren, where she was head designer of the men's Purple Label. In 2000, she moved to Gucci, where she worked as a senior designer under Tom Ford, and alongside future stars such as Burberry's Christopher Bailey and Calvin Klein's Francisco Costa. Five years later, she moved back to the UK to take the helm at Pringle of Scotland, in her first stint as a creative director. There, Waight Keller was able to make use of her knitwear expertise (after receiving a Bachelor's degree in fashion from Ravensbourne College of Art, she had completed a Master's in fashion knitwear at the Royal College of Art in London), and her transformation of the heritage house into a contemporary fashion player won acclaim.

At Chloé, she was praised for making use of this experience: her knitwear was applauded, as was her tailoring, which critics related to her previous work in menswear. But her real success was in the easy femininity that underpinned her collections, which were rich with flowing gowns, silk blouses and hippie-ish elements. Waight Keller's collections included many nods to the 1970s, including in her debut showing, where her pleats paid tribute to the legacy of Karl Lagerfeld, and in the success of wafting layers and hand-painted dresses for the house. 'My work at Chloé has been about exploring the tension between a boyishness with a femininity,' Waight Keller told reporters in 2016.

On the subject of femininity, she told the *Evening Standard* in 2013, 'For many years femininity has been considered a bit girlie, frivolous, and not intelligent, but we know from our amazing results of the ready-to-wear that this isn't true. I believe most women feel beautiful when they are at their most feminine. Of course, one wants to do this with coolness and an edge, but essentially women gravitate towards easy-to-wear, feminine clothes that are flattering and that complement their skin and personality.' Her conclusion: 'The Chloé woman is someone empowered by being feminine.'

Born in Birmingham, England, in 1970, Waight Keller's early inspiration came from her mother, who was herself a keen dressmaker and introduced her daughter to the art of fabric-sourcing. 'I used to go to the old rag market with my mother, who would make clothes for the family and things for the house,' Waight Keller told the *Telegraph* in 2014.

Of her formative years, growing up during an era of skinheads, punks, New Romantics and goths, she recalled to *Libération* newspaper: 'The house was full of sewing and knitting accessories. I fell in love with fashion. Back then I would buy *Vogue* and be transported flicking through the pages, looking at the models. But I was also excited by everything I was seeing on the street. From the outset I saw fashion as a back-and-forth between these two things.' The *Guardian* reported that during her time at Chloé, Waight Keller was 'responsible for a string of hits', including billowing dresses decorated with tiny tassels and widely copied luxe tracksuits.

In January 2017, after six years at the head of the house, Waight Keller's departure from Chloé was announced. In March 2017, she was appointed the first female artistic director of Givenchy, succeeding Riccardo Tisci. The following year she made the high-profile move of designing the royal wedding dress for the Duchess of Sussex. Some six months later, the duchess presented Waight Keller with the British Designer of the Year Award.

PLEATED DRESSES
AND RETRO HUES

'The challenge at Chloé, which will celebrate
its 60th anniversary next year, will be which
roots to return to – the Karl Lagerfeld years?
Philo's heyday?' said Nicole Phelps on
Style.com in October 2011, on the occasion
of Clare Waight Keller's debut for Chloé.

In the end, it was Lagerfeld whom Waight
Keller paid homage to, with pleated dresses,
wide bottoms and retro hues. There were
references to his famous hand-painted
garments (see, for example, p. 62): here, a craft
technique was used for the show's opening
looks (see right), whereby colour was applied
onto pre-pleated textiles, creating vibrant
stripes. Waight Keller also nodded to
Lagerfeld's innovative layering (see p. 120),
with silk crepe T-shirts worn under flowing
dresses (see p. 514, right).

The 'hyperreal flower embroideries on
crisp shirts and flowy shorts' also dated to
Lagerfeld's era, Phelps noted. Those florals
were a hit with photographers. Daria
Werbowy appeared in Chloé's floral pants,
shot by Inez van Lamsweerde and Vinoodh
Matadin, in the February 2012 edition of *Vogue
Paris*. Lara Stone wore the floral shirt (shown
opposite, bottom right) in the March edition,
photographed by Mikael Jansson.

The house regarded Waight Keller's collection
as the perfect interpretation and expression
of the 'flou' at Chloé. So, too, the colour palette,
which Waight Keller described in an interview
with *WWD* the day before the show as 'a
palette of makeup shades accented with soft
brights'. This, too, was perfectly in sync with
the house palette – those beiges and pinky
beiges – as previously defined by Hannah
MacGibbon (see p. 481).

Le Monde noted: 'the sorbet colours go
perfectly with sunray-pleated skirts or
structured jackets'. Pleats were everywhere.
As US *Vogue* commented: 'Waight Keller
showed fluid pleats in myriad ways, including
a grown-up take on the schoolgirl's knife-pleat
skirt.' She also played with sizing. *Vogue* noted:
'Oversizing one element at a time, either top or
pants is the way it works, for her, one extreme
against the other.'

Backstage, Waight Keller talked of 'fluidity
and femininity, but boyish'. Born in England,
but a frequent traveller, she had only recently
relocated to Paris. 'It's great to be in a French
house,' she told the *Telegraph*, 'because you
have the opportunity to work with an atelier.
I just moved here, but already am feeling the
energy of the city, and that has really
influenced me.'

SPORTSWEAR
AND DUSTY PASTELS

For her second season at the helm of Chloé,
Clare Waight Keller was still considering
her position as an Englishwoman in Paris –
a heritage that connected her with many of
Chloé's former leaders, from Stella McCartney
and Phoebe Philo to, more recently, Hannah
MacGibbon. Backstage, she explained that
she had tried to mix the casual sensibility of
English sportswear with the chic, considered
appropriateness of the French, hence the
liberal mixing within the styling: red knit
sweatpants with a lace blouse, a floral
embroidered sweatshirt worn with a satin
pencil skirt (see opposite, right), an oversized
parka worn over neat tailoring.

In the *New York Times*, Cathy Horyn was
impressed, calling it 'a very strong collection
full of distinctive color – pale pink, lemon,
dusty blue, deep red, camel – and standout,
pretty sportswear'.

For Style.com, Nicole Phelps praised the
knitwear (Waight Keller's area of expertise),
as well as the dresses. 'Waight Keller has a
good handle on the breezy, uncomplicated
frock that is Chloé's claim to fame,' she
wrote. 'She proved that last season [see p. 512],
and she confirmed it here with a deep red
drop-waist T-shirt dress [see p. 518, right]
and an ivory shirtdress with a lace skirt
[p. 519, bottom right]. These would be a
good place to start when she sets to work
on next season.'

As with her debut, there were whiffs of Karl
Lagerfeld and his 1970s era at the house. On
SHOWstudio.com, Alexander Fury called
Chloé's collection 'probably the best they've
shown for a number of years'. 'You were at
least halfway through the foamy, structured
daywear before you hit anything that jarred
against the eye,' Fury explained. 'Otherwise,
it was sleek sailing through a dusty pastel
palette of faded turquoise, fleshy pink and a
rainbow of taupes. Those were the age-warped
hues of a seventies Chloé advertisement
mouldering in an old issue of Paris *Vogue*.
Strange as it may sound, that's a compliment.'

TRANSPARENT AND OPAQUE LAYERING

'It is a tall order to be the creative director of a house during its 60th anniversary,' wrote Jo-Ann Furniss for Style.com. 'And to do that in only your third season is an even taller one. Yet Clare Waight Keller came through this challenge with suitable aplomb for Spring.'

Nearby to the Tuileries, where the show was held, was a new exhibition, 'Chloé. Attitudes', curated by Judith Clark at the Palais de Tokyo, and featuring many highlights from the Chloé Archive. And yet, according to Furniss, Waight Keller 'appeared unbowed by the weight of history – what was shown today was not a greatest-hits collection'. The mood was assured, fresh and modern, and in step with what was becoming Waight Keller's signature: a boyish take on classic separates, plays on volume and on layering (particularly through experiments with the transparent and the solid), and new forward-thinking materials, such as pleated polyester. (That said, those with a keen eye could argue that some of the flouncier dresses had whiffs of '70s Lagerfeld, Waight Keller's favourite Chloé inspiration.)

Waight Keller told reporters backstage that she was inspired not by details or surfaces, but instead by an ethos: the liberated state of mind that Gaby Aghion, the founder of the brand, had brought to fashion, in her quest to release women from restrictive and heavy haute couture. Ahead of the show, Waight Keller spent time revisiting transcripts of interviews with Aghion. One line stood out: 'I don't explain anything. I lived the life I wanted.'

Critics and buyers were impressed with the confidence. 'Honestly, I think this past show was the most spot-on I have seen in terms of capturing the spirit of the Chloé girl, which had waned in the years before Clare took over,' Daniella Vitale, then chief merchant of Barneys New York, told the *New York Times*. 'She embodies that Chloé spirit herself,' Vitale added of Waight Keller.

TOUGH GIRLS
AND TOMBOYS

'Cold nights, tough girls' was the final line of the show notes handed out to guests at this season's Chloé show, which made uniform its key focus, including bibbed shirts, pinafores and pleated skirts that recalled rebellious British schoolgirls, smoking in secret. (Indeed, other listed inspirations included night buses, dorm rooms, bike sheds, bare legs and independent spirit.)

The look was, according to a *Los Angeles Times* review, 'Tomboy. Nubbly wool felt coat. Patchwork fur pullover worn with leather sweatpants. Pinafore dresses with straps that resembled utility belts. High waist, cropped pants. Chain-link fence T-shirts. Hiking boots and lace-up, lug-sole oxfords.' The paper mourned the absence of Chloé's signature softness, but other critics were impressed with the conviction, and the playful sense of rebellion. 'In presenting a somewhat tougher girl than is expected for Chloé, [Waight Keller] made it her best collection yet,' wrote Jo-Ann Furniss for Style.com.

Furniss theorized that Waight Keller's history as an accomplished menswear designer had shaped the strength of this collection, noting the success with which she had, in just four seasons, brought 'a certain English and boyish discipline' to the house.

Backstage, Waight Keller told reporters that the show was a tribute to growing up and gaining confidence. It was, she said, 'essentially about girls creating independence through the way they dress'.

LACE, V CUTS AND PLEATS

Backstage after this show, Clare Waight Keller
told reporters that she was imagining a more
feminine, sensual muse than usual when
working on the collection. Romance was in
and, thus, so too were its fashion bedfellows:
transparency, lace, deep V cuts.

But this was sex appeal done in the French,
refined way, said Jo-Ann Furniss for Style.com.
'The music might have been loud drum and
bass, with all of its hard, mid-nineties London
connotations, but this collection felt decidedly
rooted in Paris.'

Pleats, a Waight Keller go-to since her debut
for the house (see p.512), remained big news,
appearing both on gowns and tapered-leg
trousers with ankle ties. (Pleats were an
unexpected mega trend that season, with
Phoebe Philo at Céline and Raf Simons at
Dior also showing them.) '[T]he most sensual
garment of the collection was pleated, too –
a white dress with arm ties, split high at the
sides, worn with silk cami-knicker-style shorts
[see opposite, right],' noted Furniss. 'Clare
Waight Keller has not produced anything
quite that sexy before.' (Alongside the shift
in look was a shift in venue. Rather than the
usual Tuileries tent, this show was held at
the Lycée Carnot.)

Critics praised the summery attitude, and the
way the garments flowed elegantly across the
body. In her 'On the Runway' blog for the *New
York Times*, Cathy Horyn called the collection
'exceedingly calm and pretty, in a season that
has tended to be brassy'.

BOLD PRINTS AND
WILD TEXTURES

Regular attendees at Clare Waight Keller's
shows for Chloé had, by now, come to
recognize a familiar balance: English
boyishness with French refinement.
And yet, wrote Jo-Ann Furniss for Style.com,
'this Fall there was perhaps an injection
of a new element: something wild'.

Printed wild-cat furs and a rainbow leopard-
spot jacquard (see opposite, bottom right)
offered 'a notion of letting loose', Furniss said.
Indeed, many critics felt that Waight Keller
herself was loosening up, given the new
foray into bold print and pattern, and the
experiments with textures and tufting. Furniss
was particularly taken with the footwear,
including sheepskin ankle-strap shoes.

Outerwear was also praised. British *Vogue*'s
Sarah Harris admired the voluminous coats.
'Outsize would be an understatement, these
are broad sweeping wrap coats that could
happily house a small family,' she said of the
look. Other ensembles included a duvet-like
padded leather puffer and a longer coat
covered in tufts of marabou feathers.

There was 'quite an English spirit to this
figure who exchanged her sensible slim line or
shrug-on coats in beige or lavender for a wilder
leather coat, "pillowy padded," as [Waight
Keller] described it,' wrote Suzy Menkes in the
New York Times. A toughness ran throughout
the show, she argued: 'A tunic decorated with
metallic cutouts ... looked positively fierce
[see p.535, right].'

Backstage, Waight Keller gave attendees the
Twitter-friendly soundbites that had come to
define this fast-paced era of fashion reporting.
'She's wilder and more mysterious,' she said of
the Chloé woman. 'She has an urban mystery.'

FOLK-INSPIRED FLUIDITY

The news of the death of Gaby Aghion, founder of Chloé, on 27 September 2014, just a day before the house's S/S 2015 show, put this collection on the front page of the *New York Times*. 'At Chloé, a Bittersweet Day', read the 30 September headline, alongside a photograph from the show, which was dedicated by Clare Waight Keller to Aghion's memory.

Inside the paper, Vanessa Friedman noted that the 'airy volumes' of wafting cheesecloths, draped crepes and flouncing babydolls, with waists defined by rows of lacy links, 'paid homage to Ms. Aghion's initial imperative to create a freer, more fluid femininity'. 'I was interested in fabrics with history, almost a folklore,' Waight Keller said before the show.

Key to this collection, alongside Waight Keller's signature boyish workwear, was the classic Chloé 'flou'. Waight Keller explained to reporters, 'I wanted that one amazing shape that just hung off thin spaghetti straps.' White was the dominant hue of the collection, and the pretty gowns, in broderie, were in step with the summer trend for skimpy yet virginal 'gypsy'-style dresses (Waight Keller's stringy-strapped designs appeared in numerous editorials by photographers such as Peter Lindbergh, for US *Vogue*, and Ellen von Unwerth for *Vogue Italia*, as well as in the Chloé advertising campaign, by Inez van Lamsweerde and Vinoodh Matadin, which saw models striding barefoot along the beach, leading horses by hand, manes and gowns matching and flowing). Additional colours – dusty blue, terracotta, turquoise, ivory, mint green – had an ethereal mood, and were, according to the show notes, deliberately 'sun-faded' and 'folk'-inspired, like the collection's fabrics.

GENTLEMEN'S CLOTHING AND 'FLOU'

The show notes for the A/W 2015–2016 collection told guests that this season's Chloé look 'celebrates whimsical classicism as a modern-day movement'. Of the Chloé woman: 'Her nonchalant spirit evokes the essence of the outdoors for a soft yet strong femininity.'

The first look featured a sweeping military coat, with sharp peaked shoulders, worn over a softer, feminine blouse (see right). This balance of 'flou' and tailoring continued throughout: waistcoats were layered over billowing chiffon gowns, or a cape over a floaty mini-dress.

Jo-Ann Furniss called it 'the most confident collection that creative director Clare Waight Keller had produced to date', noting, 'The Chloé girl lost much of her pouty, superfluous French folderol: Despite her penchant for voluminous cheesecloth, she became precise, measured, and a much tougher creature – not the type to burst into tears if her boyfriend was caught flirting, say, with a Givenchy girl or even a Céline woman.'

Backstage, Waight Keller told reporters, 'I really wanted to capture something confident, but still with a carefree spirit. I can only describe the Chloé girl as a "gentlewoman", wearing guardsmen's coats and gentlemen's clothing, but still with the flou and lingerie lace.'

This season, she dedicated the show to International Women's Day, held yearly on 8 March, a move that highlighted Waight Keller's focus on reaffirming Chloé's history as a woman-founded brand, built with the needs and realities of modern women in mind. It was a history that other brands could only dream of, in a moment where the entire fashion industry seemed keen to prove its feminist credentials. Indeed, this period saw a growth in pro-women messaging on runways, and in images – from slogan T-shirts to campaigns focused on 'empowerment' – leading to a rapid entwinement of pop culture, consumer culture and feminism, and a new drive, within the press, for celebrating women designing for women.

TECHNICOLOUR ELEGANCE

The invitation for the Chloé S/S 2016 show featured a photograph by Ryan McGinley, known for ethereal yet exuberant shots, usually featuring young bodies, heady movements and bright, sparkling lights. The chosen image was dreamy, trippy: a woman floating, or falling, with a sun-lit glow around her, through an expanse of purple light. It was fitting, then, that Clare Waight Keller told guests, via her show notes, that the collection would capture 'the spirited optimism of the Chloé girl through a technicolour lens'. The look, she said, would be 'embodying a sense of carefree sexiness', adding, 'the silhouette floats light as air'.

The technicolour, sun-glared look of McGinley's images was captured in the clothes – flowing blouses in ombré stripes, wide '90s rave pants, halter tops, acid-wash denim separates, and pastel rainbow dresses, the colours of which were defined by the show notes in sorbet terms: 'lemon, pistachio, lavender, vermillion and palest rose'. The mood was festival chic, a sportier, modern take on the eternal fashion muse: the lithe groupie, in her thrown-together boho ensembles. There was a zip-up sports top thrown on over a chiffon gown, trackpants worn with romantic off-the-shoulder blouses, peasant tops worn with micro shorts.

'The 1990s is one of Spring's big stories, but no one has put forward her interest in the decade more explicitly than Clare Waight Keller at Chloé,' wrote Nicole Phelps for US *Vogue*. On seats, Waight Keller had left a note declaring the collection 'a tribute to girls named Kate, Chloé, Cecilia, Corinne, Rosemary, Emma, and Courtney, who embody the liberty and the elegance of a perfectly mastered and excessively lived simplicity'.

Backstage, Waight Keller told reporters that, to her, such muses represented a freer time: 'There's such a fast pace to fashion now; I think we've lost the innocence of the spirit of fashion, the youthful optimism that it portrays. And I think there's something quite joyful about fashion that's been missing.'

BIKER CHIC

For her A/W 2016–2017 collection, Clare
Waight Keller named her muse as Anne-
France Dautheville, who, in the 1970s, rode a
motorcycle solo across the Middle East, and
went on to become the first woman to ride solo
around the world. The runway was a dirt track;
a baked-mud path for models to stride down in
moto-trousers (a direct homage to a pair worn
in a photo of Dautheville), leather culottes,
billowy dresses with Middle Eastern-style
embroideries, knitted caftans and
cashmere djellabas.

'I was taken with the idea of a woman just
deciding to go on her own journey,' Waight
Keller told reporters backstage before the
show. 'That attitude, that sense of courage,
and cultural discovery. It felt right for now.'
Indeed, as Vanessa Friedman wrote in the
New York Times, this show took place against
a backdrop of uncertainty and fear, provoked
by the November 2015 terrorist attacks
in Paris.

The invitation came with a quote from the
stylish Dautheville: 'Up high, fall was waiting
for me – dry, clear and crisp. I was waiting for
it, and in my saddlebag I'd packed a big jumper
and a scarf. The track wasn't easy... But
the countryside was a thousand times more
beautiful, because we'd earned it.' On Vogue
Runway, Nicole Phelps commented, 'Waight
Keller has turned Chloé into a top brand
through her keen appreciation of the
wanderlust in so many of us. We want to
channel the festival girl and the free-spirited
biker chick precisely because the reality is
we spend our days hunched over our phones,
developing text neck and complaining about
our fading eyesight. We'd like to feel the wind
whipping through our hair.'

URBAN FRENCH STYLE

With this collection, Clare Waight Keller talked about 'going back to the roots and simplicity of French style'. After last season's wild motorcycle trip (see p.548), and past forays into festival dress, Waight Keller was keen to make things more formal, and urban. 'I wanted to bring it back to the city. It was time to clean it up,' she told reporters backstage.

Tailoring was a key component of this new vision, encompassing suits with collarless jackets and slouchy pants, including a new style, modelled on sailors' uniforms, which came with buttons at the waist and volume through the calves, before cinching above the ankles. But, for the more romantic Chloé woman, there was still plenty of 'flou', including flouncy layered mini-dresses and midi-frocks, in hues and floral prints that were inspired by vintage 1970s sheets.

This season was marked by continued excitement for the many female designers now helming Parisian fashion houses. 'Paris Fashion Week SS17: Let's Hear It For The Girls', read a headline on *Elle*'s website, above a piece which noted, 'Clare Waight Keller, Isabel Marant, Maria Grazia Chiuri, Bouchra Jarrar, Phoebe Philo, Miuccia Prada, Rei Kawakubo... when was the last time we saw so many women leading the women's wear calendar in Paris? From fashion to politics, it's been a big year for women bosses.'

Waight Keller told Jo Ellison of the *Financial Times* that the collection was inspired, in part, by the women around her – those she saw each day in her travels around Paris – hence the classic French palette of white, navy, cream and black. This collection marked five years since Waight Keller moved to the French city. 'I've been looking at the essence of French style, the women on the metro, and in daily life. And I wanted to bring that same easy simplicity and relevance into the collection,' she said, explaining that she wanted to 'change the pace' at Chloé – a comment that would prove prescient, given her imminent departure from the house, rumoured throughout the end of 2016, and formally announced in January 2017.

PSYCHEDELIC CHLOÉ GIRLS

This collection would mark Clare Waight Keller's final show for the house, the end of a five-and-a-half-year tenure. Fittingly the show focused, according to its press release, on escapism and 'psychedelic optimism'.

The notes talked of the Chloé woman – or 'Chloé girl', as the house then referred to her in many communications, including a popular hashtag accompanying shots of the brand's clothing on social media – disappearing down 'a rabbit hole of decades'. The press release continued: 'Short dresses bloom with organza puff sleeves or come traced with star lace, zig zag edging, and cloud forest embroideries on tulle.' Prints were suitably trippy: mushrooms, butterflies, opium poppies, night skies.

Fittingly, given the 1960s mood of some pieces, Marianne Faithfull sat front row, watching as mini-dresses, retro knit cardigans and brogue Mary Janes appeared. For those who loved Waight Keller's past forays into the '90s, there were track pants in rave hues. And, unsurprisingly, there was still the whiff of the '70s, especially elements of Karl Lagerfeld's tenure at Chloé.

'Waight Keller's influence in steering sales at the Richemont-owned house has been indisputable,' wrote Jo Ellison in the *Financial Times* of the designer's exit. 'Her unpretentious message and easily digestible trends – gentle athleisurewear, pretty femininity, tactile luxury and a knowing-but-unthreatening cool, not to mention hit accessories – have been best sellers and her looks have been powerfully influential on the high street. This collection synthesised her key codes, and some of her favourite themes.'

Rumours were rife across front rows about the next move for Waight Keller (she would eventually be appointed creative director at Givenchy, a role she held for three years between 2017 and 2020) and about who would be her replacement in steering the Chloé girls into their new chapter.

Natacha Ramsay-Levi

A Short Biography

Shortly after the appointment of Natacha Ramsay-Levi in March 2017, Geoffroy de la Bourdonnaye, chief executive of Chloé, told the press, 'It was obvious it had to be her from the moment I met her.' Born in Paris in 1980, to an interior designer mother and a publisher father, Ramsay-Levi had grown up on the city's storied Left Bank. 'Natacha utterly embodies my idea of the Chloé girl,' continued de la Bourdonnaye. 'She is creative and daring, refined and sophisticated, beautiful and with a fierce point of view. She is cool; she is streetwise and very French in her approach. Also, she is extremely well trained in the art of couture and has extensive experience of the pressures of working for a big international brand.'

Indeed, before arriving at Chloé, Ramsay-Levi, who was not at the time widely known in the press, was the right-hand woman to Nicolas Ghesquière, of Balenciaga and Louis Vuitton, who was celebrated, not for the girlish romance of Chloé, but for a futuristic hardness. The *New York Times* called Ghesquière 'a devotee of an aesthetic defined by resolute modernism and absolute cool'. Their interview with Ramsay-Levi, on her appointment, noted that, 'While she was at pains to stress that she would not bring black PVC and sexually charged androgyny to Chloé, it is hard to imagine that some of that futuristic grit will not make its way into this next chapter for the house.'

Many other critics agreed that Ramsay-Levi had an 'edgier' profile than the women who came directly before her (Clare Waight Keller, Hannah MacGibbon, Phoebe Philo and Stella McCartney), all of whom had embraced the youthful, bohemian side of Chloé, building on, as the *New York Times* put it, 'the image of Chloé as a house that saw the world through a gauzy lens, with clothes full of the easy, breezy bohemian sensibility of the 1970s. (The Chloé woman, historically, has been a [very] expensively clad free spirit, a playful flirt in lashings of flounce, suede and ... lace.)'

Before beginning her career in fashion, Ramsay-Levi once dreamed of being a historian. Her tenure at Chloé was marked by her interest in the house's past, and her clever use of archive references, including prints lifted directly from Karl Lagerfeld's 1970s collections for the house as well as horses that nodded to McCartney's motifs. Ironically, given that many critics argued that Ramsay-Levi's collections were not sufficiently 'Chloé', she was – of the many contemporary designers who have helmed the house – undoubtedly the most interested in spending time in the Chloé Archive and in recreating past designs in new, unexpected ways. Her interest in cinema, art and sculpture also shaped her epoch at Chloé, which saw various women artists invited to collaborate on sets and prints.

Ramsay-Levi studied history at the Paris 8 University, before enrolling at the prestigious fashion institute Studio Berçot, in 2000. In 2018, as the new head of one of Paris's most storied fashion houses, she discussed her approach to fashion with *Elle* magazine: 'For me, fashion is a way to participate in the world. I want clothes that reveal the personality of the women who wear them. It's a dialogue; the vector of precious emotions. It's the idea of strength versus power.' Underlining her convictions, she placed a note on every seat at her first show, which read: 'I want to give women the possibility of showing their strength, not their power.'

Having won wide praise for her confident, eclectic, cool-girl propositions, which the *New York Times*'s *T Magazine* referred to as having 'that same, endlessly worshiped *je ne sais quoi* that the brand was built upon, when its founder Gaby Aghion introduced Chloé – and the concept of luxury prêt-à-porter – to the world in 1952', Ramsay-Levi reconsidered her role in the light of the turmoil triggered by the Covid-19 pandemic. In December 2020, after a nearly four-year stint, her departure was announced.

ECLECTIC ATTITUDE

Following her appointment in 2017, Natacha Ramsay-Levi became the first French woman to lead Chloé since Martine Sitbon was made creative director in 1987 (see p.240). The house had, since its foundation, developed a reputation as a great launch pad for the young – and for sharp-eyed (especially British) women with a taste for an insouciant 'It girl' look – but critics were now keen to see a youthful, French take on Chloé codes.

This collection marked Ramsay-Levi's first as a sole creative director: in the past she had worked at Balenciaga and Louis Vuitton under Nicolas Ghesquière (who now sat front row to cheer for her). It was also a shift for Chloé, given Ramsay-Levi's past employers were known for stricter, edgier and more overtly intellectual designs than those associated with the cheerful haute-bohemia of Chloé.

Reviews were positive. Nicole Phelps, reviewing for Vogue Runway, called it 'a super-confident debut, bubbling over with variety and distinctive pieces that will be instantly identifiable as Chloé when they start parading around next year'. Many critics complimented the way Ramsay-Levi managed to tie together the rich history of the house: 'From Lagerfeld came the idea for the painted dresses, only hers are ... painted with auspicious symbols like eyes and hands,' wrote Phelps, in reference to a bespoke collaboration with the Indian artist Rithika Merchant, whom Ramsay-Levi had discovered online (see opposite page). 'McCartney and Philo both liked horses,' Phelps continued, 'and Ramsay-Levi's *chevaux* were embroidered on trim velvet tailoring. She said she took a sense of lightness from Waight Keller, indicating the floaty micro-floral print dresses. Even Hannah MacGibbon got a nod via a pair of slouchy camel pants' (see p.567, left, for Ramsay-Levi's interpretation in white silk crepe with lace inserts).

Additional praise came for Ramsay-Levi's conviction in her own ideas. In the *New York Times*, Vanessa Friedman noted that the house codes had been given an 'update and essential toughness', in part thanks to their styling with cut-out cowboy-style boots, the addition of 'steel loops for no-fuss decoration', and Merchant's vaguely surreal illustrations on silk poplin. The *New York Times*'s *T Magazine* praised Ramsay-Levi's eclectic mix of inspirations, noting that she 'is informed by everything from New Wave cinema to Cycladic artifacts'.

'I always like to have something that is a bit wrong – nothing too bourgeois,' Ramsay-Levi said. 'I call it vintage in the future.'

CUT-OUTS AND SKIN

In explaining the ideas and icons behind her
second collection for Chloé, Natacha Ramsay-
Levi, a committed cinephile, name-checked
1970s actresses such as Anjelica Huston,
Sissy Spacek, Isabelle Huppert and Stéphane
Audran (who, Ramsay-Levi noted, often wore
Lagerfeld for Chloé) as muses, praising their
majesty and talent. 'I want her to be very
strong, but you can't really reach her,' she
told reporters, of this season's Chloé woman.

A key theme was twisting of conformity.
'Her process was to take quite straightforward
bourgeois pieces – like a shirtdress, say – and
de-normalize them,' said Nicole Phelps for
Vogue Runway. 'She did it by removing shirt
buttons and creating a skin-baring, open-V
neckline accentuated by a long pendant
necklace; by dropping the waist; by adding
knife pleats or embroideries; and, sometimes,
by placing substantial cut-outs at the hip.'

Phelps was impressed by the confidence on
display, noting how quickly Ramsay-Levi had
'moved Chloé away from the festival-chick-on-
holiday vibes of her predecessor'. She added,
'Ramsay-Levi's are not clothes for Glastonbury.
They're for wearing to the Frieze Art Fair or
a fashion happening…'

Others remarked on the strong 1970s mood,
and the slightly tricky impenetrability of
Ramsay-Levi's Chloé woman. 'Like most
Nicolas Ghesquière alumni, Natacha Ramsay-
Levi's woman has a regal aloofness to herself,
often something closer to a fantasy character –
like the female robot in Fritz Lang's
Metropolis – than to actual human beings,'
read a report in *Wallpaper*. Nearly all critics
noted that the key message was skin. Both
Wallpaper and *Vogue* called the defining
element of the collection the cut-outs: 'present
everywhere and revealing new and unexpected
erogenous zones, including the top of the
stomach, the hipbones and the shoulders',
according to the former.

HIPPIE MODERNISM

Nicole Phelps for Vogue Runway called Spring 2019 Natacha Ramsay-Levi's 'Chloé-est runway collection yet', thanks, in part, to the given theme of bohemianism, and the festival-style clothes that paid tribute to escapism and wild jaunts abroad. 'Hippie modernism' was how Ramsay-Levi put it.

The look was sarong-style skirts, trousers with knotted pareo details, Persian rug motifs, and heaps of jewelry. Paisley and flower prints had been sourced from vintage silk scarves, bought at flea markets, and transformed into bias-cut silk dresses and flowing skirts. Other garments, namely T-shirts printed in sunset hues (see opposite, bottom left), came with a motif of hands raised in a triangular gesture – a symbol of the 'sacred feminine', according to the show notes.

The notes also referred to handkerchief hems, tunics cascading in 'goddess pleating', and 'ikat, laddered linen and plissé mousseline' used to create 'a sensory overload of wrapped and bias-cut layering'. The whole collection was defined as having a 'solar energy', thanks to its fabrics, colour palette and shapes.

In the *New York Times*, Vanessa Friedman joked that Ramsay-Levi had taken 'a virtual van down to the beach at sunset on Ibiza (or Crete or Capri or Essaouira; take your pick), and then pulled an assortment of urban folklore out of her magic trunk'.

EASY MODERN DRESSING

On 19 February 2019, shortly before the A/W 2019–2020 Chloé show, the designer Karl Lagerfeld – who served as creative director of Chloé twice (see pp. 110 and 296), a role that stretched across some twenty-five years – died. In tribute, postcards showcasing images of some of his most adored collections for the house were placed on every seat at the Chloé show. On the back, guests found comments from Lagerfeld about his work and vision. Nicole Phelps, writing for Vogue Runway, was particularly struck by one note, written about a 1975 collection: 'The essence of modern dressing – unstructured, weightless, totally feminine.' This comment, Phelps said, encapsulated what Natacha Ramsay-Levi offered her guests at the show: 'an array of the kind of breezy but polished dresses that women have looked to Chloé for since Karl's days'.

Some of the dresses were cut with asymmetrical hems and voluminous shoulders and sleeves. In terms of tailoring, there were flippy pencil skirts with sailor-style buttons, trousers that blended the look and fit of a cargo pant with a formal bootleg, and mariners' coats and capes. Jackets and coats with furry lapels, and silk pussy-bow blouses, nodded to Chloé's 1970s styles, and Lagerfeld's heyday.

Le Monde called this the 'least complicated' of Ramsay-Levi's collections for Chloé, praising the way she managed to balance house signatures – flowing silk blouses, chic shirts – with 'the sophistication which is dear to her, and which is also the trademark of Nicolas Ghesquière', her former boss, known for his often futuristic-feeling designs. The latter *Le Monde* identified in Ramsay-Levi's 'play on volumes, with bias cuts, puffed sleeves, and knots that redraw the contours of a skirt'.

UNSTUDIED SOPHISTICATION

Many critics interpreted this collection
as a shift for Natacha Ramsay-Levi. Gone
were the bold, swirling, artistic prints and
the over-layered hippie-ish accessories of
past seasons. The look was neater, cleaner.
'I'm thinking of it as chapter two for myself.
I've tried a lot of different things; I thought,
let's simplify – be honest and true,' Ramsay-
Levi told reporters.

Indeed, the mood was sophisticated; even,
at points, vaguely business-like, thanks to the
heavy use of pinstripe. There were silk shirts,
mannish tailored trousers with matching suit
jackets, a wrap-over shirt dress in black and
white stripes (see p. 582, left). The collection
was also very French, thanks to twists on the
classic striped Breton top and updates on
classic ditsy floral prints. For the more daring
shopper, there were bustier tops in lace;
and for the younger, there were a couple
of Ramsay-Levi's familiar printed T-shirts,
one printed – fittingly, given the collection's
elegance – with the slogan 'Handle with Grace'
(see opposite).

While the collection was true to Ramsay-Levi,
it was also true to Chloé. The show ended
with two long pleated dresses in the brand's
distinctive hue (see, for example, p. 583, right):
the elegant shade of creamy peach that had
become a lasting signature following Karl
Lagerfeld's era leading the house.

'Unstudied sophistication' was how Ramsay-
Levi summarized this season's look, presented
on a runway with décor inspired by Antiquity
(this had also informed the staging for the
S/S 2019 show, see p. 572, and that season's
advertising). The S/S 2020 show notes referred
to the new collection as a lesson in balance
between tailoring and 'flou': 'a fundamental
vision of femininity anchored in reality'.

FASHION MEETS ART

This would be Natacha Ramsay-Levi's penultimate collection for the house of Chloé. After her exit, Chloé chief executive Riccardo Bellini told press, 'She is an important member of that proud tradition of women who have designed at Chloé.'

It was fitting, then, that this show was a tribute to female creativity. The invitations came with mini-posters of paintings by the Hungarian-American artist Rita Ackermann, accompanied by the caption, 'If you listen carefully...I'll show you how to dance'. Five additional paintings by the artist, created in the 1990s and 2000s, were used as prints on a shirt, a shawl and a flowing shirt dress (see right). ('Fashion-art collaborations don't typically seem so effortless,' noted Nicole Phelps for Vogue Runway.) Another female artist, the French sculptor Marion Verboom, created golden totems to decorate the catwalk. And the English singer and actress Marianne Faithfull rasped her way through a series of poems, including Byron's 'She Walks in Beauty', on the soundtrack. 'Yes, clothes are great, but I love creative women,' Ramsay-Levi told reporters ahead of the show. 'It's about a community of creative spirits.'

The clothes themselves served as a summary of Ramsay-Levi's vision for the house, which tended to combine Chloé essentials – silk blouses; romantic, wafting dresses – with modern twists on 1970s tailoring, alongside a smattering of off-beat counter-cultural details (see this season's pins, reading 'Girls Forward', attached in threes across models' chests).

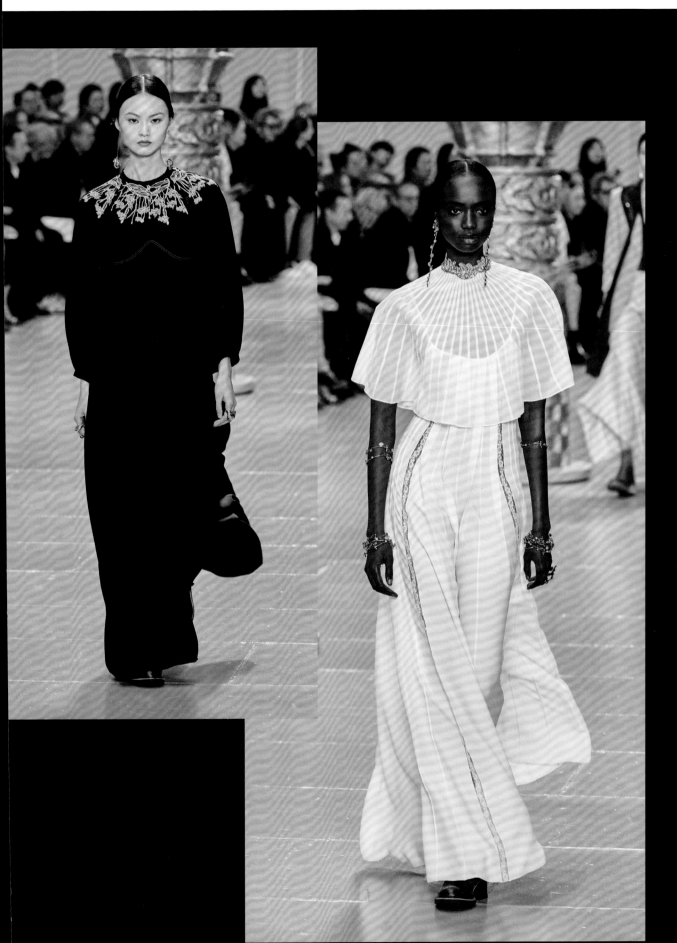

SLOGANS AND OPTIMISM

In a *New York Times* piece on Natacha
Ramsay-Levi's departure, which was
announced on 3 December 2020, Vanessa
Friedman wrote of Chloé's transition under
Ramsay-Levi's leadership 'from the Provençal
windswept romanticism established by the
founder Gaby Aghion to a harder edged,
more complicated hipness'.

Ironically, this collection, her last, was perhaps
the simplest, most grounded of all of her shows
for Chloé, in terms of wearability. (This sense
of ease and real-life appeal was emphasized by
the arrangement of three giant screens in the
courtyard of the Palais de Tokyo, where the
show was held, which streamed live footage
of her models making their way to the runway;
crossing the street, exiting buildings or
walking up the banks of the River Seine.)

The *Washington Post* called it a 'calmer vision'
for contemporary youthful dressing than that
presented by many other designers on the
Paris schedule, praising 'crisp shorts over silky
bloomers, flowing pleated dresses and a good
number of grounded flats for pounding the
pavement'.

As with her A/W 2020–2021 show (see p.584),
Ramsay-Levi used this as a chance to
champion women artists, who – like peers
such as Maria Grazia Chiuri at Dior – she
believed deserved more attention. This season,
invitees received posters featuring Corita
Kent, an educator and former religious sister
who won praise in the Sixties for her slogan-
based works about social justice, Christianity,
poverty, racism and war, and her broader
message of peace and solidarity. The featured
slogans included 'Get with the action' and
'Powerful enough to make a difference'.

Ramsay-Levi offered her own form of
sloganeering, placing wording on her
clothing, including: 'Hope' (Kent's serigraph
from 1965) on the hip of a white shift dress,
and 'I can handle it' (Kent's 1966 serigraph)
on a long-sleeved top. 'I picked those,' she told
reporters, 'because I think they're very strong
messages of optimism. But also of actions.'

Gabriela Hearst

A Short Biography

The Uruguayan designer Gabriela Hearst told reporters, ahead of her first show for Chloé in March 2021, that she saw the house as the 'Aphrodite' to her own label's 'Athena' – the former the goddess associated with lust and love (and, of course, the symbol of scallops – a Chloé signature); the latter with wisdom and war. In other words, to Hearst, Chloé could be feminine, playful, sensual even, while her own brand, which she founded in 2015, could continue to offer the dignified refinement and specific elegance so beloved by many professional women in her customer base.

And yet, after beginning her work for the house, Hearst brought a sense of strength and purpose to Chloé, offering not just whimsy and romance, but also vigour, depth and a strong attention to hand-crafted techniques, including ones under threat of being neglected or forgotten due to increased reliance on machines. Hearst's focus on showcasing ways in which fashion's approach to sustainability can be improved – the cornerstone of her eponymous label – is now a central value at Chloé: under Hearst, it has become the first luxury house to earn a B Corp Certification. 'I think the job of a designer is not just to make something beautiful; it has to be more than that,' she said, when interviewed for this book in June 2022. 'I have to do more than just send clothes down a runway. It's a job for telling stories that need to be told.'

Born in the Paysandú department of Uruguay in 1976, Hearst (née Perezutti) grew up surrounded by nature, cattle, horses and sheep on her family's 17,000-acre ranch, Santa Isabel. There, she has said, 'the notion of luxury meant things were beautifully crafted and made to last'. She attended the British School in Montevideo, before studying Communications at the O.R.T. University of Uruguay and, eventually, relocating to New York.

Hearst's appointment – which she took on alongside continuing her own label and her role as manager of her father's ranch – marked a change for Chloé. Firstly, Hearst became the first non-European to hold this position (though one could draw a parallel between Hearst and fellow non-European Gaby Aghion, the house's founder). And secondly, she was known not just for her aesthetic abilities, but predominantly for her strong advocacy of recycling, regularly using deadstock and reworked materials within her own collections. Chloé's CEO Riccardo Bellini told reporters that he was looking forward to Hearst's leadership in this area, and her role in holding the company accountable. 'What a brand stands for, its beliefs and values, will become as relevant as products and aesthetics,' he said. British *Vogue* commented, 'For many brands sustainability has become a talking point, but Hearst's appointment cements Chloé as one of the most environmentally-minded luxury goods companies in the world.'

On the announcement of her appointment in December 2020 – three months after she had won the prestigious CFDA Award for Womenswear Designer of the Year – the *New York Times*'s headline referred to her as someone 'Refashioning the Luxury Business' in her commitment to balancing style with sustainable practices. Indeed, Hearst's focus has been on two vital elements: 'the materials that we have, and who makes our things'. Cross-industry collaboration is also key: 'It's really about taking things out of the fashion arena.' Hearst's team regularly engage with charities, scientists, researchers and advocates, 'cross-pollinating worlds that would never usually speak to each other'.

Hearst also informed reporters that she was excited to build on the 'purposeful vision of Gaby Aghion' and the legacy of the many talented women who had preceded her (she has notably reused a buckle introduced by Hannah MacGibbon, and now works with members of MacGibbon's former team). 'I was not subtle about how much I wanted that job!' she told the *New York Times*, who reported that she went into her interview at Chloé with a 92-page dossier on her ambitious goals – both aesthetic and environmental – for the house. In fact, Hearst's connection to Chloé runs deep. Her first perfume was a Chloé scent, and her first handbag was by the house. She also identified with Aghion: their backstories both began far from fashion metropolises, and Aghion's Chloé was also about re-thinking wider societal issues. In addition, Hearst shares Aghion's minute attention to detail: 'We have the best button game in fashion,' she said recently, of Chloé's handmade buttons, often in delicate ceramic.

Hearst's debut show incorporated influences from her own South American heritage (indeed, the show made clear how often fashion's take on bohemianism borrows liberally from other cultures, repackaging local attire as something hippie-ish or exotic). Here, her collaboration with Manos del Uruguay, a non-profit organization that has provided work to artisan women from rural areas since 1968, gave Chloé's signature 'boho-chic' an authentic backstory. Of Hearst's second collection for Chloé, US *Vogue* wrote that 'when you consider how many women's organizations and communities Chloé is benefiting ... it almost begins to seem possible that this work could even be marking a shift in the entire purpose of a luxury brand's existence'.

Hearst's take: 'I have tried to augment the value system of the founder.' Her aim – in acknowledging the climate crisis, and working with diverse voices and skilled workers – remains to move things forward. 'So we are continuing – continuing to fight for the empowerment of women, whether it's through our work with non-profits, women-led craft techniques, or businesses that are more ethical and more balanced.' In Hearst's vision for Chloé, the clothes are simply one part of the complex puzzle.

SOUTH AMERICA
AND SUSTAINABILITY

This collection marked the debut of
Uruguayan-American designer Gabriela
Hearst as creative director of Chloé. And, as
was becoming customary when a new designer
presented their first collection for the house,
the show was rich with nods to Chloé's history
and the vision of founder – and Hearst's
namesake – Gaby Aghion. 'I wanted to begin
my time with Chloé by first paying honour
to her,' Hearst recently stated. 'It was really
essential to start this journey that way.'

Brasserie Lipp, the site where so many
of Chloé's earliest shows were staged, was,
poignantly, the selected venue for this show,
which was presented digitally via video
without a physical audience. Models
strolled in front of the restaurant, across
the cobblestones of Saint-Germain-des-Prés
(a route engineered, in part, to comply with
COVID regulations), and invitees, unable to
be in Paris in person due to travel restrictions,
were sent boxes of swatches – 43 in all,
encompassing knits, silks and tweeds – so
they could feel the quality of materials by
hand. The scallop, another archive go-to
for designers making their Chloé debut (see
pp. 414 and 484), was also present, appearing
as a decoration on blouses and on petals of
leather or denim, patchworked together to
form coats.

Elsewhere, there was fringing on bags
and dresses, ruffles across tops, and even
intarsia butterflies on sweaters and scarves.
Particularly popular among critics was the
earthy colour palette, used on striped dresses,
and the introduction of the puffcho, a type of
poncho that combined a blanket poncho and
a puffer jacket. The show was a nod to Hearst's
heritage, as much as Chloé's.

This collection also marked the acceleration
of the house's sustainability strategy. Hearst,
who is committed to improving fashion's
environmental impact, announced that she
had eliminated polyester and viscose from
the collection and had created knitwear from
recycled cashmere. She also showed sweeping
coats, crafted from silks sourced from waste
fabrics from the Chloé Archive, which, when
zipped up, became a Sheltersuit, a technical
garment created by a Dutch non-profit to
double as a sleeping bag for the homeless.
Though the Chloé Sheltersuit was simply
a catwalk piece, not for sale, it marked a
collaboration with the non-profit to create
1,000 backpacks, also made from deadstock.
Chloé announced that for each one sold, two
Sheltersuits would be donated. 'The Chloé
Girl Has Grown Up – And Grown a Social
Conscience', said the *New York Times*.

LOVE AND LACE

'The first collection we did [see p. 596] was about showcasing Gaby Aghion's values and paying respects. Your job is to be a link in the chain to make sure that this brand, which has lived nearly 70 years, continues. The second collection had to be about what is my driving force – what pushes me – and it's love: a love for craft,' Gabriela Hearst told British *Vogue*.

The publication called the show a 'push for social entrepreneurship', thanks to the inclusion of pieces crafted by a myriad of non-profit artisans, to be sold under the umbrella of a new label, Chloé Craft. Hearst spoke of a desire to reconnect shoppers with things that are handmade, or even rustic, questioning associations between perfection, gloss and the fresh-from-the-factory-belt look of much modern luxury. 'It's the antithesis of industrialized "luxury" – which, to me, is not luxury,' she said recently.

Shells on jewelry and dresses were crafted by Akanjo in Madagascar; colourful woven bags were created by the teams of women at Mifuko in Kenya; and Ocean Sole, a Kenyan-based non-profit that removes flipflops from the ocean and presses them into new forms, provided one-of-a-kind soles for many of the shoes. Finally, the set, which furnished a sunny bank of Quai de la Tournelle in Paris, was created by Les Bâtisseuses, a non-profit that involves refugee and immigrant women in the construction of houses, giving them employment and purpose, while challenging the norms of an industry whose workforce is typically male. 'It's all about: how can we lift up others, how can we empower others,' Hearst said, of her vision for Chloé, in June 2022. 'We are focused on the social impact.'

The show was tightly edited, to limit waste and over-production – only 31 looks, rather than the 50 or so typical of modern fashion shows, and far, far fewer than the days of Lagerfeld, where shows could last for hours and feature some 200 looks. And yet each felt in keeping with the light, airy history of the brand, and the connotations of festivals, beaches and bohemianism that have appeared consistently on Chloé runways across the decades, despite the unique perspectives of the house's many creative directors. 'What with its summer-holiday caftans, ponchos, lacy dresses, and smattering of boyish pantsuits, the collection is fully in the tradition of the free-spirited Chloé girl brand identity that has been passed down from hand to hand by a succession of women designers, from Stella McCartney and Phoebe Philo onward,' said US *Vogue*.

'As cheesy as it sounds, this collection is about love,' Hearst told reporters. 'It's really about the love of so many things: the love of craft, the love of friendship, the love of fellow humans.'

PATCHWORKS OF HOPE

The Paris A/W 2022–2023 fashion shows
took place against a backdrop of turmoil
and distress: in the middle of fashion month,
on 24 February 2022, Vladimir Putin of Russia
invaded Ukraine, beginning a war that quickly
claimed hundreds of civilians' lives and caused
millions to flee their homes. Elsewhere, while
COVID regulations were widely lifting,
the pandemic was still at large, and citizens
worldwide continued to experience fear,
financial uncertainty, and the threat of
new waves or new variants. Additionally,
environmental concerns were – after two years
of headlines dominated by the virus – firmly
back on the agenda. Many involved in the
shows expressed confusion and doubt about
the relevance of fashion in such troubling
times; what could the industry offer?

Hope, was Gabriela Hearst's answer. This
season, she focused her Chloé collection on
visualizing what she called 'climate success',
telling reporters that positive imagining
is crucial to turning climate anxiety into
action. 'The past two years have not left
many optimists still standing but Gabriela
Hearst … is among the few who remain,' said
the *Guardian*. As a way of picturing a better
future, Hearst printed, wove and hand-painted
motifs of 'landscape catastrophes' versus
'landscape successes' – melted glaciers and
burning landscapes contrasted, on the reverse
of garments, with pictures of polar bears,
green mountain ranges, bountiful forests.

Hearst said the collection was inspired by the
British conservationist Isabella Tree, a pioneer
of restorative rewilding. 'My mom's place is
full of wildlife, because she never overgrazes,
so it's regenerative,' Hearst told reporters,
of her family ranch in Uruguay.

The general look of the collection was clean,
minimal, with a palette focused heavily on
black, alongside a smattering of earthy tones
such as burnt red, brown, tan, orange. Hearst
said her silhouette was inspired by Franco
Zeffirelli's 1972 film *Brother Son, Sister Moon*,
about the life of Francis of Assisi, hence the
stripped-down, modest look. Excitement came
in a handful of patchwork pieces, such as a
gilet modelled by Amber Valletta (see right),
created in a collaboration with the celebrated
Gee's Bend women quilters of Alabama, who
used Chloé deadstock scraps to create pieces
for the show.

Many reviewers noted that the venue – a large
glass structure, the ground of which had been
scattered with soil – felt like a greenhouse;
a fitting space for a show committed to nature,
hand-work and growth.

Bibliographic Note

In order not to disrupt the flow of reading, we have decided not to include references or footnotes in the main body of the text. Sources for quotations can be found below.

AnOther Magazine, 21 April 2021

Asahi Evening News (Tokyo), 24 November 1980

Chicago Daily News, 2 April 1974

Chloe. Attitudes (foreword by Gaby Aghion, text by Sarah Mower), New York, 2013

Clark, Judith, interview with Gaby Aghion, 28 August 2012

Coddington, Grace, *Grace: A Memoir*, London, 2012, p.128

Collections, Spring/Summer 1963; Winter 1965/66

Contacts Franco-Italiens, April 1968

Country Life, 14 October 1982

Crash, Summer 2006

Daily Express (London), 15 October 1979; 23 October 1981

Daily News (New York), 21 December 1960

Dazed & Confused (*Dazed*), July 2006; March 2010; March 2011

Drapers Record, 19 April 1975

Drapery & Fashion Weekly (London), 10 May 1968; 2 November 1973

Elle (France), September 1958; September 1959; May 1960; February 1962; November 1962; November 1964; September 1982; December 1990; October 1991; February 1992; 30 September 2016 (Elle.com); February 2018

Evening Standard (London), 10 April 1975; 13 September 2013

Fashion Weekly (London), 4 November 1977

Fashion Wire Daily, 8 October 2002; 11 March 2003

Femme, January 1984

Financial Times, 29 September 2016; 2 March 2017

France-Soir, 8 January 1959; 2 July 1959; 1 December 1959

Guidicelli, Tan, interview, Chloé Archive, 13 September 2017

Harper's Bazaar (London), August 2010

Harper's Bazaar (New York), September 1969

Hourcade, Patrick, *Karl: Une si longue complicité*, Paris, 2021, p.158

Houston Chronicle, 13 May 1981

International Herald Tribune, 24 March 1984; 20 October 1984; 22 March 1986; 9 March 1994; 12 October 1994; 17 October 1995; 10 October 1996; 16 October 1997; 7 October 2002; 15 October 2009

International Textiles, October 1974

Jardin des Modes, February 1963; February 1965; Special Ed. 1970; January 1987

Journal du Pas-de-Calais (Boulogne-sur-Mer), 30 November 1962

Journal du Textile, 4 April 1978; 7 November 1978

L'Est Éclair, 15 January 1963

L'Indépendant Franc-Parleur, August 1964

L'Officiel, September–October 1965 (*L'Officiel du Prêt à Porter*); Spring/Summer 1971 (No. 582); Autumn/Winter 1988 (No. 741); Autumn/Winter 1991 (No. 765)

L'Orient (Beyrouth), 5 July 1967

La Dépêche du Midi (Toulouse), 12 September 1967

La Dépêche Mode, May 1968

La Lanterne (Brussels), 28 October 1968

La Nouvelle République du Centre Ouest (Tours), 4 March 1959

La Patrie (Montreal), 25 January 1959

Le Figaro, 7 May 1964; 5 May 1966; 17 April 1979; 22 March 1986; n.d. [*c.* 9 March 2003]

Le Matin, 21 March 1980

Le Méridional Marseille, 18 December 1962

Le Monde, 5 July 1962; 7 April 1973; 6 November 1976; 30 October 1988; 3 March 2000; 24 May 2000; 11 October 2001; 6 March 2006; 12 March 2009; 4 October 2011; 1 March 2019

Le Populaire du Centre (Limoges), 22 December 1965

Le Télegramme (Morlaix), 19 February 1963

Les Nouvelles de Paris, May 1964

Libelle (Brussels), 4 February 1963

Libération (Paris), 8 March 2012

Los Angeles Times, 26 October 1975; 13 April 1976; 4 March 2013

Midi Libre, 19 January 1977

New York Herald Tribune, 4 June 1959; 1 December 1960; 3 April 1974; 22 October 1974; 8 April 1975; 22 October 1975; 6 April 1976; 6 April 1981

New York Times, 7 December 1960; 26 February 1962; 13 September 1964; 30 October 1972; 3 April 1974; 26 October 1976; 2 November 1976; 16 February 1979; 16 October 1979; 20 October 1980; 18 October 1982; 21 March 1983; 28 August 1983 (*New York Times Magazine*); 17 October 1983; 29 March 1992; 6 December 1992; 17 October 1993; 17 March 1995; 17 October 1995; 13 March 1998; 15 October 1998; 8 October 1999; 3 March 2000; 11 June 2000; 26 November 2000; 21 January 2001; 15 March 2001; 14 March 2002; 10 March 2003; 8 March 2004; 11 October 2004; 8 October 2007; 4 March 2008; 7 October 2008; 19 March 2009; 15 October 2009; 18 October 2009; 6 December 2009; 7 February 2010; 28 February 2010; 6 March 2011; 3 October

2011; 5 March 2012; 2 October 2012; 18 October 2012; 24 January 2014 ('On the Runway' blog); 4 March 2014; 28 September 2014; 30 September 2014; 3 March 2016; 27 September 2017; 28 September 2017; 15 February 2018 (*T Magazine*); 27 September 2018; 3 December 2020; 1 October 2021

News-Free Press (Chattanooga, TN), 27 March 1984

Palm Beach Daily News, 20 October 1984

Penticton Herald, 6 April 1961

Philadelphia Inquirer, 25 October 1981; 25 March 1985

Racing, April 1963

San Francisco Chronicle, 21 October 1985

SHOWstudio.com, 6 March 2012

Silhouettes, no. 87, 1967

Style.com, 8 March 2003; 10 October 2003; 8 March 2010; 3 October 2010; 6 March 2011; 2 October 2011; 4 March 2012; 30 September 2012; 2 March 2013; 28 September 2013; 1 March 2014; 8 March 2015

Tatler (London), February 1976

The Christian Science Monitor, 29 April 1974

The Cut, 9 May 2011

The Daily Telegraph (*The Telegraph*) (London), 4 April 1977; 24 October 1977; 19 October 1981; 22 October 1984; 21 October 1985; 15 October 1998; 3 December 2002; 3 October 2011; 11 January 2014

The Glasgow Herald, 23 July 1979; 19 October 1981

The Guardian (London), 7 October 2002; 12 October 2006; 30 January 2017; 4 March 2022

The Independent (London), 24 March 1995

The Japan Times (Tokyo), 7 June 1979

The Observer (London), 4 April 1982; 31 March 1985

The Sunday Bulletin in Philadelphia, 5 December 1965

The Sunday Times (London), 28 November 1965

The Times (London), 21 October 1979; 7 April 1981; 27 March 1984; 26 October 1998

The Washington Post, 21 October 1979; 6 April 1981; 9 April 1981; 27 March 1982; 24 October 1982; 21 October 1985; 22 March 1988; 16 October 1992; 15 March 1993; 29 August 1993; 13 October 1993; 12 October 1994; 3 March 2000; 15 March 2001; 13 March 2002; 12 October 2004; 7 October 2008; 14 March 2009; 10 October 2010; 28 September 2019

Toulouse Informations, October 1967

Vogue (American), April 1971; March 1972; July 1972; August 1972; March 1973; July 1973; January 1974; July 1976; September 1976; January 1977; March 1977; July 1978; August 1979; December 1979; January 1981; July 1982; December 1986; April 1990; October 1990; January 1993; July 1993; July 1997; October 1999; May 2001; August 2001; February 2002; April 2004; June 2004; September 2004; May 2005; June 2005; August 2005; March 2006; April 2007; April 2012; 1 October 2015 (Vogue.com)

Vogue (British), August 1967; March 1973; October 1973; January 1974; March 1975; March 1977; August 1977; March 1989; February 1990; February 1992; July 1999; 2 March 2014

Vogue (French), February 1961; August 1971; August 1973; November 1973; February 1974; August 1976; February 1977; March 1977; February 1978; August 1978; February 1984; Fall/Winter 2010 Special

Vogue (Italian), January 1973; January 1974; February 1987

Vogue Runway, 3 March 2016; 28 September 2017; 1 March 2018; 27 September 2018;

28 February 2019; 27 February 2020

Wallpaper, 2 March 2018

Women's Wear Daily (*WWD*), 16 December 1958; 30 July 1959; 1 December 1959; 1 June 1960; 11 December 1961; 29 March 1962; 11 June 1962; 31 October 1968; 8 December 1969; 13 April 1970; 20 October 1970; 4 November 1971; 18 April 1972; 27 September 1972; 3 April 1973; 5 April 1973; 22 October 1974; 5 May 1977; 25 October 1977; 27 October 1977; 2 March 1978; 11 April 1978; 20 October 1978; 24 October 1978; 15 October 1979; 1 April 1980; 20 October 1980; 3 April 1981; 6 April 1981; 19 October 1981; 4 January 1984; 7 June 1984; 22 October 1984; 22 January 1985; 24 March 1986; 4 June 1986; 20 October 1986; 30 January 1987; 24 March 1987; 6 May 1987; 14 May 1987; 1 September 1987; 20 September 1988; 17 October 1988; 24 October 1988; 6 February 1989; 17 March 1989; 20 March 1989; 1 June 1989; 19 September 1989; 16 October 1989; 23 October 1989; 19 March 1990; 22 October 1990; 2 January 1991; 19 March 1991; 22 October 1991; 23 March 1992; 2 June 1992; 16 June 1992; 12 October 1992; 15 March 1993; 13 October 1993; 9 March 1994; 12 October 1994; 17 March 1995; 17 October 1995; 10 October 1996; 17 December 1996; 17 March 1997; 14 October 1997; 16 October 1997; 12 March 1998; 27 May 1998; 12 October 1998; 11 March 1999; 29 March 1999; 7 October 1999; 5 October 2001; 11 October 2001; 13 March 2002; 8 October 2002; 13 October 2003; 11 October 2004; 14 February 2005; 7 March 2005; 10 October 2005; 5 January 2006; 24 August 2006; 19 September 2006; 28 September 2006; 9 October 2006; 12 October 2006; 1 March 2007; 5 March 2007; 8 October 2007; 3 March 2008; 20 March 2008; 3 October 2008; 12 March 2009; 5 October 2009; 2 October 2011

Variant spellings of Chloé (Chloe, Chlöe, Chloë) have been silently amended in quotations.

Collection Credits

Names and descriptions have been supplied, where available in the Chloé Archive, for the period of the house's 'Alphabet' system for naming garments (A/W 1958–1959 to S/S 1987).

NB In some collections, pieces of the same category, such as hats, knitwear and jewelry, are named according to a theme (musical instruments, boats, Disney characters, etc.) and are exceptions to the alphabetical naming system.

A/W 1958–1959
n.d.; Brasserie Lipp, Paris
pp.30 and 31, left Silk faille cocktail dress in *chiné à la branche* (resist-dyed) floral print (*p.30* catwalk model in front of Brasserie Lipp, with Saint-Germain-des-Prés church in the background); *p.31, right* 'Amphore' dress with visible ruffled petticoat

S/S 1959
4 and 8 December 1958; Chloé HQ, 15 rue de Miromesnil, 75008 Paris
p.32 'Bêtise' dress in navy flannel, with white shirt-front by Judith Barbier; *p.33, left* 'Bon point' dress in black and white tweed by Hurel, with white shirt-front by Judith Barbier; *p.33, right* 'Babillage' shirt dress in wool by Raimon, with white shirt-front by Judith Barbier

A/W 1959–1960
29 May 1959;
Brasserie Lipp, Paris
p.34 Formal dress in wool fibre and black mohair, with bertha collar and cuffs trimmed with pleated taffeta ribbon; *p.35, left* 'Caïd' masculine-style suit, with elongated jacket in black and white herringbone wool by Labbey; *p.35, right* Cocktail dress in orange Rhodia faille by Bianchini-Férier, tied and low-cut in the back, low-rise skirt with two tiers of puffed flounces

S/S 1960
25 November 1959;
Brasserie Lipp, Paris
p.36 Sleeveless dress in wool fabric by Wébé, with patent-leather corset belt; *p.37, top left* 'Devoir' dress in black and white wool muslin tartan by Gérondeau, with starched collar and shirt-front, flared skirt and patent-leather corset belt; *p.37, top right* Dress in silk cloqué by Sekers; *p.37, bottom left* Pleated dress in printed silk muslin by Tacosa; *p.37, bottom right* Dress in bright red organdy embroidered with polka dots by Pierre Brivet, with scalloped flounces and a bodice embellished at the back with five flat satin bows

A/W 1960–1961
19 May 1960;
Closerie des Lilas, Paris
Hats by Florence René Pochet; jewelry by Jacques Gautier; gloves by Helanca; flowers by Fromentin.
p.38 (left) Double-breasted wool coat, with shawl collar, raglan sleeves, double fastening and patch pockets, and a hat by Florence René Pochet; (right) 'Épinard' collarless dark green coat in wool by Lalonde, with hidden fastening and patch pockets, and a hat by Florence René Pochet; *p.39, top left* Suit with pleated pocket flaps and a hat by Florence René Pochet; *p.39, right* 'Ébéniste' coat in flecked black and white wool fabric by Raimon, trimmed with black braiding; *p.39, bottom left* 'Empire' suit in reversible flecked green, blue and black tweed by Dormeuil, decorated with silver buttons and dark braiding at the outer edges of the fabric, and a hat by Florence René Pochet; *p.40, left* 'Escudos' shirt dress in gold lace by Pierre Brivet, over a matching satin sheath; *p.40, right* 'Écume' sheath cocktail dress, with a low back in white tulle embroidered with a silver ear of wheat motif by Pierre Brivet; *p.41, top* Drop-waist sheath dress in jersey, with flared skirt in chiffon taffeta; *p.41, bottom* 'Esprit' suit in chestnut-brown *point d'esprit* nylon tulle by Pierre Brivet, lined with silk, collar with tightly gathered ruffles

S/S 1961
n.d.; Closerie des Lilas, Paris
p.42 Dress in Everglaze cotton satin with print in pastel shades by Tacosa, with detachable apron in white organdy trimmed with braiding matching the dress; *p.43, left* 'Fantasio' suit in sugar-pink heavy crepe wool by Gérondeau, with blouse in white crepe buttoned at the back, collar and cuffs embellished with a soft flounce; *p.43, right* 'Flou-flou' wrap dress in white satin-backed silk crepe by Ducharne, with neckline and cuffs edged with a soft gathered flounce

A/W 1961–1962
3 and/or 16 May 1961; Paris
p.44 Shirt dress in iron-grey jersey, with silver lamé collar and cuffs; *p.45, left* Cape and skirt in jade and yellow tartan by Dormeuil, with navy lining, navy waistcoat, tie and shirt in honan silk; *p.45, top right* Sleeveless sheath dress in black shantung by Tacosa, over a blouse in black muslin with white polka dots by Bianchini-Férier; *p.45, bottom right* Skirt suit and blouse, with jacket lapels and pockets in the same striped fabric as the blouse

S/S 1962
n.d.; Hôtel du Palais d'Orsay, Paris
p.46 Backless long-sleeved sheath dress in red embossed crepe; *p.47, right* 'Indigo' dress in silk muslin, with neckline, bust, cuffs and skirt adorned with gathered ruffles; *p.47, bottom left* Dress in silk muslin, the bottom of the skirt adorned with satin stripes

A/W 1962–1963
n.d.; Paris
p.48 Dress in paisley-printed wool and silk by Brochier; *p.49* Narrow skirt entirely ruffled in black crepe by Brochier, worn with blouse in white crepe satin by Véron, with wide sleeves and pearl buttons and cufflinks

S/S 1963
n.d.; Brasserie Lipp, Paris
p.51, left Jacket and dress ensemble, 'sport' jacket in white shantung lined with gold, worn with long sleeveless dress; *p.51, right* 'Lilium' suit in light canvas, with lining and blouse in daisy-print silk muslin by Tacosa

A/W 1963–1964
n.d.; Brasserie Lipp, Paris
p.52 Suit in white wool tweed, with pearl cotton collar and facings, and matching cotton blouse; *p.53, top left* 'Maille' wool dress; *p.53, right* Sheath dress in prune crepe, with chainmail *fichu* in gold metal; *p.53, bottom left* Dress in pink Tergal lamé, brocaded with silver by Léonard, neckline embellished with rhinestones

A/W 1964–1965
n.d.; Brasserie Lipp, Paris
p.56 Evening coat in silver lace, Mylar and Courtelle by Marescot, with concealed buttons, worn with long-sleeved sheath dress in black silk satin organdy by Bodin; *p.57, left* Long evening

dress in silk, with floaty sleeves and darted bust panel; *p. 57, right* Dress in metallic Lurex lace by Pierre Brivet, with underskirt in pastel-green muslin

S/S 1965
n.d.; Paris
p. 58 'Radar' halter-neck dress tied at the back, in black viscose Rhodia crepe inlaid with white crepe by Buche

A/W 1965–1966
n.d.; Paris
p. 59 Evening look, cuffed at the ankles, in bright yellow Rhodia crepe embroidered with large white plastic sequins

S/S 1966
18 November 1965;
Brasserie Lipp, Paris
Hair and make-up by Desfossé; hats by Monique Dofny; jewelry by Jacques Gautier; shoes by Charles Jourdan.
p. 61 'Tertulia' long dress in ivory dupion silk muslin, hand-painted with coral motifs by Le Besnerais

A/W 1966–1967
n.d.; Brasserie Lipp, Paris
p. 60 Dress in pink, turquoise and pale-green Tergal cloqué lamé by Bucol with wide stripes embellished with rhinestones, jewelry by J. C. Brosseau

S/S 1967
n.d.; Paris
Hats by Jeannine Montel; jewelry by Jeanne Do, Peladan, Scemama; shoes by Charles Jourdan.
p. 62 Dress in silk shantung, hand-painted in yellow and orange shades by Nicole Lefort

A/W 1967–1968
n.d.; Paris
p. 63 'Ballet' sheath dress in orange silk cloqué woven with copper Lurex yarn by Lyon Nouveautés Textiles

S/S 1968
n.d.; Paris
p. 64 Jacket and dress ensemble, short blouson jacket and shoulder-baring sheath dress in wool by Verzoletto, with vertical breast pockets and inlaid belt

A/W 1968–1969
n.d.; Paris
p. 65 Blouse in white silk crepe by J. B. Martin, pleated skirt in black alpaca by Dormeuil

S/S 1969
n.d. [before 31 October 1968];
Paris
p. 66 'Entracte' tunic dress in coffee silk jersey by Leleu, stand-up collar gathered under a yoke, puffed sleeves buttoned at the cuffs, soft waistband draped at the hips

A/W 1969–1970 6
n.d.; Paris
p. 67 'Fausse alerte' tunic and trousers in hand-painted Moroccan crepe, tunic hemmed with marabou feathers

S/S 1970
10 November 1969;
Restaurant Laurent, Paris
Make-up by Harriet Hubbard Ayer; hats by Jeannine Montel; gloves by Neyret; shoes by Charles Jourdan.
p. 68 Long dress in crêpe de Chine, hand-painted with geometric motifs

A/W 1970–1971
13 April 1970;
Restaurant Laurent, Paris
p. 69, top left Blouse in crêpe de Chine by Bini, printed with striped triangular motifs in red, beige and brown, and a hat by Jeannine Montel; *p. 69, top right* 'Inauguration' pinafore dress in silk ivory, hand-painted with black stripes and a motif of men in top hats by Nicole Lefort, over a black silk muslin blouse; *p. 69, bottom left* 'Informatique' pinafore dress and shawl in chestnut-brown muslin with silver lamé by Boileau, over a plain silk muslin blouse; *p. 69, bottom right* 'Iréel' embroidered dress in nude silk jersey

S/S 1971
19 October 1970;
Restaurant Laurent, Paris
Hair by Jean-Marc Maniatis; make-up by Harriet Hubbard Ayer; gloves by Neyret; shoes by Charles Jourdan.
p. 70 'Lahore' halter-top tied at the neck in black silk jersey and wrap skirt in crêpe de Chine hand-painted by Nicole Lefort; *p. 71, top left* 'Latitude' black jersey top and skirt hand-painted by Nicole Lefort; *p. 71, top right* 'Liberté' blouse with low-cut back in hand-painted silk muslin by Tacosa and crêpe de Chine skirt; *p. 71, bottom* Fringed shawl in crêpe de Chine hand-painted by Nicole Lefort

A/W 1971–1972
19 April 1971;
Restaurant Laurent, Paris
Hair by Jean-Marc Maniatis; make-up by Harriet Hubbard Ayer; shoes by Charles Jourdan.
p. 72 'Minaret' jacket with petal collar in shocking-pink textured mohair by Dumas-Maury and jodhpur trousers in black wool by Moreau; *p. 73, left* Long dress in crêpe de Chine hand-painted by Nicole Lefort, design inspired by Albert Gleizes's painting *Danseuse espagnole*; *p. 73, right* Shawl and short halter-neck dress tied at the neck in crêpe de Chine by Hurel, hand-painted and trimmed with marabou feathers; *p. 74, left* 'Mephisto' tunic in satin with raglan sleeves, printed with playing cards by Bosch, elastic grosgrain belt; *p. 74, right* 'Minerve' long pleated dress in muslin by Hurel, embroidered with rhinestones; *p. 75, left* Long dress embroidered with sequins and flower motifs; *p. 75, right* 'Météore' long dress in black georgette, large collar in white satin, body embroidered with rhinestones

S/S 1972
25 October 1971;
Restaurant Laurent, Paris
p. 76 'Nadja' short jacket with batwing sleeves in plain black and white checkered wool by Wurmser and wide high-waisted trousers; *p. 77* 'Norvège' short jacket with batwing sleeves in plain white wool flannel and pink tennis stripes by Agnona and wide high-waisted trousers

A/W 1972–1973
17 April 1972;
Restaurant Laurent, Paris
Hair by Jean-Marc Maniatis; make-up by Harriet Hubbard Ayer; pearls by Wolloch; gloves by Neyret; shoes by Mario Valentino.
p. 78 'Porcelaine' halter-neck tied at the neck with shirt-front and white pleated silk muslin skirt; *p. 79, top left* 'Play-Boy' smoking jacket in shocking-pink flannel embroidered with gold, and long skirt in black crepe; *p. 79, top right* 'Pélican' halter-neck tied at the neck in white organza, with velvet straps, black ribbed trim and sheath skirt in black silk crepe by Hurel; *p. 79, bottom left* 'Praline' long dress in brown silk jersey by Hurel, with 'diamond-point' cut-out at the back, cuffs embroidered with gold and silver

sequins; *p. 79, bottom right* 'Publicité' pleated dress in black wool cheesecloth

S/S 1973
n.d.; Restaurant Laurent, Paris
p. 80 'Ressac' printed blouse and high-waisted trousers; *p. 81, left* 'Riz' long jacket with short sleeves and patch pockets, and skirt in flannel by Wurmser, bra in printed silk crepe; *p. 82, left* 'Réconciliation' skirt and scarf in silk hand-painted with motifs of doves and roses by Nicole Lefort, bra in black silk jersey; *p. 82, right* Blouse with short sleeves in ivory crepe, skirt and bra in draped black silk jersey, handkerchief in checkerboard print; *p. 83* 'Rhodes' top and skirt ensemble in ivory crêpe de Chine printed with brown shells, blouse tied at the front and pleated skirt, both buttoned along the spine; *p. 84* 'Rachmaninoff' long dress and scarf in crêpe de Chine hand-painted with geometric motifs and characters from the Commedia dell'arte by Nicole Lefort; *p. 85* 'Revue' top (with detachable straps) embroidered with black sequins, loose trousers, and shawl in ivory Moroccan crepe hand-painted by Nicole Lefort with a design inspired by tiles created by Armand Albert Rateau for Jeanne Lanvin in 1924

A/W 1973–1974
Between 1 and 4 April 1973; Restaurant Laurent, Paris
p. 86 'Sumatra' backless dress in prune silk jersey, Art Deco-inspired embroidery with white and pink rhinestones, long draped panels crossed at the back and tied at the waist; *p. 87, left* 'Soyeuse' skirt suit in mastic (cream-coloured) crêpe de Chine printed with burgundy Art Deco motifs by Staron, sleeveless knitted sweater and scarf in matching colours; *p. 87, top right* 'Scottish' wool coat, two-tone belt; *p. 87, bottom right* 'Stuart' blouse in hand-painted crêpe de Chine, 'Santal' skirt in black crepe; *p. 88* 'Sketch' backless midnight-blue evening dress embroidered with 'old gold' tube beads; *p. 89* 'Starter' blouse in hand-painted silk satin, and 'Santal' skirt in black crepe

S/S 1974
22 October 1973; Restaurant Laurent, Paris
Hats and large flowers in crêpe de Chine by Jeannine Montel;

jewelry by Patrick Hourcade. *p. 90* 'Tiercé' jacket in white wool gabardine with patch pockets and edges outlined in black braiding, black dress with white belt, scarf in printed silk, hat with large crêpe de Chine flower by Jeannine Montel; *p. 91, left* 'Surf' long cardigan in knitted Lisle yarn, 'Coquelicot' blouse in striped crêpe de Chine by Hurel, and 'Vacances' trousers in wool gabardine; *p. 91, top right* 'Caspienne' beachwear; *p. 91, bottom right* 'Torpédo' coat and trouser ensemble in white wool gabardine, scarf belt in crêpe de Chine, Bibi hat by Jeannine Montel; *p. 92* 'Tarasque' cardigan and skirt in raspberry knitted Lisle yarn, dress and scarf in crêpe de Chine printed with Art Deco motifs by Bini, flower by Jeannine Montel; *p. 93* 'Tourmaline' dress with low-cut back in crêpe de Chine printed with a glass marble motif, flower by Jeannine Montel; *p. 94* 'Thésée' dress in beige silk crepe printed with brick-red Art Deco motifs by Bini, slit sleeves, matching parasol, jewelry by Patrick Hourcade, flower by Jeannine Montel; *p. 95* 'Baltique' poncho dress in ivory crêpe de Chine hand-painted with black and sea-green Art Deco motifs, matching parasol

A/W 1974–1975
1 April 1974; Grand Foyer, Palais de Chaillot, Paris
Hair by Jean-Marc Maniatis; make-up by Harriet Hubbard Ayer; jewelry by Patrick Hourcade; tights by Chesterfield; boots by Walter Steiger.
p. 96 'Vésinet' raincoat in steel-grey grosgrain lined with plum faux fur, wide belt in matching leather, plum wool scarf, boots by Walter Steiger; *p. 97, left* Cape coat in unlined woolen whipcord, wide cuffs and scarf-sleeves in contrast knit; *p. 97, right* Loose sky-blue coat and skirt in flannel by Wurmser, sleeveless coat in black rabbit fur, silk blouse; *pp. 98–9* 'Vizir' belted coat with patch pockets, white cashmere sweater with corolla collar, silk crepe beret, wool scarf; *p. 100, left* 'Vipère' striped and belted dress; *p. 100, right* Striped and belted dress; *p. 101* 'Villefranche' belted jacket and skirt in wool gabardine

S/S 1975
21 October 1974; Grand Foyer, Palais de Chaillot, Paris
p. 102 'Accessit' polo shirt and skirt in fine flannel by Wurmser, tank top in crêpe de Chine; *p. 103, top left* 'Abri' raincoat; *p. 103, right* 'Arsenic' dress in ivory crêpe de Chine by Bini, Chantilly lace inserts, double collar and pleated flounces, black crepe bow; *p. 103, bottom left* Cardigan in black knitted cotton, blouse in ivory crêpe de Chine with pleated ruff and cuffs, pleated skirt; *p. 104* 'Album' backless dress with cape collar in pearl-grey crêpe de Chine printed with pink spots; *p. 105, top* 'Albanie' tunic and skirt in candy-pink cashmere and silk, tank top in matching crêpe de Chine; *p. 105, bottom* 'Amélie' dress in beige-pink crêpe de Chine with boat neckline, elasticated waist and cuffs, puffed sleeves embellished with rows of pearly ball buttons; *p. 106* Cape in crêpe de Chine hand-painted with Art Deco-style floral motifs and stripes; *p. 107* Dress and scarf in ivory crêpe de Chine hand-painted with blue floral motifs inspired by porcelain decoration; *pp. 108–9* Show finale

A/W 1975–1976
7 April 1975; Palais des Congrès, Paris
Shoes by Mario Valentino.
p. 114 'By Night' dressing gown in black crêpe de Chine by Bini printed with floral motifs and orange illuminated Cs inspired by 19th-century male dressing gowns, 'Michel-Ange' blouse in white crêpe de Chine and black tie, 'Brooklyn' hemless trousers in silk velvet; *p. 115, left* 'Billard' tunic dress with striped cashmere and silk shirt-front, and 'Sonate' plain underskirt; *p. 115, right* 'Break' tunic dress with cashmere and silk shirt-front, and 'Rabelais' trousers, feather boa; *p. 116, top* 'Bourgogne' lilac dress and plum shawl in silk jersey; *p. 116, bottom* 'Beaumanoir' dress in rosewood silk jersey; *p. 117, left* 'Bijoutier' dress in coral crêpe de Chine with gathered neckline and waist, skirt with slit in front, V-shaped neckline in the back, and 'Opérette-bis' reversible shawl in coral and grey crêpe de Chine; *p. 117, right* 'Pulcinella' hand-painted blouse in silk crepe embroidered with gold sequins, and 'Beach' skirt in black silk jersey; *p. 118, left* Kimono, tunic

and scarf in black crêpe de Chine by Bini printed with plum and lilac floral motifs, black silk trousers; *p.118, right* 'Allegra' dress, cape and long skirt in hand-painted silk crepe; *p.119, left* 'Atlanta' dress, blouse and shawl ensemble; *p.119, right* 'Fioventina' blouse, sleeveless tunic and long skirt hand-painted with designs inspired by the Vienna Secession

S/S 1976
20 October 1975;
Palais des Congrès, Paris
p.121, top left Vest and bathing suit in white knitted silk, with veil and scarf belt; *p.121, top right* Sleeveless striped tunic, scarf and black bathing suit; *p.121, bottom left* 'Cannes' bathrobe coat in white flannel with red piping by Wurmser, bathing suit in red garter-stitch knit cut out in the back; *p.121, bottom right* Short dungarees in printed crêpe de Chine, blouse with stand-up collar; *p.122, left* 'Coralie' dress and trousers in pale pink and beige striped silk, lace insert, pleated ruffles and pearly ball buttons; *p.122, right* 'Conquistador' halter-neck tied at the neck and trousers in printed silk by Bini, apron in plain silk by Cattin, and printed border by Bini; *p.123, top left* Floaty trousers and bikini top in light grey crêpe de Chine printed with red, black and white flags, sleeveless jacket in edge-to-edge white cotton piqué; *p.123, right* 'Cuvillier' belted dress in black crêpe de Chine printed with cornucopias by Bini, pleated collar; *p.124* 'Caraco' dress; *p.125* 'Croquis' belted dress with Peter Pan collar in ivory silk printed with blue arabesques by Bini, lace insert, underdress by Cattin

A/W 1976–1977
5 April 1976;
Palais des Congrès, Paris
p.126 'Dandy' jacket, waistcoat and culotte-skirt ensemble in steel-grey flannel lined with cardinal-red satin; *p.127, left* 'Discours' black and white checked coat; *p.127, right* 'Démarché' red and white checked coat; *p.128, left* 'Dialogue' striped wool dress, leather belt, turtleneck sweater; *p.128, right* 'Lotion' long blouse in printed silk crepe, silk pussy-bow shirt, crewneck sweater in brown cashmere, plaited leather belt, 'Enghien' flannel skirt; *p.129, left* Jacket

and dress in silk crepe printed with different motifs in the same colours, leather belt, brown cashmere scarf, fabric flower brooch; *p.129, right* Jacket and trouser ensemble in sand-coloured silk crepe, lining of jacket and long tunic in gold Lurex, leather belt; *p.130* 'Derain' quilted coat in hand-painted silk crepe by Nicole Lefort with stitched flowers, lined with gold Lurex; *p.131* 'Durêve' dress in ivory silk crepe hand-painted with motifs inspired by 'coromandel' lacquer panels

S/S 1977
25 October 1976; Hall Concorde, Palais des Congrès, Paris
Hair by Jean-Marc Maniatis; make-up by Jacques Clemente for Elizabeth Arden; tights by DIM; shoes by Walter Steiger; espadrilles, perfume and accessories by Chloé.
p.132 'Écorce' rosewood gabardine jacket with small chevrons, 'Catch' 'waist-maker', 'Pâquerette' blouse, 'Abricot' trousers; *p.133, top left* 'En compétition' faux sporty evening ensemble, T-shirt with bright yellow and black stripes, skirt in sheer black lace; *p.133, top right* 'Étienne' jacket and skirt ensemble; *p.133, bottom left* 'Enfouie' T-shirt dress in silk printed with aubergine, teal, ivory and ochre stripes, 'waist-maker' in silk with leaf patterns in colours matching the dress; *p.133, bottom right* 'Échancrée' waistcoat-wrap in black crêpe de Chine worn open over a T-shirt and skirt printed with pink, green and blue floral motifs on a black background; *p.134, left* 'Eldorado' 'terrace' dress in fire-red silk crepe with teal trim, comet pleats; *p.134, right* 'Érable' T-shirt dress, scarf tank top tied over the top of the dress, box-pleated skirt in silk hand-painted with coral stripes on an off-white background; *p.135, left* 'Enfance' T-shirt dress in crêpe de Chine hand-painted with a Chinese shadow motif by Nicole Lefort and embroidered by Chaste with glass beads, 'waist-maker' (scarf tank top) tied around the top of the dress; *p.135, right* 'Étrusque' T-shirt and pleated skirt hand-painted by Nicole Lefort with stripes and spots, fan-shaped belt; *p.136, left* 'Europe' T-shirt dress in ivory silk cloqué pleated on the front, 'waist-maker' in fire-red silk;

p.136, right Dress in Roman crepe by Bini with full comet pleats; *p.137, left* 'Effrontée' cotton cardigan, top and skirt in embroidered ivory cotton tulle; *p.137, right* 'Ever-green' coat in St Gallen lace by Forster Willi, embroidered on an ivory cotton georgette dress encrusted with lace inserts

A/W 1977–1978
28 March 1977; Hall Concorde, Palais des Congrès, Paris
Hair by Jean-Marc Maniatis; make-up by Jacques Clemente for Elizabeth Arden; tights by DIM; shoes by Guido Pasquali.
p.138 'Flagrant' velvet waistcoat with empire collar, French-style breeches, Casanova-style 'Figaro' blouse in satin by Cattin and lace; *p.139, top* 'Fardée' dress, high-heeled thigh-high satin boots; *p.140, right* 'Finlande' cape; *p.141, left* 'Forain' dress in black muslin printed with grey-mauve and blue heliotropes by Bini, trimmed with marabou feathers, belt in crepe satin; *p.141, top right* 'Fontanges' dress in Roman crepe by Bini, embroidered by Chaste, neckline trimmed with marten fur and Chantilly lace, sleeves embroidered with gold sequins; *p.141, bottom right* 'Funambule' dress in fine wool printed with flowers by Bini, trimmed with velvet at neckline and cuffs; *p.142, left* Wool coat, turtleneck sweater with embroidered lace shirt-front; *p.142, right* 'Fontenelle' skirt and jacket in lichen-coloured flannel embroidered with pearl-grey lace; *p.143, top left* 'Frondeuse' skirt and jacket with moveable sleeves in almond-green *drap de cocher* (felted coated wool), 'old silver' embroidery by Chaste; *p.143, top right* Bolero in black velvet adorned with ivory guipure appliqués, satin riding boots; *p.143, bottom* 'Faust' bolero in black velvet adorned with ivory lace appliqués

S/S 1978
24 October 1977; Hall Concorde, Palais des Congrès, Paris
p.144 'Galon' ivory tulle dress adorned with appliqués of embroidered lace; *p.145, top left* 'Gadoue' jacket in white basket-weave tweed; *p.145, right* 'Gabon' dress in cotton voile with embroidered appliqués; *p.145, bottom left* 'Génoise' jacket in basket-weave linen and cotton, skirt and T-shirt

in ecru mesh canvas; *p.146, top left* 'Grenadier' jacket in caramel and white pekin stripe tricotine, dress in caramel and white milleraies silk toile; *p.146, right* 'Géométrie' dress in salmon-pink wool cheesecloth; *p.146, bottom left* 'Gap' ensemble in silk crêpe de Chine printed with flower motif by Bini; *p.147* 'Gorge' dress in ivory chintz embroidered with flowers and foliage

A/W 1978–1979
10 April 1978;
Palais de Chaillot, Paris
Hats by Jeannine Montel; jewelry by Ugo Correani; shoes by Guido Pasquali.
p.148 'Métronome' spencer jacket with big shoulders and shawl collar in black bouclé wool, 'Galion' trousers in black velvet, 'Étoile' brooch by Ugo Correani; *p.149, top left* 'Harmonie' cape and trousers ensemble, 'Caravelle' jacket in velvet by Wurmser; *p.149, top right* 'Herbier' jacket by Dormeuil, 'Hêtre' waistcoat and trousers in tweed by Wurmser, 'Si' hat in check tweed by Dormeuil; *p.149, bottom left* 'Harvard' jacket in checked tweed by Dormeuil, waistcoat and trousers by Wurmser; *p.149, bottom right* 'Hidalgo' dress in sand-coloured silk crepe by Galtrucco; *p.150, top left* 'Ivoire' pussy-bow dress and flounced skirt in ivory silk crepe by Galtrucco; *p.150, right* 'Ilion' embroidered jacket and trousers ensemble by Galtrucco, blouse tied at the front in silk by Galtrucco, 'La' fascinator; *p.150, bottom left* 'Ivan' dress in cheesecloth fabric printed with motifs inspired by Vladimir Lebedev; *p.151, left* 'Impression' jacket in printed silk by Bini, 'Vent' skirt; *p.151, right* 'Hironimus' blouse and skirt in printed silk by Bini, 'La' fascinator; *p.152* 'Instrument' quilted bolero in silk by Cattin, embroidered by Vermont with geometric motifs made from multicoloured thread, rhinestones and tubular pearls, 'Mistral' tulip skirt in silk by Cattin, 'Fa' fascinator with velvet visor; *p.153, top* (centre) 'Golfe' sweater, 'Vent' skirt; *p.153, bottom* 'Ilôt' short edge-to-edge jacket in white flannel by Wurmser, embroidered with black jet motifs and trimmed with quilted velvet, flannel trousers, 'Mi' fascinator with visor in quilted velvet

S/S 1979
n.d.; Paris
Hats by Jeannine Montel; jewelry by Ugo Correani; bags by Robert's; shoes by Guido Pasquali.
p.154 'Lustre' jacket in black velvet, trousers in white cotton by Wurmser, yellow leather belt, 'Balance' cockerel brooch in white lacquered plexiglass by Ugo Correani; *p.155, top* 'Logique' jacket and skirt ensemble by Wurmser, 'Roulette' hat, 'Lézard' jacket and skirt ensemble by Moreau, 'Borsalino' belt, 'Cluedo' headband; *p.155, bottom* 'Leader' jacket, 'Jeudi' bag, 'Pocker' hat, 'Poisson' flower brooch in white lacquered plexiglass by Ugo Correani pinned onto the hat; *p.156, top* 'L'été' dress in silk printed with poppies by Galtrucco; *p.156, bottom* 'Laos' dress in silk printed with robots by Bini; *p.157, top* 'Roupie' jacket with big shoulders in bouclé wool, dress in silk printed with flowers by Galtrucco; *p.157, bottom* 'Libation' evening dress in crêpe de Chine by Bini printed with flying saucers, bust entirely embroidered by Vuillaume with black tubular beads except for the motifs; *p.158, top left* 'Las cases' jacket in white wool embroidered with black tulips by Wurmser, narrow trousers in black *grain de poudre* by Wurmser, 'Hennin' belt; *p.158, right* 'Luna Park' corset and trousers in crêpe de Chine printed by Moreau, 'Pocker' hat; *p.158, bottom left* Twin set in silk printed with tulips; *p.159* (left) 'Leaf' long dress in printed crêpe de Chine by Bini; (right) 'Lagune' long dress in printed crêpe de Chine by Bini

A/W 1979–1980
9 April 1979;
Carreau du Temple, Paris
Hats by Jeannine Montel; jewelry by Ugo Correani.
p.160 'Mazurka' puffed frock-coat dress in emerald-green silk taffeta by Taroni, 'Terre' hat by Jeannine Montel, probably inspired by traditional Russian *kokoshnik* headdress, 'Albatros' brooch by Ugo Correani; *p.161, top left* 'Mérignac' coat in wool by Wurmser, 'Saturne' hat by Jeannine Montel, 'Colibri' brooch by Ugo Correani; *p.161, right* 'Panthère' jacket in black velvet, 'Jaguar' trousers in black velvet, 'Épagneul' collar in astrakhan by Swakara, 'Saturne' hat by Jeannine Montel, 'Vahine' belt;

p.161, bottom left Turtleneck dress in wool, 'Terre' hat by Jeannine Montel; *p.162, top left* 'Léopard' jacket in velvet by Samt, 'Terre' hat by Jeannine Montel, 'Tourterelle' necklace and 'Papagayo' bracelet by Ugo Correani; *p.162, right* 'Montespan' dress in silk crepe by Cattin embellished with lace flounces by Chantiss and rows of imitation pearls, 'Satellite' tambourin hat; *p.162, bottom left* 'Mac Donald' evening cape in brushed silk printed with ducks, bustier in black velvet by Samt, breeches in black silk satin, 'Luge' gaiters by Guido Pasquali, 'Terre' hat by Jeannine Montel; *p.163, top* 'Marivaux' jacket by Bini embroidered with wings in shiny white sequins; *p.163, bottom* (left) 'Marivaux'; (right) 'Murmure'; *p.164, top* (right) 'Leopard' suit in wool by Wurmser; *p.164, bottom left* 'Terre' hat by Jeannine Montel, 'Hirondelle' brooch by Ugo Correani; *p.164, bottom right* 'Terre' hat by Jeannine Montel, 'Plume' and 'Plumeau' hat accessories; *p.165* 'Murillo' dress in midnight-blue silk satin by Taroni embroidered with an appliquéd lightbulb motif, 'Lune' hat by Jeannine Montel

S/S 1980
15 October 1979; Paris
Hats by Jeannine Montel; jewelry by Ugo Correani; shoes by Walter Steiger.
p.166 'Jerk' scalloped strapless swimsuit in knitted pearl cotton; *p.167, top* (left) 'Nantua' blouse and short skirt in silk printed with black and white motifs by Bini; (centre) 'Next' spencer jacket in black and white cotton-blend by Bini, skirt in silk crepe by Cattin; (right) 'Nippes' dress in silk printed with black and white floral motifs by Bini; *p.167, bottom left* 'Nu pieds' tunic and skirt in pale yellow silk crepe printed with turquoise and purple stripes by Galtrucco, 'Lindbergh' hat; *p.167, bottom right* 'Network' dress in silk, 'Lindbergh' hat; *p.168, top left* 'Nord-Express' short raincoat in yellow polyester and rubber; *p.168, right* 'Narcisse' jacket and trousers in wool by Wurmser; *p.168, bottom left* 'Java' asymmetric top and Bermuda shorts in knitted pearl cotton, necklace by Ugo Correani; *p.169, left* 'Jerk' scalloped strapless swimsuit in knitted pearl cotton, necklace by Ugo Correani; *p.169,*

right 'Blues' dress in knitted pearl cotton, buttoned in the back, 'Auriol' hat; *p.170, left* 'Nigeria' dress in silk crepe by Bini; *p.170, right* 'Nysten' asymmetric dress in silk crepe by Bini, bodice entirely embroidered with sequins and glass beads, 'Lindbergh' hat; *p.171, left* 'Nonza' dress in silk by Cattin embroidered with a hot air balloon motif; *p.171, right* 'Nageoire' T-shirt-shaped tunic in fine gold shimmering lamé by Diochon

A/W 1980–1981
31 March 1980;
Palais de Chaillot, Paris
Hair by Jean-Marc Maniatis; make-up by Jacques Clemente for Elizabeth Arden; 'hair hats' by Karl Lagerfeld; jewelry by Ugo Correani; bags by Robert's; tights by Fogal; shoes by Walter Steiger. *p.172* 'Philadelphie' dress in silk crepe by Cattin, turtleneck collar and cuffs in lace by Solstiss, skirt with lightly pleated tiered flounces; *p.173* 'Ecrin bis' sweater in cotton and nylon; *p.174, left* 'Pergame' tunic dress and Bermuda shorts in silk crepe by Taroni, standing collar, cut-out shoulders, embroidered by Montex Ateliers with gold and silver metallic sequins; *p.174, right* 'Pâturage' dress in silk crepe by Cattin, pussy-bow collar, shirt-front and cuffs in tulle embroidered with flower motifs; *p.175, left* 'Pneumatique' raincoat in elastomer and polyester; *p.175, right* 'Protocole' quilted evening jacket in silk and black and gold polyester lamé by Diochon-Lurex with Medici collar and gigot sleeves, 'Poppée' dress in gold lamé by Diochon with V-shaped neckline and gigot sleeves, worn over an orange lamé slip, with matching scarf; *p.176* 'Platine' jacket in gold lamé by Diochon, lined with vermillion silk, 'Puerto Rico' dress in gold lamé by Diochon, shirt-front in lace by Solstiss; *p.177* 'Pavillon' dress in finely striped silver silk and polyester lamé by Diochon with stacked collar, 'boudin' around the waist, quilted bust and sides of skirt mimicking a panier dress

S/S 1981
19 October 1980; Quonser hut, Porte de Versailles, Paris
Hair by Jean-Marc Maniatis; make-up by Jacques Clemente for Elizabeth Arden; jewelry by Ugo Correani; tights by Fogal; shoes by Walter Steiger.

p.178 (left) 'Renoir' ensemble in wool crepe by Agnona: edge-to-edge spencer jacket and matching pleated Bermuda shorts; (right) 'Raffinement' edge-to-edge jacket and pleated Bermuda shorts in wool crepe by Agnona; *p.179, top left* 'Raphia' jacket and Bermuda shorts ensemble in straw-coloured wool, blouse in acetate and viscose by Stunzi; *p.179, top right* 'Rocambole' waistcoat and trousers ensemble in wool; *p.179, bottom left* 'Rouge-gorge' pleated top and skirt in viscose and acetate by Bini, with white trim around the square neckline and bottom of the short sleeves; double-layer skirt, one pleated on another longer straight skirt; necklace by Ugo Correani; *p.179, bottom right* 'Renouveau' top and skirt in viscose and acetate by Bini, with lightly quilted boat neckline; double-layer skirt, one pleated on another longer straight skirt; *p.180, left* 'Londres' short-sleeved knit sweater with geometric pattern, 'Truffe' trousers; *p.180, right* 'Robespierre' boat-neck dress in silk by Bini, two motifs of leaves and diagonal stripes in the same colours; *p.181, left* 'Réveil' top and skirt in printed black silk crepe by Bini, with lightly padded white boat neckline, double-layer skirt; *p.181, top right* 'Rengaine' dress in navy crêpe de Chine printed with multicoloured spots by Bini, boat neckline and hem bordered with white cotton by Stunzi; *p.181, bottom right* 'Roumanie' top and skirt in silk by Galtrucco, with boat neckline and lightly quilted hemlines; *p.182, left* (left) 'Reliure' dress in floral-printed cotton by Bini, over trousers in silk by Cattin; (right) 'Redoublée' tunic in floral-printed cotton by Bini, over trousers in striped crepe in the same colours by Bini; *p.182, right* 'Réunion' waistcoat, top and skirt in cotton by Bini printed with orchid motifs and stripes in the same colours; *p.183* (from left to right) 'Rimini', 'Ronsard' and 'Ravin' dresses in crêpe de Chine by Cattin embroidered with lightning bolts of sequins, rhinestones and silver thread

A/W 1981–1982
5 April 1981;
Tent, Les Halles, Paris
Hair by Jean-Marc Maniatis; make-up by Jacques Clemente for Elizabeth Arden; hats by Jean Barthet; jewelry by Ugo Correani

for Chloé and Isadora for Chloé; tights by Fogal for Chloé; shoes by Walter Steiger for Chloé. *p.184* 'Science' coat and trousers in wool by Wurmser; *p.185, top left* 'Salzbourg' jacket and trousers; *p.185, top right* 'Séverine' dress and bodice belt in wool by Wurmser; *p.185, bottom left* 'Safari' coat-dress and trousers in wool gabardine; *p.185, bottom right* 'Scott' coat and trousers in rayon; *p.186, left* 'Suzanna' dress in printed wool and silk by Bini, sautoir necklace by Ugo Correani; *p.186, right* 'Slave' coat-dress and straight trousers in steel-grey flannel by Wurmser, decorated with gold braid trimmings and embroidered with appliqués; *p.187, left* 'Spectacle' dress with puffed sleeves in black silk crepe with vermillion lining, decorated with gold braid trimmings, embroidered with gold lamé appliqués and red faceted imitation stones; *p.187, right* 'Tokyo' sautoir necklace by Ugo Correani; *p.188, left* 'Solveig' dress with boat-neck collar and trousers in wool decorated with gold braid trimmings, ears of wheat embroidery and brass ball buttons; *p.188, right* 'Saké' dress in silk printed with chrysanthemuns and lined with gold lamé by Bini; *p.189, left* 'Scylla' dress in printed crepe by Diochon, high lace collar; *p.189, right* 'Senso' dress with boat-neck collar lined with black fox fur, bust in organza brocaded with geometric motifs in gold, red, salmon and black lamé, skirt in black organza by Hurel

S/S 1982
17 October 1981;
Palais des Congrés, Paris
Hair by Jean-Marc Maniatis; make-up by Jacques Clemente for Elizabeth Arden; hats by Jean Barthet; jewelry by Tess-Designs New York and Ugo Correani; shoes by Walter Steiger for Chloé; music included Soft Cell. *p.190* 'Talc' jacket in cotton, 'Mistigri' culotte-skirt in cotton, 'Russule' hat; *p.191, top left* 'Trève' dress and trousers in printed silk crepe by Bini, cuffs and hems edged with layers of pointed organza, 'Guêpe' belt, 'Russule' hat; *p.191, top right* 'Trocadéro' dress in printed cotton by Bini, 'Amanite' hat; *p.191, bottom* 'Tric-Trac' dress and jumpsuit in printed georgette crepe by Bini, 'Bolet' hat; *p.192, left* 'Tangente' dress in silk crepe by Bini,

chrome ball-beading embroidery, 'Guêpe' belt; *p.192, right* 'Thory' dress in printed silk by Bini, 'Guêpe' belt; *p.193, bottom left* 'Thyrse' dress over tunic in printed silk crepe by Bini, embroidered with black tube beads and blue and red sequins; *p.193, top right* 'Tableau' bustier dress in printed silk crepe by Bini, organza embroidery and sequins by Vermont; double-layer skirt, the top one open at centre front

A/W 1982–1983
26 March 1982;
Cour du Louvre, Paris
Jewelry by Ugo Correani.
p.194 (centre) 'Vis-à-vis' jacket in vermillion wool by Wurmser; (right) 'Vendôme' jacket in electric-blue wool by Wurmser; *p.195, top left* 'Variété' dress in printed silk by Bini; *p.195, right* 'Vermillion' dress in printed silk by Bini; *p.195, bottom left* 'Vigny' jacket and skirt in anthracite wool with silver Lurex stripes by Galtrucco; *p.196, left* 'Ultimatum' dress in pearl-grey silk by Cattin, with silver sequin embroidery and batwing sleeves; *p.196, right* 'Vivaldi' jacket in black wool by Wurmser, with silver demi-sphere embroidery by Vuillaume on sleeves, brooch by Ugo Correani attached to hat; *p.197, left* (left) 'Victoria' dress in silk crepe by Cattin, decorated with lace inserts, batwing sleeves and ruffled skirt; (right) 'Young et Uzès' ensemble in silk crepe by Cattin, decorated with lace inserts; *p.197, right* (left) 'Vanini' strapless dress in black silk by Cattin, with silver sequin embroidery; (right) 'Vertige' strapless dress in black silk by Cattin, with silver sequin embroidery, brooch by Ugo Correani

S/S 1983
15 October 1982; Paris
Hair by Alexandre de Paris; make-up by Jacques Clemente for Elizabeth Arden; hats by Jean Barthet; jewelry by Ugo Correani for Chloé; shoes by Walter Steiger for Chloé.
p.198 'Architect' straight dress in houndstooth linen with large rectangular yoke on the bust and frill on the back, hips highlighted by loose pockets; *p.199, top left* 'Anémone' dress in silk crepe by Cattin, vermillion lining of the panels to tie at the waist and black wrap skirt; *p.199, right* 'Arizona' jacket and skirt

ensemble in white-striped cotton by Wurmser, necklace and brooch attached to belt by Ugo Correani; *p.199, bottom left* 'Amitié' ensemble in wool by Wurmser; *p.200, top left* 'Adagio' evening dress in crêpe de Chine by Bini, embroidery on open back of electric guitar in sequins by Lanel; *p.200, bottom* 'Angkor' open-back evening dress in black acetate crepe and viscose, straight stand-up collar, batwing sleeves, front embroidery of violin in threads, rhinestones, and gold and silver beads by Vermont; *pp.200–1* (left) 'Archer' evening suit in linen by Moreau, shawl-collar jacket with silk satin lapel by Cattin, embroidery of electric guitar in sequins, rhinestones and tube beads by Lanel; (centre) 'Aurélien' open-back dress in silk crepon by Galtrucco, embroidery of electric guitar in sequins, rhinestones and tubular pearls by Lanel; (right) 'Arcole' jacket and skirt in wool and polyester by Wurmser, silk lapel by Galtrucco, embroidery of violin in sequins and tubular beads by Lanel; *p.202, left* 'Arpège' top and skirt in silk by Mantero, embroidery by Montex; *p.202, right* 'Ariane' wrap skirt dress in silk by Bini, embroidery by Montex; *p.203, top* (left) 'Anouchka' dress in tulle and lace embroidered with sequins by Hurel; (right) 'Argent' dress in nylon tulle by Wurmser, finely pleated collar and sleeves, silver and gold sequin embroidery by Hurel; *p.203, bottom* 'Atoll' dress in cotton tulle and embroidered rayon, top of sleeves embellished with a row of faux cultured pearls

A/W 1983–1984
18 March 1983;
Cour du Louvre, Paris
Hair by Alexandre de Paris; make-up by Jacques Clemente for Elizabeth Arden; hats by Jean Barthet; jewelry by Ugo Correani; shoes by Walter Steiger.
p.204, left (left) 'Ivry' sweater in cabled wool; (right) 'Adverbe' straight skirt in wool and mohair by Wurmser; *p.205, bottom left* 'Bois de rose' three-quarter-length coat in bouclé wool by Wurmser, large collar plunging towards the hem, large matching scarf; *p.205, bottom right* 'Building' dress in printed wool and silk blend by Bini, with high collar and batwing sleeves, 'Impératif' petticoat in black

wool; *p.206, left* 'Bénédictine' cape and dress in printed wool and silk blend by Bini, 'Mandrin' leather belt, 'Brunch' coat in Woolmark wool; *p.206, right* 'Badge' cape coat, shawl-collared spencer jacket with knotted panels at the front, and straight skirt in alpaca and wool blend with light Prince of Wales motifs, 'Impératif' petticoat in black wool; *p.207* 'Bungalow' dress in printed silk by Bini, 'Flèche' necklace; *p.208, left* 'Bath' dress in royal-blue silk by Cattin, buttoned at centre front and V-neck at the back, embroidery by Lanel of taps and water jets in tubular pearls, sequins, and silver and black rhinestones; *p.208, right* 'Bruissante' long dress in silk, embroidery by Lanel of taps and water jet in tubular pearls, sequins, and silver and black rhinestones; *p.209, left* Necklace by Ugo Correani in the shape of a showerhead from which spout water jets in rhinestones, ending in pearl beads; *p.209, top right* 'Beaulieu' dress, embroidery by Montex, 'Tilbury' hat; *p.209, bottom right* 'Bugatti' dress in black jersey, silver faceted-cabochon embroidery by Hurel in the shape of arrows on the collar, sleeve tops and centre front; *p.210* 'Brise' long halter-neck dress in midnight-blue silk crepe by Stunzi, bust embroidered with a trompe l'œil of double rows of buttons, straps ending in the back with embroidery by Chaste of showerhead and water jet in tubular pearls, sequins and silver rhinestones; *p.211, left* 'Bijou' bow dress in silk taffeta by Diochon, large shells secured at the waist with jewel-embroidery; *p.211, right* 'Bain' dress in red, blue and black acetate and viscose by René Manoha, embroidered by Lanel with a motif of showerhead and silver water jet

S/S 1984
14 October 1983; Paris
Hair by Alexandre de Paris; make-up from Elizabeth Arden; hats by Jean Barthet for Chloé; jewelry by Ugo Correani for Chloé.
p.213, top left 'Costume' jacket and trousers in wool by Wurmser; *p.213, top right* 'Caractère' dress with ecru cotton appliqués by Tacosa on black linen background by Moreau; *p.213, bottom left* 'Caprice' jacket, blouse, overskirt and mid-calf skirt in black and white cotton by Cuccirelli; *p.213,*

bottom right 'If' three-quarter-length jacket with shawl collar, tank dress in black and white mercerized cotton; *p. 214, left* 'Cigogne' dress by Cattin, top and tie-on overskirt in silk printed with pixellated landscape motifs by Bini; *p. 214, top right* 'Ciné Club' dress by Cattin, top and tie-on overskirt in printed silk by Bini; *p. 214, bottom right* 'Calicot' jacket, top, overskirt and skirt in printed cotton and viscose by Bini; *p. 215, left* 'Cabriole' bustier and overskirt in silk crepe by Bini, embroidered with Circassian figures and animals, pleated mid-calf skirt; *p. 215, right* 'Carnaval' halter-neck top with overskirt in silk by Bini, embroidered with Circassian figures and animals, pleated mid-calf skirt; *p. 216, top left* 'Chardin' jabot top and skirt in silk crepe by Cattin, decorated with lace flounces; *p. 216, right* 'Carpeaux' dress in crepe, embroidery by Hurel of trompe l'œil of garments draped in pearls and gold sequins; *p. 216, bottom left* 'Childéric' dress in cream silk crepe by Cattin, lace trims, 'kolpos' pleated blouse; *p. 217, left* 'Crétoise' dress in ivory crepe, trompe l'œil embroidery of chiton and himation in beads and sequins, and piece of black muslin draped asymmetrically like a himation; *p. 217, right* 'Crétoise' dress in ivory crepe, trompe l'œil embroidery of chiton and himation in pearls and sequins; *p. 218* (left) 'Coïncidence' linen jacket by Moreau, trompe l'œil embroidery of T-shirt on hanger in sequins and glass beads on the back, over a plain short-sleeved dress; (right) 'Cintre' dress in black acetate crepe and viscose by Stunzi, trompe l'œil embroidery of dress on hanger in sequins and glass beads on the bust; *p. 219* 'Cobra' asymmetrical long dress in black acetate crepe and viscose by Stunzi, trompe l'œil embroidery of scissors in silver tubes creating triangular cutouts of red sequins

A/W 1984–1985
23 March 1984; Salle Sully, Cour Carrée, Palais du Louvre, Paris
Hair by Valentin for Jean-Louis David; make-up from Elizabeth Arden; hats by Jean Barthet for Chloé.
p. 222 (left) 'Mathurin' knitted jacket with large contrasting lapels, 'Goelette' skirt in light silk by Cattin, 'Arpagon' grey sweater with large lapels [Guy Paulin]; (centre) 'Mathurin' knitted coat with large contrasting lapels, 'Goelette' skirt in light silk by Cattin, 'Chimène' beige sweater with lapels, shoes in beige satin [Guy Paulin]; (right) 'Gymnase' long wool jersey cardigan with large lapels, 'Goelette' trousers in grey silk crepe by Cattin, 'Cléante' peplum sweater in taupe with pale yellow lining [Guy Paulin]; *p. 223, top left* 'Damas' blazer and 'Péniche' trousers in Prince of Wales lamé in black silk and gold Lurex by Galtrucco [Guy Paulin]; *p. 223, bottom left* 'Debutante' long dress in Prince of Wales lamé in lavender silk and gold Lurex by Galtrucco [Guy Paulin], 'Basket' belt; *p. 223, right* (left) 'Défini' bustier dress in Moroccan crepe by Cattin, sheer chiffon top and sleeves, trompe l'œil embroidery of bow tie [Philippe Guibourgé]; (right) 'Dîner' dress in Moroccan crepe by Cattin, transparent chiffon back, trompe l'œil embroidery of necklace [Philippe Guibourgé]

S/S 1985
19 October 1984;
Jardin des Tuileries, Paris
First part by Philippe Guibourgé: hats by Stephen Jones and Jean Barthet; jewelry by La Porte Bleue for Chloé; shoes by Sidonie Larizzi. Second part by Guy Paulin: hats by Jean Barthet, Michel and Gelot; jewelry by Patrick Retif for Chloé; shoes by Maud Frizon; ballerina shoes by Heaston.
p. 224 'Eliot' coat and jacket in wool by Wurmser, 'Origan' trousers in wool by Wurmser, 'Dallas' sweater, 'Chatou' hat [Guy Paulin]; *p. 225, top* (left) 'Élysée' dress in silk by Hurel; (right) 'Ébène' top and skirt in silk by Bini [Guy Paulin]; *p. 225, bottom* 'Excitante' top, skirt and shorts in silk crepe by Cattin, shorts embroidered with sequins [Philippe Guibourgé]

A/W 1985–1986
22 March 1985; Salle Sully, Cour Carrée, Palais du Louvre, Paris
p. 226 'Fidèle' spencer jacket and skirt in black wool, 'Sisley' white blouse, 'Agra' necklace in brass and rhinestones, 'Grenade' black hat; *p. 227, left* 'Forfait' long coat in black cashmere, 'Forgeron' jacket in fuchsia wool by Wurmser, skirt in black wool by Wurmser, blouse in taupe silk by Cattin, 'Grenade' black hat [Luciano Soprani]; *p. 227, top right* (left) 'Fable' top in black silk by Cattin, dress in printed silk by Galtrucco; (right) 'Faïence' top in printed silk by Galtrucco, dress in black silk by Cattin, 'Gin' belt in pink lamb's leather; *p. 227, bottom right* 'Franche' halter-neck dress in black silk crepe by Cattin, embroidery by Lanel

S/S 1986
19 October 1985;
Tent, Jardin des Tuileries, Paris
Hair by Romain and Patrick Ales; make-up from Elizabeth Arden; hats by Jean Barthet for Chloé; jewelry by Monty Don and F. Van de Casteele; shoes by Maud Frizon for Chloé.
p. 228 'Gay Lussac' bomber, jacket and skirt ensemble; *p. 229, top* For the three central silhouettes, (left) 'Gavroche' bomber jacket, blouse and skirt in silk, all buttoned in front; (centre) 'Grigi' (in wool) or 'Gaucho' (gabardine) jacket, blouse and skirt ensemble in silk, all buttoned in front; (right) 'Gagman' red dress; *p. 229, bottom left* 'Caravane' bralette and belt ensemble in red knit, culotte-skirt in printed silk; *p. 229, bottom right* 'Girasol' bustier and skirt

A/W 1986–1987
21 March 1986; Salle Sully, Cour Carrée, Palais du Louvre, Paris
Hair by Romain and Patrick Ales; make-up from Elizabeth Arden; hats by Jean Barthet for Chloé; jewelry by F. Van de Casteele; shoes by Robert Clergerie for Chloé.
p. 230 'Habanera' coat in banker-grey flannel by Wurmser, 'Fusil' pleated skirt in wool by Wurmser, 'Biche' tie-neck blouse in silk satin by Cattin, 'Rembrandt' amber necklace, 'Van Gogh' amber bracelet, 'Vlaminck' earrings, 'Pique' hat; *p. 231, left* 'Hauban' coat in wool and polyamide by Moreau, 'Javelot' skirt in wool, 'Antilope' blouse in silk by Cattin, 'Utrillo' earrings; *p. 231, right* (model seen from the front) 'Histoire' long black jacket and skirt with striped effect in anthracite-coloured acetate and viscose by Stunzi, jacket decorated with rhinestone buttons, 'Ouistiti' blouse in pure silk by Cattin, 'Manet' earrings with rhinestones; (model seen from behind) 'Hit-parade' long grey jacket and skirt with striped

effect in acetate and viscose by
Stunzi, 'Biche' blouse in pure
silk by Cattin

S/S 1987
17 October 1986; Paris
Hair by Mod's Hair; make-up
from Helena Rubinstein; jewelry
by Chloé and Christian Migeon;
tights and lace socks by Exciting;
shoes by Camille Unglick for
Chloé; production by Stephen
Jones, Jacques Lecorre and
Michel; set by Lamberto Deho;
music by Laurent Godard;
coordination by Bernard Trux.
p. 232 'Imper' overcoat in
resin-coated cotton by LIM;
p. 233, left 'Indéniable' jacket in
wool and mohair, dress in lace by
Marescot; *p. 233, top right* (left)
'Ici' jacket in grey pure wool
by Wurmser, 'Blaise' cuffed
Bermuda shorts in linen by
Dormeuil; (right) 'Iceberg' jacket
by Wurmser, 'Blaise' cuffed
Bermuda shorts in linen by
Dormeuil; *p. 233, bottom right*
'Image' short strapless dress
in polyester and cotton

A/W 1987–1988
20 March 1987; Salle Sully, Cour
Carrée, Palais du Louvre, Paris
Hair by Marc-Vincent for Chloé;
make-up from Helena
Rubinstein; hats by Stephen
Jones for Chloé; jewelry by Wiga
for Chloé; gloves by Lavabre-
Cadet; tights by Exciting; shoes
by Camille Unglick; fur by The
Fur Vault; glasses by Calamand;
music by Laurent Godard;
coordination by Bernard Trux

S/S 1988
16 October 1987; Paris
Hair by Orlando Pita; make-up
from Elizabeth Arden; hats by
Philippe Model and Jacques
Lecorre; jewelry by Martine
Chenail and Maison Gripoix;
gloves by Maison Buscarlet;
tights by Elizabeth de Ginisty;
shoes by Robert Clergerie;
glasses by Calamand; artistic
director of the show Marc Ascoli;
music by Henri Flesh; lighting
by Pascal Lagreze

A/W 1988–1989
18 March 1988; Salle Sully, Cour
Carrée, Palais du Louvre, Paris
Hats by Philippe Model; tights
by DIM; canes by Madeleine Gely

S/S 1989
21 October 1988; Paris

A/W 1989–1990
17 March 1989; Paris

S/S 1990
20 October 1989; Paris
Hair by Valentin for Jean-Louis
David; make-up by Linda
Cantello; shoes by Philippe
Model by Monique; illustrations
by James Dignan

A/W 1990–1991
16 March 1990; Salle Sully, Cour
Carrée, Palais du Louvre, Paris

S/S 1991
19 October 1990; Paris
Hair by Valentin; make-up
by Linda Cantello; shoes by
Philippe Model by Monique;
glasses by IDC; artistic director
of the show Marc Ascoli;
music by Thierry Planelle
and Christian Fourteau;
illustrations by James Dignan

A/W 1991–1992
15 March 1991; Paris
Hair by Valentin; make-up
by Mary Greenwell; shoes by
Philippe Model by Monique;
artistic director of the show
Marc Ascoli; music by Thierry
Planelle and Christian Fourteau;
illustrations by James Dignan

S/S 1992
18 October 1991; Paris

A/W 1992–1993
20 March 1992; Paris
Hair by Valentin and Jean-Louis
David team; make-up by Linda
Cantello; shoes by Philippe
Model by Monique; artistic
director of the show Marc Ascoli;
music by Frédéric Sanchez;
set by Aimé Deudé

S/S 1993
14 October 1992; Salle Sully, Cour
Carrée, Palais du Louvre, Paris
Hair by Julien d'Ys; make-up by
Stéphane Marais; hats by Maison
Michel and Stefan Lubrina
for Chloé; jewelry by Spok and
Aventurine for Chloé; bags by 31
Février and Maison Desrues for
Chloé; belts by Maison Desrues
and Hervé Masson for Chloé;
gloves by Lavabre Cadet for
Chloé; shoes by Rodolphe
Menudier, Philippe Model and
Massaro for Chloé; glasses by
IDC for Chloé; embroidery
by Montex for Chloé

A/W 1993–1994
13 March 1993; Salle des Arts,
Cour Carrée, Palais du Louvre,
Paris
Hair by Julien d'Ys; make-up by
Stéphane Marais; hats by Maison
Michel, Stefan Lubrina, Natalie

Spiteri for Chloé; jewelry
by Spok, Delphine Charlotte
Parmentier for Chloé; shoes
by Rodolphe Menudier/Delage,
Massaro for Chloé; bags by
Maison Desrues and Natalie
Spiteri for Chloé; belts by
Maison Desrues for Chloé;
gloves by Lavabre Cadet, Stefan
Lubrina, Natalie Spiteri for
Chloé; embroidery by Montex
for Chloé

S/S 1994
12 October 1993; Cour Carrée,
Palais du Louvre, Paris
Hair by Julien d'Ys, assisted by
Tamaris; make-up by Stéphane
Marais; hats by Maison Michel
for Chloé; jewelry by Spok and
Delphine Charlotte Parmentier
for Chloé; shoes by Rodolphe
Menudier/Mercadal for Chloé;
bags by Jamin Puech and Lesage
for Chloé; glasses by Optical
Affairs for Chloé; hand-painted
embroideries by Montex for
Chloé; embroidery by Simonnot-
Godard for Chloé; sound stylists
Michel Gaubert and Steven
Brinke; paper work by Marie
Farge

A/W 1994–1995
8 March 1994; Salle Le Nôtre,
Carrousel du Louvre, Paris
Hair by Julien d'Ys, assisted by
Tamaris; make-up by Stéphane
Marais; hats by Maison Michel
for Chloé; jewelry by Spok,
Delphine Charlotte Parmentier
and Taher Chemirik for Chloé;
shoes by Rodolphe Menudier/
Mercadal and Robert Clergerie
for Chloé; bags by Jamin Puech
for Chloé; belts by Maison
Desrues and Hervé Masson for
Chloé; gloves by Lavabre Cadet
for Chloé; glasses by Optical
Affairs for Chloé; embroidery
and hand-painting by Montex
for Chloé; sound stylists Michel
Gaubert and Steven Brinke

S/S 1995
11 October 1994; Salle Le Nôtre,
Carrousel du Louvre, Paris
Hair by Julien d'Ys, assisted by
Tamaris; make-up by Stéphane
Marais; hats by Carolin
Schuster-Böckler for Chloé;
glasses by Antony Meimaroglou
for Chloé; jewelry by Spok,
Delphine Charlotte Parmentier
and Taher Chemirik for Chloé;
bags by Jamin Puech and
Delphine Charlotte Parmentier
for Chloé; tights by Wolford;
shoes by Rodolphe Menudier/
Mercadal for Chloé; embroidery
by Montex for Chloé; hand-

painting by Stefan Lubrina and
Stéphane Fenestre for Chloé;
sound stylists Michel Gaubert
and Steven Brinke

A/W 1995–1996
16 March 1995; Salle Le Nôtre,
Carrousel du Louvre, Paris
Head and hair styling by Julien
d'Ys, assisted by Tamaris;
make-up by Stéphane Marais;
jewelry by Spok, Delphine
Charlotte Parmentier, Françoise
Klein, Lemarié for Chloé; gloves
by Lavabre Cadet for Chloé;
shoes by Rodolphe Menudier
for Chloé; bags by Jamin Puech
for Chloé; glasses by Antony
Meimaroglou for Chloé;
embroidery by Montex for Chloé;
tights by Wolford; sound stylists
Michel Gaubert and Steven
Brinke

S/S 1996
16 October 1995; Paris
Hair by Julien d'Ys, assisted by
Tamaris; make-up by Stéphane
Marais; hats by Maison Michel
and Stefan Lubrina for Chloé;
jewelry by Spok and François
Klein for Chloé; flowers by
Lemarié for Chloé; gloves by
Lavabre Cadet for Chloé; tights
by Wolford; shoes by Rodolphe
Menudier for Chloé; bags by
Stéphanie Vedrenne-Trebbi
for Chloé; glasses by Antony
Meiraroglou 'Beau soleil' for
Chloé; embroidery by Montex
for Chloé; sound stylists Michel
Gaubert and Steven Brinke

A/W 1996–1997
13 March 1996;
Salle Gaveau, Paris
Embroidery by Montex for Chloé

S/S 1997
9 October 1996; Salle Le Nôtre,
Carrousel du Louvre, Paris

A/W 1997–1998
14 March 1997; Salle Le Nôtre,
Carrousel du Louvre, Paris
Hair by Odile Gilbert; make-up
by Stéphane Marais; jewelry
by Pascal Arthus-Bertrand for
Chloé; gloves by Lavabre-Cadet
for Chloé; tights by Wolford;
shoes by Rodolphe Menudier
for Chloé; embroidery and
hand-painting by Montex for
Chloé; music by Michel Gaubert
and Stephen Brinke

S/S 1998
15 October 1997;
Opéra Garnier, Paris
Hair by Sam McKnight; make-up
by Linda Cantello; jewelry by

Stella Cadente for Chloé; glasses
by Essilor for Chloé; corsets by
Hubert Barrère for Chloé; tights
by Wolford; shoes by Christian
Louboutin for Chloé; embroidery
by Montex for Chloé; crochet by
Nathalie Spiteri for Chloé;
pleating by Lognon for Chloé;
music by Frédéric Sanchez;
direction and lighting by
Thierry Dreyfus; production
by W.A.B. Production

A/W 1998–1999
11 March 1998; Paris
Hair by Sam McKnight;
make-up by Linda Cantello

S/S 1999
14 October 1998;
Palais Brongniart, Paris
Hair by Sam McKnight; make-up
by Linda Cantello; jewelry by
Note d'Élégance for Chloé; hair
ornaments by N.P. Didier Poncet
for Chloé; glasses by Marcolin
for Chloé; corsets by Hubert
Barrère for Chloé; shoes by
Christian Louboutin for Chloé;
embroidery by Montex for Chloé;
crochet and embroidery by
Nathalie Spiteri for Chloé;
floral décor by Guillon Fleurs;
production by W.A.B.
Production; music by
John Carter

A/W 1999–2000
10 March 1999; Conservatoire
National des Arts et Métiers,
Paris
Hair by Marc Lopez; make-up
by Linda Cantello; hats by Ets
Michel for Chloé; corsets by
Hubert Barrère for Chloé; shoes
by Ernesto Esposito for Chloé;
glasses by Marcolin; hook by
Natalie Spiteri for Chloé;
music by Seb Chew; flowers
by Christian Tortu; production
by W.A.B Production

S/S 2000
5 October 1999;
Petit Palais, Paris
Hair by Marc Lopez; make-up by
Linda Cantello; straw hats and
bags by Ets Michel for Chloé;
gold chains by Loumen for
Chloé; shoes by Ernesto Esposito
for Chloé; rhinestone diamonds
by Natalie Spiteri for Chloé;
music by Seb Chew

A/W 2000–2001
1 March 2000;
Opéra Garnier, Paris
Make-up by Linda Cantello

S/S 2001
11 October 2000;
Petit Palais, Paris
Glasses by Marcolin

A/W 2001–2002
14 March 2001; Union Centrale
des Arts Décoratifs, Paris
Hair by Eugene Souleiman;
make-up by Val Garland; metal
engraving and resin by Antoine
Jeannot for Chloé; glasses by
Marcolin; bags by Maison André
Renaud for Chloé; shoes by Iris
for Chloé; music by Seb Chew;
video clip by Seb Janiak,
Cassandra Casanove and
Audrey Bitbol

S/S 2002
10 October 2001;
Carreau du Temple, Paris

A/W 2002–2003
12 March 2002; Petit Palais, Paris

S/S 2003
6 October 2002;
Carreau du Temple, Paris
Hair by Guido Palau;
make-up by Linda Cantello

A/W 2003–2004
9 March 2003;
Carreau du Temple, Paris
Hair by Guido Palau; music
included David Bowie, 'Fame'
(rap version)

S/S 2004
11 October 2003; École Nationale
Supérieure des Beaux-Arts, Paris
Hair by Guido Palau; make-up
by Charlotte Tilbury

A/W 2004–2005
6 March 1994; Espace
Éphémère Tuileries,
Jardin des Tuileries, Paris
Hair by Luigi Murenu

S/S 2005
9 October 2004; Espace
Éphémère Tuileries,
Jardin des Tuileries, Paris

A/W 2005–2006
5 March 2005; Espace
Éphémère Tuileries,
Jardin des Tuileries, Paris
Hair by Luigi Murenu;
make-up by Charlotte Tilbury

S/S 2006
8 October 2005; Espace
Éphémère Tuileries,
Jardin des Tuileries, Paris

A/W 2006–2007
4 March 2006; Espace
Éphémère Tuileries,
Jardin des Tuileries, Paris
Hair by Luigi Murenu;
make-up by Charlotte Tilbury

S/S 2007
7 October 2006; Espace
Éphémère Tuileries,
Jardin des Tuileries, Paris
Hair by Guido Palau;
make-up by Diane Kendal

A/W 2007–2008
3 March 2007; Espace
Éphémère Tuileries,
Jardin des Tuileries, Paris
Hair by Orlando Pita; make-up
by Tom Pecheux for M.A.C.

S/S 2008
6 October 2007; Espace
Éphémère Tuileries,
Jardin des Tuileries, Paris
Hair by Guido Palau;
make-up by Diane Kendal

A/W 2008–2009
1 March 2008; Espace
Éphémère Tuileries,
Jardin des Tuileries, Paris
Hair by Guido Palau;
make-up by Lucia Pieroni

S/S 2009
4 October 2008; Espace
Éphémère Tuileries,
Jardin des Tuileries, Paris
Hair by Luigi Murenu; make-up
by Charlotte Tilbury; shoes by
Iris for Chloé; sunglasses by
L'Amy; music direction by
Seb Chew and John Gosling;
casting and production by KCD;
technical production by OBO;
lighting by Jan Kroeze

A/W 2009–2010
11 March 2009; Espace
Éphémère Tuileries,
Jardin des Tuileries, Paris
Hair by Guido Palau; make-up
by Charlotte Tilbury; shoes by
Iris for Chloé; sunglasses by
L'Amy; music direction by
Seb Chew and John Gosling;
casting and production by KCD;
technical production by OBO;
lighting by Jan Kroeze

S/S 2010
6 October 2009; Espace
Éphémère Tuileries,
Jardin des Tuileries, Paris
Hair by Guido Palau; make-up
by Diane Kendal; shoes by Iris
for Chloé; sunglasses by L'Amy;
music direction by Seb Chew
and John Gosling; casting and

production by KCD; technical
production by OBO; lighting
by Jan Kroeze

A/W 2010–2011
9 March 2010; Espace
Éphémère Tuileries,
Jardin des Tuileries, Paris
Hair by Guido Palau for Redken;
make-up by Charlotte Tilbury;
shoes by Iris for Chloé; music
direction by Seb Chew and John
Gosling; casting and production
by KCD; technical production
by OBO; lighting by Jan Kroeze

S/S 2011
4 October 2010; Espace
Éphémère Tuileries,
Jardin des Tuileries, Paris
Hair by Luigi Murenu; make-up
by Charlotte Tilbury; shoes by
Iris for Chloé; music direction
by Seb Chew and John Gosling;
casting and production by KCD;
technical production by OBO;
lighting by Jan Kroeze

A/W 2011–2012
7 March 2011; Espace
Éphémère Tuileries,
Jardin des Tuileries, Paris
Hair by Luigi Murenu; make-up
by Charlotte Tilbury; casting
director Michelle Lee; shoes by
Iris for Chloé; music direction
by Seb Chew and John Gosling;
production by KCD; technical
production by OBO; lighting
by Jan Kroeze

S/S 2012
3 October 2011; Espace
Éphémère Tuileries,
Jardin des Tuileries, Paris
Hair by Eugene Souleiman;
make-up by Lucia Pieroni;
stylist Tabitha Simmons; casting
director Michelle Lee; shoes by
Iris for Chloé; music direction by
Steve Mackey and John Gosling;
production by KCD; technical
production by OBO; lighting
by Jan Kroeze

A/W 2012–2013
5 March 2012; Espace
Éphémère Tuileries,
Jardin des Tuileries, Paris
Hair by Paul Hanlon; make-up
by Aaron de Mey; stylist Camille
Bidault Waddington; casting
director Michelle Lee; music by
Steve Mackey and John Gosling;
production by OBO; lighting by
Jan Kroeze

S/S 2013
1 October 2012; Espace
Éphémère Tuileries,
Jardin des Tuileries, Paris
Hair by Guido Palau; make-up by
Diane Kendal; casting director
Michelle Lee; music by Steve
Mackey and John Gosling;
lighting by Jan Kroeze

A/W 2013–2014
3 March 2013; Espace
Éphémère Tuileries,
Jardin des Tuileries, Paris
Hair by Anthony Turner;
make-up by Diane Kendal and
the M.A.C. Pro team; shoes by
Iris for Chloé; casting director
Michelle Lee; casting by KCD;
production by OBO; music
direction by Steve Mackey
and John Gosling; lighting
by Jan Kroeze

S/S 2014
29 September 2013;
Lycée Carnot, Paris
Hair by James Pecis; make-up by
Diane Kendal; casting director
Michelle Lee; shoes by Iris for
Chloé; live music direction by
Steve Mackey and John Gosling;
production by OBO; lighting by
Jan Kroeze

A/W 2014–2015
2 March 2014; Salon
d'Honneur, Grand Palais, Paris
Hair by James Pecis; make-up by
Diane Kendal; casting director
Michelle Lee; nails by Odile
Sibuet; live music direction by
Michel Gaubert; production
by OBO; lighting by Philippe
Cerceau; video by La Mode
en Images

S/S 2015
28 September 2014; Salon
d'Honneur, Grand Palais, Paris
Hair by Eugene Souleiman;
make-up by Lucia Pieroni;
nails by Odile Sibuet; casting
directors Michelle Lee and
Shawn Dezan; shoes by Iris for
Chloé; live music direction by
Steve Mackey and John Gosling;
production by La Mode en
Images; lighting by Philippe
Cerceau; video by La Mode
en Images

A/W 2015–2016
8 March 2015; Salon
d'Honneur, Grand Palais, Paris
Hair by Eugene Souleiman;
make-up by Lucia Pieroni; nails
by Odile Sibuet; stylist Jane How;
shoes by Iris for Chloé; casting
directors Michelle Lee and

Shawn Dezan; live music direction by Michel Gaubert; music included Fleetwood Mac; production by La Mode en Images

S/S 2016
1 October 2015; Salon d'Honneur, Grand Palais, Paris
Hair by Eugene Souleiman; make-up by Lucia Pieroni and the M.A.C Pro Team; nails by Odile Sibuet; stylist Jane How; shoes by Olg for Chloé; casting directors Michelle Lee and Shawn Dezan; production by La Mode en Images; artistic direction by Aude Delerue and Patrick Roppel; live music direction by Michel Gaubert; lighting by Philippe Cerceau; video by Walter Films

A/W 2016–2017
3 March 2016; Salon d'Honneur, Grand Palais, Paris
Hair by Eugene Souleiman; make-up by Aaron de Mey and the M.A.C. Pro Team; nails by Odile Sibuet; stylist Jane How; casting by Elodie Yelmani and Arianna Pradarelli for Creartvt; production by La Mode en Images; live music direction by Michel Gaubert; lighting by Philippe Cerceau; video by Walter Films

S/S 2017
29 September 2016; Salon d'Honneur, Grand Palais, Paris
Hair by Eugene Souleiman; make-up by Aaron de Mey; casting directors Arianna Pradarelli and Elodie Yelmani

A/W 2017–2018
2 March 2017; Salon d'Honneur, Grand Palais, Paris
Hair by Eugene Souleiman; make-up by Aaron de Mey; nails by Odile Sibuet; stylist Jane How; casting directors Arianna Pradarelli and Elodie Yelmani; production show video by Walter Films; production by La Mode en Images

S/S 2018
28 September 2017; Maison Chloé, Paris
Hair by Paul Hanlon; make-up by Lauren Parsons; stylist Max Pearmain; casting director Ashley Brokaw; sound design by Allegria Torassa; multimedia artist Sofia Mattioli

A/W 2018–2019
1 March 2018; Maison de la Radio, Paris
Hair by Paul Hanlon; make-up by Pat McGrath; stylist Max Pearmain; casting director Ashley Brokaw; production show video by Walter Films; accessories consultant Ligia Dias; sound design by Allegria Torassa; documentary by Sofia Mattioli; show backstage coverage by Sherman McMinn

S/S 2019
27 September 2018; Foyers E and F, Maison de la Radio, Paris
Hair by Paul Hanlon; make-up by Pat McGrath; stylist Max Pearmain; casting director Ashley Brokaw; production by La Mode en Images; video and photography by Bureau Future

A/W 2019–2020
28 February 2019; Foyers E and F, Maison de la Radio, Paris
Hair by Paul Hanlon; make-up by Pat McGrath; nails by Odile Sibuet; stylist Max Pearmain; casting director Ashley Brokaw; production by La Mode en Images; music by Jackson Fourgeaud; sound design by Allegria Torassa; videos and photographs by Freecaster, Picto, Rep, Catwalk pictures

S/S 2020
26 September 2019; Galerie Courbe, Grand Palais, Paris
Hair by Guido Palau; make-up by Pat McGrath; stylist Camille Bidault Waddington; casting director Ashley Brokaw; music by Jackson Fourgeaud; design, show production and set by La Mode en Images

A/W 2020–2021
27 February 2020; Galerie Courbe, Grand Palais, Paris
Hair by Guido Palau; make-up by Pat McGrath; stylist Camille Bidault Waddington; casting director Ashley Brokaw; soundtrack by Jackson Fourgeaud, featuring Marianne Faithfull; sculptures (on set) by Marion Verboom; design and show production by La Mode en Images

S/S 2021
1 October 2020; Parvis Bas, Palais de Tokyo, Paris
Hair by Guido Palau; make-up by Pat McGrath; stylist Camille Bidault Waddington; casting director Ashley Brokaw; music by Jackson Fourgeaud;

set by Random Studio; design and show production by La Mode en Images

A/W 2021–2022
3 March 2021; Chloe.com, filmed in Saint-Germain-des-Prés, Brasserie Lipp, Les Deux Magots, Paris
Hair by Holli Smith for Bobbi Brown; make-up by Hannah Murray; stylist Camilla Nickerson; casting director Jess Hallett; film director Alexandre de Betak; director of photography Daniël Bouquet; design and show production by Bureau Betak; film production by Bureau Future; music composed and performed by Juan Campodónico; music production by Danilo Astori Sueiro

S/S 2022
30 September 2021; Quai de la Tournelle, Paris
Hair by James Pecis; make-up by Hannah Murray; bags by Mifuko; shoes by Ocean Sole; shell decorations by Akanjo Madagascar; stylist Camilla Nickerson; casting director Jess Hallett; show setting by Les Bâtisseuses; music soundtrack production by Danilo Astori Sueiro; music by Juan Campodónico; design and show production by Bureau Betak

A/W 2022–2023
3 March 2022; Parc André Citroën, Paris
Hair by James Pecis; make-up by Hannah Murray; patchworks by Gee's Bend; shell decoration by Akanjo Madagascar; bags by Mifuko and Sarah's Bag; stylist Camilla Nickerson; casting director Jess Hallett; music soundtrack production by Danilo Astori Sueiro; music by Juan Campodónico; music production and programming by Pablo Bonilla; mix and mastering by Julio Berta; design and show production by Bureau Betak

Credits included reflect the information available at the time of publication. We would be pleased to insert an appropriate acknowledgment for missing credits in any subsequent reprint.

Picture Credits

a = above; b = below; c = centre; l = left; r = right

A.D.P. – Agence Diffusion Presse: 2, 30–31, 35–7

Agence de Presse Dalmas: 46–7

Raymond Aghion: 27

Paolo Roversi/Art + Commerce: 563

Niall McInerney, Photographer. © Bloomsbury Publishing Plc.: 1982: 199 (bl), 200 (bc), 202–3; 1983: 208 (l), 209 (ar); 1991: 282–4, 285 (ar, br), 287, 288 (l); 1996: 350 (l)

© Guy Bourdin: 66

Ronnie Burg: 48

© André Carrara / Vogue Paris: 65

© Guy Marineau & Étienne Tordoir/ Catwalkpictures: 141 (b), 143 (b), 161 (bl), 162 (al, bl), 163 (b), 164 (a, bl), 191 (al), 195–7, 204–5, 209 (br), 211, 213 (ar, br), 214 (ar, br), 216 (bl), 217 (l, r), 223 (al, r), 226, 227 (l), 229 (br), 230, 231, 234–5, 240–43, 248, 249 (al, bl), 251, 254, 255 (al, r), 256 (ar, l), 257–9, 272, 273 (r), 274, 275 (r), 276–9, 280 (l), 281 (l), 285 (l), 286, 288 (r), 289–91, 292 (l), 293, 294 (r), 295–304, 305 (r), 306–33, 341 (ar), 346–9, 350 (r), 351 (b), 352, 353 (r), 354 (l), 355 (l), 356 (l), 375 (al, bl), 389, 395 (r, bl), 429 (l)

© Duffy/Vogue Paris: 58

FIDM Museum Special Collections, Gift of Arnaud Associates. Photo Michel Arnaud: 162 (r), 164 (br), 171, 179 (ar), 180, 198, 199 (al, r), 200 (al), 209 (l), 210 (r), 213 (bl), 214 (l), 215, 216 (r), 218–19, 244–7

© firstVIEW/IMAXtree: bellyband (c, r), 340, 341 (al, bl, br), 342–5, 351 (a), 353 (l), 354 (r), 354–5 (background), 355 (r), 356–7 (background), 356 (r), 362–74, 375 (r), 376–8, 379 (r), 380–88, 390–94, 395 (al), 396–409, 414–28, 429 (r), 430–79, 484–507, 512–59, 564–88, 589 (al, br), 590–91, 596–602, 603 (l, ar), 604–7

© Boo George: 511

Getty Images: Arnal/Garcia/Gamma-Rapho: 294 (l); Estrop: 589 (ar, bl); Cynthia Johnson: 239; Thierry Orban/Sygma: 292 (r); Daniel Simon/Gamma-Rapho: 113, 194, 201, 207, 222, 228, 229 (a, bl), 233 (l, br), 256 (br), 275 (l), 305 (bl); Kristy Sparow: 603 (br); Victor Virgile/ Gamma-Rapho: 249 (r), 250, 255 (bl), 273 (l), 281 (r)

© Zoë Ghertner: 595

Jean-Luce Huré: bellyband (l), 80–85, 96–109, 115, 120–25, 139–40, 142

Keystone-France/Gamma Rapho: 38–41

Photo Hermann – Studio Hollenstein: 44

© Steve Hiett: 413

© Jardin des Modes/March 1961, Louis-R. Asire: 42; December 1969 by Louis Faurer: 67; June 1970 by Claude Pataut: 68; November 1968 by John Stember: 64

Jacqueline Melzassard: 32, 33 (r)

J.C. Nicolas: 57 (l)

Courtesy the estate Karen Radkai/ Vogue Paris: 56

Shutterstock: Chris Barham/ANL: 138; Neville Marriner/ANL: 280 (r); Paul van Riel/ Hollandse Hoogte: 166–70, 174 (r), 175 (l), 178, 179 (al, bl, br), 181 (br), 182–7, 188 (l), 190, 206 (r), 208 (r), 210 (l), 213 (al), 233 (ar), 252–3

Trunk Archive: Paola Kudacki: 483; Mary McCartney: 361

All Rights Reserved: 33 (l), 34, 43, 45, 49, 50–53, 57 (r), 59–63, 69–79, 86–95, 114, 116–19, 126–37, 141, 143 (a), 144–60, 161 (al, r), 163 (a), 165, 172–4, 175 (r), 176–7, 181 (l, ar), 188 (r), 189, 191 (ar, b), 192–3, 206 (l), 212, 216 (al), 223 (bl), 224–5, 227 (ar, br), 232, 260–71, 334–9

Acknowledgments

The author and the publisher would like to thank the team at the Chloé Archive – Catherine Lebrun and Geraldine-Julie Sommier, as well as Camille Kovalevsky, Maud Villers and Louise Delahaye – for their expertise and enthusiasm.

Additional thanks from the author to all at Thames & Hudson, especially Adélia Sabatini, Kitty Grady and Corinna Parker; and to Jenny Wilson, for the expert eye. And to James Shaw, for the much-needed breaks from writing.

Additional thanks from the publisher to Kerry Davis and Don Ashby at firstVIEW, the team at IMAXtree, and Arnauld Colcomb.

The team at Chloé would like to thank Gabriela Hearst, Riccardo Bellini, Emmanuelle Mayer, Pauline Vandenbussche, Laïa Bonastre, Héloïse Anrep, Antoine Laumonier and Tommaso Sica. Chloé would also like to thank Jean-Luce Huré, Guy Marineau, Palais Galliera, Photothèque du musée des arts décoratifs, Agence Gamma, Louise Alexander Gallery and the Guy Bourdin Estate.

Considerable efforts have been
made to identify the models
featured in this book, but
in some cases we have been
unable to do so. We would
be pleased to insert an
appropriate acknowledgment
in any subsequent reprint.

Index

Cover bellyband: (left) Spring/Summer 1973
Ready-to-wear © Jean-Luce Huré; (centre) Autumn/
Winter 2009–2010 Ready-to-wear © firstVIEW/
IMAXtree; (right) Autumn/Winter Ready-to-wear
2021–2022 © firstVIEW/IMAXtree

Frontispiece (p. 2): contact sheet from
Spring/Summer 1960 Ready-to-wear

First published in the U.S. and Canada in 2022 by
Yale University Press
P.O. Box 209040
302 Temple Street
New Haven, CT 06520-9040
yalebooks.com

Published by arrangement with
Thames & Hudson Ltd, London

Chloé Catwalk: The Complete Collections
© 2022 Thames & Hudson Ltd, London

Preface © 2022 Suzy Menkes
Text © 2022 Lou Stoppard

Series concept by Adélia Sabatini
© 2022 Thames & Hudson Ltd, London

Photographs © 2022 firstVIEW/IMAXtree
unless otherwise stated

Design by Fraser Muggeridge studio

Library of Congress Control Number: 2022939007

ISBN 978-0-300-26408-1

Printed and bound in China by
C & C Offset Printing Co. Ltd

MIX
Paper | Supporting
responsible forestry
FSC® C008047
FSC
www.fsc.org